D1234730

Amy—
Best Wishes,
Stephen Jones
Joanne Mael

Tort Reform,

Plaintiffs' Lawyers,

and Access to Justice

Tort Reform, Plaintiffs' Lawyers, and Access to Justice

STEPHEN DANIELS

AND

JOANNE MARTIN

 University Press of Kansas

Published by the University Press of Kansas (Lawrence, Kansas 66045), which was organized by the Kansas Board of Regents and is operated and funded by Emporia State University, Fort Hays State University, Kansas State University, Pittsburg State University, the University of Kansas, and Wichita State University

Library of Congress Cataloging-in-Publication Data

Daniels, Stephen, 1951– author.
Tort reform, plaintiffs' lawyers, and access to justice / Stephen Daniels, Joanne Martin.
pages cm
Includes index.
ISBN 978-0-7006-2073-9 (hardback)
ISBN 978-0-7006-2074-6 (ebook)
1. Torts—Texas. 2. Law reform—Texas. 3. Torts—Economic aspects—Texas.
I. Martin, Joanne, author. II. Title.
KFT 1395.D36 2015
346.76403—dc23   2015004137

British Library Cataloguing-in-Publication Data is available.

Printed in the United States of America

10 9 8 7 6 5 4 3 2 1

The paper used in this publication is recycled and contains 30 percent postconsumer waste. It is acid free and meets the minimum requirements of the American National Standard for Permanence of Paper for Printed Library Materials z39.48–1992.

To the "true believers"—the lawyers for whom the practice of law is a calling and not just a living. They represent, as Abraham Lincoln might say, "the better angels of our nature."

Contents

List of Figures and Tables, ix

Preface, xi

Acknowledgments, xxv

1. In the Crosshairs, 1

2. "They Grabbed the Pendulum . . . and Nailed It to the Wall!": Highlights of Tort Reform, Texas Style, 31

3. A Glimpse of the Past and the Development of the Texas Plaintiffs' Bar, 70

4. The Tension between Professional Norms and the Need to Generate Business: A Window into Professional Identity, 106

5. "People Like Me Are Really the Majority of Plaintiffs' Lawyers": Structure and Hierarchy in the Texas Plaintiffs' Bar, 140

6. "If My Referring Lawyers Go Away, I'm in Trouble": Reputation, Specialization, and the Referral of Cases, 176

7. "The Juice Simply Isn't Worth the Squeeze in Those Cases Anymore": Damage Caps, "Hidden Victims," and the Declining Interest in Medical Malpractice Cases, 205

8. Conclusion: "Unless There's a Way to Make Money Practicing Law, Rights Don't Make Any Difference," 231

Methodological Appendix: Interviews and Surveys, 241

Index, 247

Figures and Tables

FIGURES

7.1. Attractiveness of Clients by Case Type in Light of Damage Caps, 221
7.2. Percent of Individual Lawyers Still Finding Different Clients Attractive in Light of Damage Caps, 227

TABLES

4.1. How Texas Lawyers Get Clients, 116
5.1. Geographic Markets for Different Groups of Lawyers, 145
5.2. Practice Characteristics and Place in the Hierarchy, 146
5.3. Nature of Change for Selected Practice-Related Characteristics: 163 Survey Repeaters, 169
5.4. Nature of Change for Selected Practice-Related Characteristics: 40 BB1 Survey Repeaters, 170
5.5. Nature of Change for Selected Practice-Related Characteristics: 41 HH2 Survey Repeaters, 171
6.1. Referrals by Case Type: Texas Referral Survey, 2004, 183
6.2. Participation in Referral Market by Referring at Least One Case: For Lawyers in Referral Survey Percent in Primary Practice Areas, 185
6.3. Reasons for Referring Cases: Lawyers in Referral Survey Making at Least One Formal Referral, 188
6.4. Criteria for Choosing a Target Lawyer: Lawyers in Referral Survey Making at Least One Formal Referral, 190
6.5. Referrals by Case Type: Plaintiffs' Lawyer Survey, 2006, 192
6.6. Reasons for Referring Cases: Lawyers in Plaintiffs' Survey Making at Least One Formal Referral, 198
6.7. Criteria for Choosing a Target Lawyer: Lawyers in Plaintiffs' Survey Making at Least One Formal Referral, 201
A.1. Respondents to the 2000 Survey and Respondents to the 2006 Survey Compared: Shared Questions in Each Survey on Practice Characteristics, 244

Preface

Thank you for sending me the questionnaire involving the study of Texas Plaintiffs'
Lawyers. . . . About a third of the way through the questions I felt my answers might
skew your results, so I decided . . . to respond to the questionnaire by writing a brief
letter explaining my involvement practicing law in the last five years.

I was licensed to practice law in Texas in 1978 and began working in a small
firm representing plaintiffs in personal injury and workers' compensation cases. In
1984, I became board certified in Personal Injury Trial Law by the Texas Board of
Legal Specialization. In November of 1986, I opened my own firm and continued to
represent plaintiffs in personal injury suits. . . . My practice was 99 percent plaintiffs'
personal injury. In 1999, I decided to close my law office due to the fact that I found
myself working harder for less money. My business expenses continued to increase,
and the value of cases continued to decline. On June 30, 1999, my lease expired and
I laid off my remaining paralegal. I had about a dozen personal injury cases and
continued to work those cases by myself out of my home. In the spring of 2001, I
settled my last personal injury case, which also happened to be the last case I had
when I closed my practice. In 2004, I decided not to renew my board certification. . . .

I believe tort reform was a major factor in my decision to close my practice. I
found jury verdicts decreased due to the propaganda disseminated by insurance
companies and big business, and this resulted in insurance adjusters offering less
money to settle cases. I began to decline representation in cases I used to accept and
was working harder and receiving less money on cases I took.

WHY SHOULD WE CARE ABOUT PLAINTIFFS' LAWYERS?

We received this letter in lieu of a completed response to a survey of Texas
plaintiffs' lawyers we conducted in 2006. The letter writer's story is simple and
stark. No doubt there are many, especially tort reform advocates, who would
be pleased to see such a lawyer bite the dust in Texas. Why should we care?

This is a book about plaintiffs' lawyers and why we should care. It is about
lawyers like our letter writer, whose practices are defined by the representation
of plaintiffs on a contingency fee basis, and the effects of tort reform on their
practices. It is set in Texas, where there is a substantial plaintiffs' bar and where
tort reform has been and remains a major political movement seeking to alter

the law as well as the broader cultural environment surrounding civil litigation. Much of tort reform, as our letter writer implies, aims to make a contingency fee practice economically unfeasible. In its wake, many plaintiffs' lawyers are changing their practices, and some are even leaving the practice area.

Plaintiffs' lawyers are squarely in the reformers' crosshairs in Texas and elsewhere, and we use the idiom with its full connotation. We should care because plaintiffs' lawyers are the civil justice system's gatekeepers, and they hold an important key to meaningful access to the rights and remedies the law provides. A second letter writer from whom we heard articulated this concept, saying, "I feel truly for the families of those that are injured that either cannot find a lawyer or because they will receive a very small recovery if they are successful in pursuing their claim." Additionally, since ours is a common law system, plaintiffs' lawyers—through the cases they handle—play a corollary role in shaping the rights and remedies the law will allow. In saying this is a book about plaintiffs' lawyers, we are saying this book is ultimately about access.

It is because of these roles, played all too well it seems, that plaintiffs' lawyers are in the tort reformers' crosshairs. One need only look at two widely touted book-length attacks by authors with ties to the staunchly pro-reform Manhattan Institute. The full title of each leaves little doubt as to the respective authors' assessment of plaintiffs' lawyers: *The Rule of Lawyers: How the New Litigation Elite Threatens America's Rule of Law* and *Lawyer Barons: What Their Contingency Fees Really Cost America*.[1] In light of the roles played by plaintiffs' lawyers, we are interested in what happens to them and their practices in the age of tort reform.

To an important extent, how these lawyers respond to changes in the legal environment, like those brought about by tort reform, will determine whether the courthouse doors will be open or closed to those seeking to avail themselves of the rights and remedies the law provides—and even what those rights and remedies will be. The key is whether plaintiffs' lawyers can respond and still make a living in this practice area. One Texas plaintiffs' lawyer's statement

---

1. Walter Olson, *The Rule of Lawyers: How the New Litigation Elite Threatens America's Rule of Law* (New York: St. Martin's Press, 2003); Lester Brickman, *Lawyer Barons: What Their Contingency Fees Really Cost America* (New York: Cambridge University Press, 2011). The Manhattan Institute has long argued for limiting plaintiffs' lawyers and contingency fees; *see* Lester Brickman, Michael Horowitz, & Jeffrey O'Connell, *Rethinking Contingency Fees* (New York: Manhattan Institute, 1994).

says it all: "Unless there's a way to make money practicing law, rights don't make any difference."

More generally, exploring how tort reform affects the practices of plaintiffs' lawyers (and hence access to rights for individuals) is important to understanding how law and politics are inexorably intertwined. Not simply in terms of partisan politics, although it is certainly this, but more generally in terms of interest group politics in the deeper sense of being about the fundamental ordering of who gets what, when, and how.[2] Tort reform is about fundamentally changing the rules and procedures surrounding the law of injuries and the rights and responsibilities that body of law lays out. The rights the lawyer quoted above has in mind—the current ones the law provides—are seen by others as intrusive, costly, and grossly unfair impediments that must be removed. Tort reform can be seen as one part of a broader political movement aimed at loosening regulation and governmental powers in the economic arena more generally.[3] At the most extreme, it can even be a challenge to law itself.

In addition, as a political movement tort reform has always been about shaping the public mind and altering the cultural environment in which civil litigation takes place—what is perceived as an injury; whether and whom to blame if there is an injury; what to do about it; and even how to respond to what others (especially plaintiffs and their lawyers) do with regard to naming, blaming, and claiming. To do so, reform interests have made a substantial investment in a relentless public relations campaign dating back at least sixty years and waged by a loosely allied group of pro-reform organizations (our letter writer characterized it as propaganda). For an example, one need only look at the mission statement for the American Tort Reform Association (ATRA): "ATRA's goal is not just to pass laws. We work to change the way

2. *See* Harold Lasswell, *Politics: Who Gets What, When, and How* (New York: World Publishing, [1936] 1968).
3. *See* Stephen Daniels & Joanne Martin, *Civil Juries and the Politics of Reform* (Evanston, IL: Northwestern University Press, 1995); Jean Stefancic & Richard Delgado, *No Mercy: How Conservative Think Tanks and Foundations Changed America's Social Agenda* (New York: NYU Press, 1996); Thomas Burke, *Lawyers, Lawsuits, and Legal Rights: The Battle over Litigation in American Society* (Berkeley: University of California Press, 2002); and William Haltom & Michael McCann, *Distorting the Law: Politics, Media, and the Litigation Crisis* (Chicago: University of Chicago Press, 2004). *See also* Brickman, *supra* note 1; Olson, *supra* note 1.

people think about personal responsibility and civil litigation."[4] Indeed, some commentators—ourselves included—argue that the reformers may have been more successful in altering the cultural environment surrounding the civil justice system than in effecting change through legislation. This can be seen in the ways in which plaintiffs' lawyers are altering their practices in the face of what they see as an increasingly hostile environment.

Our book is based on a multifaceted series of research projects begun in 1995 that allow us to do two things. The first is to systematically examine the Texas plaintiffs' bar and lawyers' practices as tort reform unfolded and progressed. The second is to provide the foundation needed to make sense of any changes in lawyers' practices—a working knowledge of the history, norms, and structure of the Texas plaintiffs' bar and the nature of plaintiffs' practice. Anchoring those projects are in-depth interviews with plaintiffs' lawyers (one hundred between 1995 and 2000, fifty-one in 2005–2006, and five in 2012–2013) and two detailed surveys of plaintiffs' lawyers (one in 2000, the other in 2006). These materials are supplemented by data from the 2004 Texas Referral Practices Survey done for the Texas State Bar's Referral Fee Task Force; the results of publicly available demographic surveys of lawyers in Texas conducted by the State Bar of Texas Department of Research and Analysis; informal observations and discussions at Texas Trial Lawyers Association (TTLA) offices and meetings, at other gatherings of plaintiffs' lawyers, and in lawyers' offices throughout the study; and archival materials related to the development of the plaintiffs' bar in Texas.

Texas has a substantial, long-standing, and differentiated plaintiffs' bar. It has a thirty-plus-year history of increasingly intense tort reform activity that includes legislative and rule changes as well as lobbying efforts and public relations campaigns on the part of interest groups with national ties. Partisan politics is a key part of the Texas story because it coincides with the Republican ascendancy in Texas and the state's rightward turn. Texas plaintiffs' lawyers are overwhelmingly Democratic and lean to the left. Finally, Texas has become the poster child for tort reform success. It provides an excellent locale for systematically examining the impact of tort reform on plaintiffs' lawyers and their practices.

---

4. American Tort Reform Association (ATRA), *ATRA's Mission: Real Justice in Our Courts*, http://www.atra.org/about/.

STARTING POINTS

Lawyers as Rational Business Actors

We have four starting points. One is rather clear-cut, at least at first glance; the second is less so but equally important; the third is semantic but also political—just what are we talking about when we talk about "reform"? The last is the matter of perspective—how we approach the issues that interest us. First is the apparently simple proposition that lawyers who rely on the contingency fee (the lawyer is paid and recoups his costs only if he wins) need to act as essentially rational business actors. This practice area has always been precarious, shaped by the relevant legal rules that define formal procedure and causes of action and by the broader and changing environment (economic and cultural). A plaintiffs' lawyer must be able to maintain a steady flow of one-shot clients with injuries the civil justice system will compensate adequately at a cost that will allow the lawyer to make a profit.

Herbert Kritzer's study of Wisconsin lawyers—*Risks, Reputations, and Rewards: Contingency Fee Legal Practice in the United States*—is the major empirical study that addresses the need for business rationality. Kritzer argues that litigators generally (plaintiffs' lawyers are a subset of litigators) can be understood in terms of portfolio theory. They must act rationally to balance the potential profit of a practice's worth of cases against the likely risks and costs. The key to the balance is diversification, rather than specialization, in providing a hedge against the risk.[5] Kritzer's book does not concentrate on tort reform or on plaintiffs' lawyers per se; nonetheless, one of the keys to understanding how tort reform may affect plaintiffs' lawyers (and whether the courthouse doors are open or closed) is grasping the need for plaintiffs' lawyers to act rationally in business terms.

Our letter writer's lament highlights the importance of the economics and the need to keep enough money coming in to—as the lawyers would say—"keep the lights on." As David Hyman and Charles Silver concisely summarize the business model, "It's the incentives, stupid."[6] Much of tort reform has the

---

5. Herbert Kritzer, *Risks, Reputations, and Rewards: Contingency Fee Legal Practice in the United States* (Stanford, CA: Stanford University Press, 2004), 9–19.
6. David Hyman & Charles Silver, *Medical Malpractice Litigation and Tort Reform: It's the Incentives, Stupid,* 59 Vanderbilt L. Rev. 1085, 1085 (2006).

effect, as indeed it is intended to, of making plaintiffs' practice much less profitable, meaning fewer lawyers in the practice area and fewer lawsuits. In talking about the decline in certain medical malpractice cases in Texas in the wake of tort reforms enacted in 2003, Hyman, Silver, and other members of their research team speculate that, in part, "the falloff in claims reflects judgments by Texas plaintiffs' lawyers (presumably as smart, motivated, and good looking as lawyers elsewhere) that many cases are no longer worth bringing."[7]

Professional Identity

While a rational actor/portfolio approach offers a concise and appealing perspective that has greatly influenced our work, it does not fully reflect what we find in Texas. At first glance, our letter writer's demise may be seen as proof of the failure to follow the rational actor/portfolio idea. Nonetheless, as later chapters will show, there is a robust plaintiffs' bar with its own professional organizations and a clear hierarchy made up of lawyers like our letter writer whose practices are almost exclusively plaintiffs' work done on a contingency fee basis. Our letter writer did have a lengthy, profitable run before retiring and closing his practice. We even found further specialization within this area of specialized practice—most noticeably medical malpractice. Not alone is the lawyer who described his practice as being almost exclusively medical malpractice—"for a while it was probably 90% of our practice, maybe as high as 95% from time to time." And, unlike our letter writer, most plaintiffs' lawyers are not going out of business, although they may be adapting their practices in various ways as conditions change.

We also find more is involved for these lawyers than just making a living, and this brings us to our second starting point. For many, there is an ideological component—a very particular professional identity—to what it means to be a plaintiffs' lawyer in Texas. It goes to the heart of how they see themselves as professionals. As one lawyer told us:

---

7. Myungho Paik et al., *How Do the Elderly Fare in Medical Malpractice Litigation, Before and After Tort Reform? Evidence from Texas*, 14 Am. L. & Econ. Rev. 561, 596 (2012). We will draw from this team's Texas research in various places in the book. They are: Bernard Black, David Hyman, Charles Silver, Myungho Paik, and William Sage. Not all team members appear as authors on each published piece.

You have true believers. . . . I put myself in that category. What has appealed to me is a family with kids whose life gets turned upside down because someone in the family gets seriously hurt or killed, and they're facing a greater than David and Goliath battle, and they need someone to fight for them. . . . I'll be in this business until the bitter end. And I hope that the bitter end is not five years from now.

This sentiment suggests that professional identity may act as a countervailing force against pure business rationality.

Here we are not talking about the long-standing dichotomy between professionalism and commercialism, with the former viewed positively and the latter negatively,[8] but something more nuanced. Although they do not use the term *professional identity*, what we have in mind is something akin to what Lynn Mather and her colleagues, in looking at divorce lawyers, call a "community of practice"—with the emphasis on community as being about things held in common. For Mather et al. it is about an identifiable set of lawyers with a shared practice area and a shared set of values or norms about professional behavior tied to that area.[9] While similar to such communities of practice, our notion of professional identity is broader. It is about a morality of aspiration—it is about ends rather than just means and behavior.[10] In other words, the question is not simply what does it mean to be *a* lawyer, but what does it mean to be *this kind* of lawyer and to make a living being this kind of lawyer. More specifically, the question is what does it mean to be this kind of lawyer in Texas with Texas's political and legal history.

As the quote about "true believers" suggests, plaintiffs' lawyers may not be best understood simply as purely rational actors. In Texas, at least, there is a unique professional identity that comes into play. Though not fully for-

8. See Jerold Auerbach, *Unequal Justice: Lawyers and Social Change in Modern America* (New York: Oxford University Press, 1976), 40–52; Carroll Seron, *The Business of Practicing Law: The Work Lives of Solo and Small-Firm Attorneys* (Philadelphia: Temple University Press, 1996). Seron's entire opening chapter is devoted to the dichotomy: "Chapter 1: Professionalism versus Commercialism," *see* 1–18.

9. Lynn Mather, Craig McEwen & Richard Maiman, *Divorce Lawyers at Work: Varieties of Professionalism in Practice* (Chicago: University of Chicago Press, 2001), 4–13.

10. Francis Zemans & Victor Rosenblum, *The Making of a Public Profession* (Chicago: American Bar Foundation, 1981), 169–170.

malized, it has a history and is reinforced—imperfectly, to be sure—by informal networks and plaintiffs' lawyers' own formal organizations. The idea of a unique identity is seen in the Texas Trial Lawyers Association's rules for full membership. It is

> limited to all members of the State Bar of Texas and all duly licensed out-of-state lawyers not licensed by the State of Texas who do not regularly and consistently represent insurance companies, corporations, utility companies and/or defendants in actions filed by individuals who have been injured or damaged and who are not associated with a law firm that regularly and consistently represents such entities or individuals; provided, however, an employee of an executive branch agency of state or federal government shall not be eligible for membership in the association.[11]

Knowing something of Texas plaintiffs' lawyers' professional identity helps us understand the culture of their practice area, what makes a professional reputation, and what defines success. It helps us understand how they try to navigate the very real challenges they face in building and maintaining a successful practice and what the boundaries may be in doing so. If plaintiffs' lawyers were purely rational actors, we might legitimately wonder why they ever decided to enter this practice area and why—in the face of tort reform in Texas—anyone would stay in it. Nonetheless, there is—and has been—a coherent plaintiffs' bar in Texas, by any measure a community of practice and then some.

All lawyers, of course, work in a world in which professional identity and economic interest necessarily coexist—not always comfortably. The issue is how lawyers who accept this kind of professional aspiration navigate the coexistence of goals that may pull them in different directions—making a good living and serving those values—in a tort reform environment. Access to the courthouse doors may depend on it.

11. Texas Trial Lawyers Association (TTLA), *TTLA Membership Application*, summarizing Article IV, Section 1A of TTLA's Bylaws, www.ttla.com/index.cfm?pg=ArticleIVSection1A. *See* www.ttla.com/index.cfm?pg=aboutmain for a statement of TTLA's mission.

Reform or "Reform"

The third of our starting points involves the semantic and politically charged question surrounding the idea of "reform." Most of those who address the topic (including us) simply use the term tort reform, a term that does carry a certain connotation. A longtime observer of tort reform in Texas—and one of our longtime informants—regularly tells us not to use tort reform, but tort "reform" instead. The quotation marks, he argues, should always be used because of the general understanding of what reform means. It carries a clear connotation, one that presumes that the current state of affairs—whatever it may be—is in dire need of improvement. There is also a certain moral judgment involved because the reason for that need is tied to the misdeeds or failures of some identifiable set of actors. Most crudely, it can be cast as the good guys versus the bad guys. Following this logic, proposed changes are not promoted as those favoring one narrow set of interests at the expense of others. Instead, the changes are presented as a needed—not merely a desired—step forward toward some more ideal or superior state of affairs that will benefit the common good.[12]

Let us turn specifically to our informant's point. The advocates for certain changes in the tort system have skillfully and strategically used the term "reform" to characterize their efforts to take advantage of the term's symbolic value. As used by its proponents, tort reform dramatically and ominously states, rather than demonstrates, that the current state of affairs is in dire need of fundamental change. It is the image of a civil justice system run amok and causing far-reaching damage—as one of the movement's long-running themes says—for which "we all pay the price." Among the key causes at the heart of the crisis are the misdeeds of a particular set of actors—plaintiffs' lawyers. Proposed changes are presented not as favoring the narrow self-interest of the reform advocates. Rather, as ATRA president Sherman Joyce asserted, "There is clearly

---

12. Other commentators would seem to agree with our informant. For instance, University of Texas law professor David Anderson said the following in 2007, reflecting on Texas tort reform: "'Tort reform' is a misnomer if the objective is merely to reduce liability. Changes that bar or reduce recovery without addressing what is wrong with the law are not reforms at all. . . . All too often, 'reforms' do nothing to simplify, clarify, or rationalize the law, and instead make it more cumbersome and irrational." David Anderson, *Judicial Tort Reform in Texas*, 26 Rev. of Litigation 1, 42–43 (2007).

broad support for tort reform as a means to rein in greedy personal injury lawyers that are manipulating our legal system for personal financial gain at the expense of the average consumer."[13]

While we will not use "reform" in our discussion (it is too cumbersome for a book-length discussion), our informant's point is well taken, and we will return to it in the book's conclusion. After all, it is about who gets what, when, and how—and that means it is about politics.

The Matter of Perspective

The issues that interest us are controversial and engender strong, differing, and often polarized views that reflect differences in professional experience, ideological viewpoint, and just plain self-interest—"you're either for us or agin us." This makes any discussion of these issues a risky proposition because there is a tendency to view any discussion through mutually exclusive sets of lenses and senses of accepted wisdom (what is "known" to be true). One can quickly be dismissed as naive—or worse, knowingly biased—for not seeing the obvious truth of things. But it is the controversy that makes the issues interesting and tells us that there is something important at stake and that it's worth the risk.

With this in mind, the last of our starting points involves the matter of perspective. More specifically, a critical perspective grounded in the insights of political science; informed by the best work in the law and social science literature; and based on extensive, systematic empirical research. We are not going to deal with the issues that interest us by offering a "balanced" approach of how side A sees those issues in the following way, whereas side B sees them in an opposing way. Critical, scholarly work is not about merely reporting and taking each side at face value—including their favorite hobbyhorse issues and political rhetoric—and leaving it at that. Instead, it is about raising and exploring questions about important issues that probe the underlying dynamics. And in regard to tort reform, it is an approach cognizant of the

---

13. ATRA, *Voters Say "Too Many Lawsuits," According to New National Poll on Tort Reform,* www.atra.org/newsroom/voters-say-too-many-lawsuits-according-new-national-poll-tort-reform. A number of scholarly commentators have examined the tort reform movement's symbolic crusade and the interests involved. *See* sources in *supra* note 3.

strategic use of "reform's" symbolic value to obviate the need for any critical examination.

The views we express in this book are ours alone. The American Bar Foundation, an independent research institute, has supported our work on plaintiffs' lawyers as it has supported our earlier work on juries and tort reform.[14] No monetary support for the research came from the American Bar Association, from any other professional organization, or from any entity with a stake in the issues we explore. We have been able to follow our findings in whatever direction they led us. The advantages of being affiliated with an institution that vigorously honors and defends independence in research are incalculable. For these advantages, we are indebted to the Board of Directors of the American Bar Foundation.

PLAN OF THE BOOK

The book is divided into seven substantive chapters, along with a conclusion and a Methodological Appendix describing the interviews and surveys at the heart of our research.

Chapters 1 and 2 serve as a general introduction and set the stage. Chapter 1 addresses the questions of why plaintiffs' lawyers are in the reformers' crosshairs and why we should care. It provides a general context for the traditionally jaundiced view of plaintiffs' lawyers that makes them an easy target for political purposes and discusses in detail the key roles of gatekeeper and shaper of the law that are the heart of the reformers' concerns. Chapter 1 also emphasizes tort reform as a political movement that goes beyond the idea of making formal changes in the law and seeks to alter the cultural environment surrounding civil litigation. In doing so, it places the discussion in the larger context of tort reform as a national political movement.

Chapter 2 adds the Texas context. Plaintiffs' lawyers have seen the Texas Legislature pass tort reform measures making it harder for them to pursue their chosen specialty profitably. They have observed a Texas Supreme Court shift in a far more conservative direction. They have also witnessed that Court flexing its political muscle beyond its rulings on individual cases—most dramatically with an attempt to fundamentally change the paid referral system

14. *See* Daniels & Martin, *supra* note 3.

that moves cases among lawyers. Additionally, they have watched an ongoing, aggressive public relations campaign waged by tort reform interests that they believe has "poisoned" the jury pool—or at least shifted public attitudes, along with jury verdicts, in a more pro-defendant direction.

These are all fronts in the reformers' multifaceted and successful battle plan, which coincides neatly with the Republican ascendancy in Texas. Chapter 2 critically discusses each of these factors and starts the discussion of how tort reform is affecting lawyers' practices, which will be continued in greater detail in later chapters.

Chapters 3, 4, and 5 focus on the Texas plaintiffs' bar and provide a needed foundation. Chapter 3 provides background on the development of the plaintiffs' bar in Texas and its own professional organizations. By no means a history, it draws from archival materials, private letters, and other materials to provide some needed context for understanding the contemporary plaintiffs' bar in Texas. It also begins the discussion of professional identity, which plays an important role in the development of the Texas plaintiffs' bar and the response to tort reform.

Chapter 4 continues the discussion of professional identity. It does so in a unique way because it was not clear to us that the lawyers being interviewed would understand the abstract ideas of professional identity found in the scholarly literature. Instead, we asked about a charged issue—the propriety of different ways in which plaintiffs' lawyers get clients, an issue that concerns them deeply and provides a window into their sense of themselves as professionals. Underlying this exploration of professional identity is the idea that these lawyers cannot be understood simply as rational business actors. Again, the important thing is how these lawyers navigate between their professional identity and business necessity—because access depends on it.

Chapter 5 presents an overview of the structure and characteristics of the contemporary Texas plaintiffs' bar. Most importantly, it shows that there is specialization and a complex hierarchy within the plaintiffs' bar. Based primarily on the findings of our two surveys of the Texas plaintiffs' bar, it also highlights the changes in plaintiffs' practice in the wake of tort reform and how lawyers navigate the coexistence of goals that may pull them in different directions in a tort reform environment. One of the key findings is the differential impact of tort reform across the hierarchy.

Chapters 6 and 7 look at two specific areas of reform activity: the referral process and medical malpractice legislation. Chapter 6 focuses on the referral system that moves cases among lawyers up and down the hierarchy, a process targeted by Texas reformers in the early 2000s. It relies on our surveys and interviews along with data from the 2004 Texas Referral Practices Survey. Importantly, it shows how the referral system underlies and reproduces the plaintiffs' bar's structure and how the referral system allows for specialization to exist. Reputation is the key to referrals and moves cases to the lawyers best able to handle them. With some sense of this system, it is easy to understand why the reformers sought major changes in the referral system as a part of their larger political agenda. The referral system is important for access to the extent it moves cases to the lawyers—often specialists—best able to handle them.

Chapter 7 examines changes in lawyers' practices in the wake of one major legislative change—caps on noneconomic damages in medical malpractice cases (a signature piece of reform passed in Texas in 2003). It shows how such a measure can close the courthouse doors—especially for the so-called "hidden victims" of tort reform. These are individuals (like the elderly) with legitimate claims for whom there will be minimal economic damages, leaving only noneconomic damages capped by the 2003 law. Given the high cost of bringing a malpractice case—costs born by the lawyer handling the case—and the risk involved, cases involving such parties are not economically viable.

Chapter 7 is built around a special section of our 2006 survey that involves a series of carefully constructed hypothetical situations designed to assess the attractiveness of different clients, holding severity of injury and liability constant. Lawyers were asked about taking each client in a medical malpractice case and in a different case not covered by the caps—one involving an accident with a tractor-trailer truck. For each case type, the lawyer was asked about taking the client before and after the 2003 caps on noneconomic damages went into effect. Needless to say, lawyers were highly unlikely to take the "hidden victim" clients in a post-2003 malpractice case, although they would have before 2003. There were no changes in the truck accident cases—all client types were economically viable before and after 2003.

Chapter 8, the Conclusion, offers a summary of the book's findings and argument by returning to the ideas underlying the starting points outlined earlier in the Preface and focuses on access.

Acknowledgments

It is not possible to acknowledge all of the people—the students, research assistants, colleagues, and people in Texas—who helped us over the years we spent researching plaintiffs' lawyers and tort reform in Texas. There are just too many, and we cannot thank them enough. A few, however, do require special thanks. John E. Collins, a Dallas lawyer, has helped and encouraged our research in Texas for well over 20 years. He was our entry point, and from him we learned things that appear in no book or academic study. When we began our research Mike Widener—now at Yale Law School—was the head of special collections at the Tarlton Law Library, University of Texas at Austin. He introduced us to and helped us exploit the treasure trove of resources in his care in Tarlton's special collections.

There are the many lawyers who took the time to sit with us for what were often lengthy interviews and to complete our surveys. Some went much further with informal discussions and acting as resources. Our promises of confidentiality prevent us from mentioning them by name.

More recently, Steve Wasby (Emeritus Professor of Political Science at SUNY-Albany) pushed, cajoled, and badgered us to complete the manuscript. He read through drafts of every chapter—or, as he would probably say, nit-picked his way through them. His comments, suggestions, and insight have been invaluable. Ginger Kimler also read through the drafts of every chapter and provided much-needed fine-tuning.

Finally are the people at the Texas Trial Lawyers Association. Over the years TTLA's leadership and staff gave us unparalleled access to them, to meetings, and to events and allowed us to just hang around and talk. In particular are Tiffany McGee, Mona Fults, and Willie Chapman. Willie remains an extraordinary resource for us. And a special acknowledgment must go to the late Tommy Townsend, who was TTLA's executive director during the time of our research.

We have been fortunate in working for an institution—the American Bar Foundation—that highly values and encourages independence in research. We have been able to follow our findings wherever they led. This would not have been possible without the significant support provided to the American Bar Foundation by the American Bar Endowment in the form of a truly unrestricted annual grant.

Tort Reform,
Plaintiffs' Lawyers,
and Access to Justice

1. In the Crosshairs

Plaintiffs' lawyers are in the reformers' crosshairs. As we will see, they are in the crosshairs because they are an easy target and wonderfully useful for symbolic purposes in the furtherance of tort reform and other political efforts. Republican strategist Frank Luntz advised conservative activists in the 1990s that they should be "making fun of the trial lawyers. . . . Make fun of them mercilessly. . . . They are truly one group in American society that you can attack with near impunity."[1]

More importantly, they are in the crosshairs because of the roles they play in the civil justice system and what happens when they play those roles well. They are the system's gatekeepers and provide meaningful access to the rights and remedies the law provides. Through the cases they handle, they also help shape what the law is and what those rights will be. In other words, in talking about their roles we are talking about politics—politics in the sense of who gets what, when, and how. And tort reform, as political scientist Thomas Burke tells us, is all about distributional politics.[2] Indeed, well-known critics of plaintiffs' lawyers like Lester Brickman and Walter Olson—both with ties to the strongly free market, individual responsibility, and pro-reform Manhattan Institute—attack plaintiffs' lawyers precisely because they can affect who gets what, when, and how through the cases they bring.[3]

In the chapter's first two sections, we address those reasons for plaintiffs' lawyers being in the reformers' crosshairs. Building on these two sections, the third places the discussion in the larger context of tort reform as a na-

---

1. Frank Luntz, *Language of the 21st Century* (Alexandria, VA: The Luntz Research Companies, 1997), 129.

2. Thomas Burke, *Lawyers, Lawsuits, and Legal Rights: The Battle over Litigation in American Society* (Berkeley, CA: University of California Press, 2002), 27.

3. *See* Lester Brickman, *Lawyer Barons: What Their Contingency Fees Really Cost America* (New York: Cambridge University Press, 2011) and Walter Olson, *The Rule of Lawyers: How the Litigation Elite Threatens America's Rule of Law* (New York: St. Martin's Press, 2003).

tional political movement, one with goals much broader than the attainment of formal legislative changes dealing with tort cases. As the mission statement of the American Tort Reform Association (ATRA) we quoted in the Preface states, "ATRA's goal is not just to pass laws. We work to change the way people think about personal responsibility and civil litigation."[4] This is important because plaintiffs' lawyers are best understood in the context of the environment in which they work. The practice of plaintiffs' law has always been a precarious business that is sensitive to both changes in the laws on the books and changes in the broader environment in which lawyers work. The tort reform movement, as ATRA's goals reflect, wants to reshape that environment.

We conclude this chapter with a short illustration drawing on Luntz's advice that nicely ties together the main points of each of the three sections. Our discussion in this chapter will touch upon the Texas experience, but a more detailed examination of the Texas context is the task of the following chapter.

THE ALL-TOO-USUAL VIEW

Calibrating the Crosshairs

Targeting lawyers for political purposes is an obvious strategy with an easy payoff. Lawyers generally are viewed—at best—with skepticism. Frank Luntz takes this characterization to the extreme, asserting that "few classes of Americans are more reviled by the general public than attorneys."[5] Opinion surveys appear to bear this out. Since the mid-1970s, the Gallup polling organization has asked people how they would rate the honesty and ethical standards of individuals working in a variety of fields. In twenty-six of these polls conducted from 1976 through 2010, no more than 27 percent of the respondents rated the honesty and ethical standards of lawyers as high or very high. By way of contrast, only once, in 1994, did fewer than 50 percent of the respondents *not* rate medical doctors' standards as high or very high

---

4. American Tort Reform Association (ATRA), *ATRA's Mission: Real Justice in Our Courts*, www.atra.org/about/.

5. Luntz, *supra* note 1, at 127.

(47 percent). Starting in 2000, at least 60 percent of the respondents rated doctors as high or very high.[6]

If lawyers generally are viewed with skepticism, plaintiffs' lawyers are viewed with derision, if not worse. For instance, an ATRA press release of February 27, 2003, announcing the results of the association's then just-completed public opinion survey, quoted ATRA's president Sherman Joyce: "There is clearly broad support for tort reform as a means to rein in greedy personal injury lawyers that are manipulating our legal system for personal financial gain at the expense of the average consumer." Among the specific findings noted were: "Personal injury lawyers are widely disliked (55% unfavorable vs. 17% favorable) . . . 80% of the electorate agrees that personal injury lawyers take too much of the money they win on behalf of their clients . . . [and] 61% of Americans feel that lawsuits against doctors result in personal injury lawyers getting rich."[7] The theme continued with the key findings in a 2012 ATRA survey, which included the following assertion: "There is widespread identification across demographic groups of personal injury lawyers as the source of problems with the system."[8] Tort reform groups across the country, including Texans for Lawsuit Reform, touted the findings of both of these surveys.[9]

Given ATRA's aggressive political stance in favor of tort reform, its poll results should be viewed with a bit of skepticism—at the very least. However,

6. As asked, the question is "Please tell me how you would rate the honesty and ethical standards of people in these different fields—very high, average, low, or very low? . . . Lawyers/Medical Doctors." *See* Roper Center Public Opinion Archives, University of Connecticut, www.ropercenter.uconn.edu, for a searchable database that includes each of the polls in the time series.

7. ATRA, *Voters Say "Too Many Lawsuits," According to New National Poll on Tort Reform*, www.atra.org/newsroom/voters-say-too-many-lawsuits-according-new-national-poll-tort-reform.

8. ATRA, *Americans Speak on Lawsuit Abuse: Results of a National Survey*, Aug. 2012, at 4, http://atra.org/sites/default/files/documents/ATRA%20SOL%20Voter%20Survey%20Summary%20FINAL.pdf.

9. "National Poll: Voters Say Litigation Is Hurting Economy, They're More Likely to Support Pro–Tort Reform Candidates," Texans for Lawsuit Reform, Aug. 21, 2012, www.tortreform.com/news/national-poll-voters-say-litigation-hurting-economy-theyre-more-likely-support-pro-tort-reform; "Voters Say—Survey Finds Tort Reform Enjoys Broad Bipartisan Support: Personal Injury Lawyers Viewed as Problem," Texans for Lawsuit Reform, www.tortreform.com/content/voters-say.

the results of other polls sponsored by groups not in the pro-reform camp are similar. Three polls conducted in the 2000s—two for Democracy Corp. (2005 and 2007) and one for Justice at Stake (2001) provide excellent examples. All used the same question with a 100-point temperature scale to ask people about their view of trial lawyers. A temperature rating of 100 degrees is the warmest, most positive evaluation a respondent could give, and 0 degrees is the coldest, most negative evaluation. The results with regard to trial lawyers are quite chilly. Among the three polls, at the highest only 31 percent of respondents in the 2001 Justice at Stake poll rates trial lawyers at least somewhat warmly at 51 degrees or higher.[10]

As if illustrating these survey results, an experienced San Antonio lawyer we interviewed told us about his perception of a change in jury behavior in the face of the tort reformers' public relations campaigns. He said, "We start with the jury box and we start with the suspicion, and it's hard to get a good verdict for a deserving victim. So very, very hard . . . [In the past] we felt a warmth in the jury box, whereas now we feel like it's a refrigerator."

Mass culture often reinforces and reflects the negative portrayal of plaintiffs' lawyers. One need only look to the novels of John Grisham, which have over the years become a running commentary on the failings of plaintiffs' lawyers and the legal profession in general. The fictitious Chicago plaintiffs' firm of Finley & Figg is described in the opening of one of Grisham's recent best-selling novels, *The Litigators*, as follows: "Finley & Figg's scam was hustling injury cases, a daily grind that required little skill or creativity. . . . Two doors away was the intersection of Preston, Beech, and Thirty-Eighth, a chaotic convergence of asphalt and traffic that guaranteed at least one good car

---

10. Available in Roper Center Public Opinion Archives, University of Connecticut, Justice At Stake Survey, Oct. 2001. Retrieved Nov. 12, 2014 from the iPOLL Databank, The Roper Center for Public Opinion Research, University of Connecticut, http://www.ropercenter.uconn.edu.turing.library.northwestern.edu/data_access/ipoll/ipoll.html; Democracy Corps Poll, Apr. 2005. Retrieved Nov. 12, 2014 from the iPOLL Databank, The Roper Center for Public Opinion Research, University of Connecticut, http://www.ropercenter.uconn.edu.turing.library.northwestern.edu/data_access/ipoll/ipoll.html; Democracy Corps Poll, May, 2007. Retrieved Nov. 12, 2014 from the iPOLL Databank, The Roper Center for Public Opinion Research, University of Connecticut, http://www.ropercenter.uconn.edu.turing.library.northwestern.edu/data_access/ipoll/ipoll.html.

wreck a week, and often more."[11] To further flesh out the character of the firm's two partners, Grisham leaves little doubt as to their legal acumen, telling the reader that each "took the bar exam three times."[12]

Of course, there is also the ubiquitous lawyer advertising on television, billboards, city buses, and almost anywhere else that advertising space is sold, along with direct-mail solicitation and the Internet. That too can reinforce the negative view of plaintiffs' lawyers. In Texas, perhaps the most prolific, long-term television advertiser is Houston's Jim "The Hammer" Adler. He also has a heavy presence on the Internet, including Facebook, Twitter, and YouTube.[13] In a 2009 *Texas Monthly* interview, Adler explained his trademark: "My trademark is 'the Texas Hammer.' A scriptwriter came up with that back in the nineties. The original ad went, 'A hammer is a valuable tool. A hammer nails hides to walls. Jim Adler will hammer and hammer and hammer until he gets you what you deserve.' Now I answer to the Hammer. Isn't that scary? I'm no longer Jim. I'm the Hammer."[14]

Even plaintiffs' lawyers worry about the image portrayed in the ads of lawyers like Adler and others. An East Texas lawyer told us, "A guy comes home from work, gets his beer, sits in front of the TV and hears this lawyer, this smarmy-looking lawyer, telling him, 'If you get hurt, I'll make you rich.' . . . And I know how I personally respond to lawyer advertising in a very negative way . . . you know, when somebody looks at that, the average person, they see graft. They see fraud. They see corruption."

In talking about direct-mail solicitation of potential clients, a San Antonio plaintiffs' lawyer told us, "The jurors know about this kind of thing, and they think that plaintiffs' lawyers are scumballs. Unfortunately, probably about one-third of them are."

As if the advertising is not bad enough, there are also the media, which William Haltom and Michael McCann see as an unwitting (although not always)

---

11. John Grisham, *The Litigators* (New York: Doubleday, 2011), 1–2. For a general examination of lawyer-bashing in the midst of the tort reform movement, *see* Marc Galanter, *Predators and Parasites: Lawyer-Bashing and Civil Justice,* 28 Ga. L. Rev. 633 (1994).

12. *Id.* at 3.

13. *See* Jim Adler & Associates, www.jimadler.com.

14. Karen Olsson, *Jim Adler, Personal Injury Attorney,* Texas Monthly, Aug. 2009, www.texasmonthly.com/story/jim-adler-personal-injury-lawyer.

ally of the reformers, reporting on exaggerated claims about the civil justice system and uncritically retelling the horror stories offered as the proof of those claims. Most prominent, of course, is the media's handling of the infamous McDonald's coffee case. Haltom and McCann show in detail how the case was portrayed in the media and mass culture in a book chapter with a title that says it all: "Java Jive: Genealogy of a Juridical Icon." It shows how "media coverage and analysis made any rational discussion of the dispute and the policy issues it raises virtually impossible, while providing a powerful boost to the dubious general claims of a partisan political reform movement."[15]

Not to be ignored are reports of the failings of and scandals involving the highest-profile plaintiffs' lawyers, like former senator and vice presidential nominee John Edwards or Richard "Dickie" Scruggs, who pled guilty in 2009 to bribing a judge in Mississippi.[16] In Texas, the exploits of the late John O'Quinn—whom *Forbes* described as a "rapacious tort lawyer"[17]—have been widely reported over the years, and he has been vilified by his enemies (and former friends). The Texas Commission for Lawyer Discipline twice tried and failed to disbar O'Quinn, both times based upon allegations of case-running (paying agents to solicit clients) in the aftermath of airplane crashes. In the 1980s, a series of scandals surrounding the Texas Supreme Court and the hefty financial contributions by high-flying plaintiffs' lawyers like Pat Maloney Sr. to the justices' elections campaigns attracted national attention that culminated in a 1987 CBS *60 Minutes* segment titled "Justice for Sale."[18] As we will explain in Chapter 2, these scandals became a major impetus for the tort reform movement in Texas and helped lead to the complete Republican control of the Texas Supreme Court.[19]

15. William Haltom & Michael McCann, *Distorting the Law: Politics, Media, and the Litigation Crisis* (Chicago: University of Chicago Press, 2004), 196.

16. Scruggs's story is told in Curtis Wilkie, *The Fall of the House of Zeus: The Rise and Ruin of America's Most Powerful Trial Lawyer* (New York: Crown Publishers, 2010).

17. Christopher Helman, *John O'Quinn, King of Torts, R.I.P.*, Forbes, Oct. 30, 2009, www.forbes.com/2009/10/30/torts-john-oquinn-business-oquinn.html.

18. *See* Ken Case, *Blind Justice*, Texas Monthly, May 1987.

19. *See* Kyle Cheek & Anthony Champagne, *Judicial Politics in Texas: Partisanship, Money, and Politics in State Courts* (New York: Peter Lang, 2004), 37–51. Allegations about alleged wrongdoing by prominent Texas plaintiffs' lawyers with strong Democratic Party ties continue. *See* John Schwartz, *BP Accuses Texas Lawyer of "Brazen Fraud"*

It's Déjà Vu All over Again

This view of plaintiffs' lawyers as hungry vultures of questionable skill and ethics is nothing new, which is one reason why they remain an easy target. Legal historians tell us that plaintiffs' lawyers have been despised and disparaged by much of the legal profession and other "respectable" people since these lawyers made their first real appearance in the later part of the nineteenth century. In Jerold Auerbach's words—talking about the stratification of the bar at the turn of the twentieth century—"the contingent fee was denigrated to the level of original sin and negligence lawyers were denounced by the professional patriciate as foreign ambulance chasers or shysters. . . . Nothing plunged the professional elite deeper into despair than contingent fees and the proliferation of negligence lawyers whose practice depended upon them."[20]

Auerbach cites a 1919 *Yale Law Journal* article by Ashley Cockrill, President of the Arkansas Bar Association, "The Shyster Lawyer." Needless to say, it was a rousing condemnation and a call for the outright elimination of such lawyers. Cockrill said that the shyster may appear in various forms, but he singled out two:

> We have the stupid, lazy shyster whose chief offense is lack of knowledge and industry. He merely ekes out a living in the scums of the law. He is a disgrace. . . . We have the "ambulance chaser," who hangs around the house of the dead and injured, seeking employment as a tinner does trade, who preys upon corporations and succeeds not only in doing great injury to his victim, the defendant, but also his other victim, his client, who so frequently is deprived of any share of the loot.[21]

These comments would not be out of place in a tort reformer's playbook.

Lawrence Friedman provides the more general picture and the image of "hungry and unscrupulous men":

in *Workers' Claims over Gulf Oil Spill*, New York Times, Dec. 17, 2013, www.nytimes .com/2013/12/18/us/bp-accuses-texas-lawyer-of-brazen-fraud-in-workers-claims-over -gulf-oil-spill.html?_r=0.

20. Jerold Auerbach, *Unequal Justice: Lawyers and Social Change in Modern America* (New York: Oxford University Press, 1976), 45.

21. Ashley Cockrill, *The Shyster Lawyer*, 21 Yale L.J. 383, 385–386 (1919).

Socially if not economically at the lowest circle of the profession were the "ambulance chasers," personal injury lawyers who raced to the scene of accidents, or to hospital rooms, to sign up victims of crashes, smashes, explosions and fires. . . . Among their clients, there were of course, a large number of fakers—con artists who specialized in slipping on banana peels, or falling off trains, and the like. . . . Sometimes, the lawyers who represented these hungry crooks were themselves hungry and unscrupulous men.[22]

This view still resonates all too well today. In his 2011 book *Lawyer Barons*, law professor and Manhattan Institute–affiliated scholar Lester Brickman bemoans the corrupting effects of the contingency fee and the lawyers who rely upon it. "Fraudulent practices associated with contingency fees simply reflect the fact that the transfers of vast sums of money in the tort system provide abundant opportunities for dishonest lawyers."[23] Among these practices, he says, are staging phony auto accidents, various kinds of medical insurance fraud and kickback schemes, and the use of paid "runners" to sign up accident victims (with nonexistent soft tissue injuries) as clients.[24]

None of what we have described in this section actually helps us understand the place of plaintiffs' lawyers in the legal profession and the role they play in the civil justice system, but it does help us to understand their attractiveness as a symbolic target useful for political purposes.

TWO KEY ROLES: GATEKEEPING AND SHAPING THE LAW

Gatekeeping

Being an easy target is not the only reason plaintiffs' lawyers are in the reformers' crosshairs. After all, the plaintiffs' bar has never had the monopoly on scoundrels in the legal profession. It is also because of the roles they play

---

22. Lawrence Friedman, *American Law in the 20th Century* (New Haven, CT: Yale University Press, 2002), 29–30.
23. Brickman, *supra* note 3, at 111.
24. *Id.* at 111–112.

in the civil justice system—roles to which the reformers strongly object. Most importantly, as political scientist Herbert Jacob observed some years ago, lawyers are the gatekeepers for the civil justice system.[25] They control meaningful access to the rights and remedies the law provides. Plaintiffs, of course, can always proceed on their own, but those who do rarely do so with success. Meaningful access requires legal representation, and if there is any doubt as to the practical importance of legal representation, a study by Charles Silver and David Hyman provides a simple Texas illustration. In analyzing data on closed Texas insurance claims for bodily injury claims in the state, Silver and Hyman find that across all lines of commercial liability insurance, claimants with lawyers received higher payments.[26] This is consistent with the findings we reported in an earlier article about medical malpractice matters in Wisconsin: those without legal representation almost never received an award, those with representation were more likely to receive an award, and those represented by the best lawyers—the medical malpractice specialists—were the most likely to receive an award (and to receive the highest awards).[27]

Although legal representation is crucially important, it is not free. Many people, perhaps most, cannot afford to pay a lawyer a retainer, to pay on an hourly basis after that, and also to pay for the expenses of preparing and proceeding with a case. The only way for most injured people to afford representation, especially in a complex matter like medical malpractice, is to hire a lawyer who will handle it on a contingency fee basis. Such a lawyer will not receive a fee unless the case is successful for the client. In addition, the lawyer almost always fronts the expenses of case review and preparation and receives no reimbursement unless there is a settlement or an award. In the words of one Texas plaintiffs' lawyer, "I front all the costs, and if we lose, I eat the costs."

25. Herbert Jacob, *Law and Politics in the United States*, 2nd ed. (New York: Harper-Collins, 1986), 118; *see also* Herbert Kritzer, *Contingency Fee Lawyers as Gatekeepers in the Civil Justice System*, 81 Judicature 22 (1997) and Joanne Martin & Stephen Daniels, *Access Denied: Tort Reform Is Closing the Courthouse Door*, Trial (July 1997), at 26. For a practitioner's perspective, *see* Philip H. Corboy, *Contingency Fees: The Individual's Key to the Courthouse Door*, 2 (4) Litigation 27 (1976).

26. Charles Silver & David Hyman, *Access to Justice in a World without Lawyers: Evidence from Texas Bodily Injury Claims*, 37 Fordham Urban L.J. 357, 364 (2010).

27. *See* Stephen Daniels & Joanne Martin, *Plaintiffs' Lawyers, Specialization, and Medical Malpractice*, 59 Vanderbilt L. Rev. 1051, 1055–1060 (2006).

The contingency fee is important, Herbert Kritzer bluntly reminds us, because it is about access to the system for those without the means to pay a lawyer to represent them. He says, "From the perspective of the average citizen, contingency fees are about 'access to justice' through the mechanism of civil litigation, or the threat of civil litigation."[28] The comments of a Texas lawyer we interviewed echoed Kritzer's point.

> Ninety percent of the people out there make their living, they pay for their kids to go to school, they pay to take care of their kids, they pay for their mortgage, they pay for their one or two cars, and at the end of the month, they may have $100 left over if they're the lucky ones. . . . And so, for someone to have the ability to go hire a lawyer on anything other than a contingency, you know, I think it's a fiction.

Access, of course, is dependent on there being lawyers willing and able to work on a contingency fee basis.[29]

As Silver and Hyman note, "tort reforms can cause the supply of legal services to contract by capping fees, reducing claim values, or making litigation riskier or more expensive for claimants."[30] If there is any doubt as to the hoped-for effect of tort reform with regard to access, Professor Brickman—the archcritic of plaintiffs' lawyers and the contingency fee—unabashedly says, "Most tort reforms will deprive some number of claimants of access to courts, and some of these claimants would have prevailed had their cases gone to

---

28. Herbert Kritzer, *Risks, Reputations, and Rewards: Contingency Fee Legal Practice in the United States* (Stanford, CA: Stanford University Press, 2004), 254.

29. A similar concern with access was a driving force behind a 2013 change in England and Wales allowing contingency fees in civil matters. Lord Justice Jackson authored the report that led to the change; in his foreword, he said, "In some areas of civil litigation costs are disproportionate and impede access to justice. I therefore propose a coherent package of interlocking reforms, designed to control costs and promote access to justice." The Right Honourable Lord Justice Jackson, *Review of Civil Litigation Costs: Final Report* (Norwich, UK: The Stationery Office, 2010), www.judiciary .gov.uk/wp-content/uploads/JCO/Documents/Reports/jackson-final-report-140110 .pdf. *See also The Conditional Fee Agreements Order 2013*, www.legislation.gov.uk /uksi/2013/689/contents/made.

30. Silver & Hyman, *supra* note 26, at 380.

trial. That, of course, is precisely the purpose of tort reform: to curtail tort litigation."[31]

It is important that Silver and Hyman—and Brickman—have in mind formal changes in the law. The plight of our letter writer in the Preface shows that tort reform efforts other than formal changes in the law also can cause the supply of legal services to contract. For bread-and-butter lawyers like our letter writer (those whose practices are built largely on small-to-modest matters), it is not the formal changes that count most. It is—to refer again to ATRA's mission statement—the reformers' efforts at changing "the way people think about personal responsibility and civil litigation." As the letter writer said, "I believe tort reform was a major factor in my decision to close my practice. I found jury verdicts decreased due to the propaganda disseminated by insurance companies and big business and this resulted in insurance adjusters offering less money to settle cases. I began to decline representation in cases I used to accept and was working harder and receiving less money on cases I took."

Shaping the Law: New Directions

The second important role played by plaintiffs' lawyers is dependent on the existence of legal recourse for injuries suffered as a result of the negligence of others and lawyers being able to provide meaningful access to that recourse. Lawyers help shape the law through the cases they handle in at least two ways, and tort reform may affect both aspects of this law-shaping role. The first is by charting new directions and expanding the law's reach, and the second is by setting the "going rate" in a given jurisdiction for the value of particular kinds of cases. Value is set through the verdicts lawyers obtain, which in turn are used to settle the vast majority of matters short of trial. In this section we discuss the idea of charting new directions, and in the next section we discuss the concept of going rates.

In a system in which courts cannot act on their own volition but must wait for litigants to present issues to them, lawyers help shape the law through the new or novel arguments they offer to courts in the course of litigation. It is the best lawyers who are likely to do this. The story told by a retired Texas appellate judge we interviewed provides an obvious example of this—the development

31. Brickman, *supra* note 3, at 121.

of strict liability in products liability law through a long series of decisions by supreme courts in a number of states dating from the early twentieth century. Texas was among these states, he said, and it judicially adopted strict liability in 1967.[32] The judge mentioned other changes as well, particularly those in medical malpractice and those that simplified and streamlined the instructions given to juries in tort cases. He talked about all of these changes dealing with tort law in Texas in the context of the development of the organized plaintiffs' bar in Texas from the late 1940s onward.

This development, in turn, helped produce a cadre of skilled plaintiffs' lawyers who shaped changes in Texas law through the cases they litigated. The judge's message was simple—if lawyers representing injured plaintiffs had not brought the cases in the first instance, and utilized their skills and resources to push their new ideas in the appellate courts, then the law would not have evolved to offer the protections for injured individuals at the time and in the manner it did. Indeed, he said that the changes in jury instructions achieved by plaintiffs' lawyers changed older rules developed through the appellate efforts of corporate and railroad attorneys in Texas earlier in the twentieth century.[33]

The judge's comments bring to mind an argument by Marc Galanter and David Luban concerning the likely effects of legislative tort reform efforts. They presume that legislative changes enacting tort reform (their particular interest is in punitive damages) are aimed at making a contingency fee practice less profitable for lawyers, especially elite lawyers. The elite plaintiffs' lawyers will also be the ones most likely to leave the market in the face of tort reform because they have the resources and skills to seek other and more lucrative opportunities in other practice areas. Less proficient lawyers will be the ones left working in the field, and this would mean, in Galanter and Luban's view, fewer top-notch lawyers devising and spreading novel legal strategies that extend the law.[34]

32. See *McKisson v. Sales Affiliates, Inc.* 416 S.W.2d 787 (1967); the Texas Supreme Court adopted strict liability for foodstuffs in 1942 in *Decker & Sons v. Capps* 164 S.W.2d 828 (1942).

33. For an excellent example of what the judge was talking about, see Kenneth Lipartito & Joseph Pratt, *Baker & Botts in the Development of Modern Houston* (Austin: University of Texas Press, 1991), 11–63.

34. Marc Galanter & David Luban, *Poetic Justice: Punitive Damages and Legal Pluralism*, 42 Am. U. L. Rev. 1393, 1452–1453 (1993).

The loss of the best plaintiffs' lawyers would also diminish the networks among plaintiffs' lawyers through which new ideas and innovations circulate, since those elite lawyers are at the heart of these networks. To the extent the better lawyers act as mentors for new lawyers entering the field, the opportunities for apprenticeship training would also be fewer, diminishing the overall quality of the plaintiffs' bar.[35] Furthermore, if the elite lawyers are the ones most likely to leave the market, then the organized plaintiffs' bar may well suffer as a result, since many of these lawyers are among its leaders and major financial backers. A less proficient plaintiffs' bar overall may mean fewer resources to pursue the plaintiffs' bar's interests, including fewer resources for practice-related programs and networking (things the judge emphasized), for lobbying and support of friendly candidates for office (executive, legislative, and judicial), for outreach and public relations campaigns, and for action by litigation groups allied with the organized plaintiffs' bar.

Professor Brickman and like-minded critics such as Walter Olson tell a story much like the judge's about the role played by plaintiffs' lawyers in expanding the law's reach. Unlike the judge's, however, their version of the story is about plaintiffs' lawyers pushing the law in new directions solely to enrich themselves while causing serious damage to the public good. In addition, they look at the judge's story as evidence of an even deeper harm to democratic institutions. In Brickman's view, pushing the law in new directions or using litigation as a form of regulation "dilutes our democratic form of government by exempting large areas of policy from legislative control. In effect, lawyers are using their positional advantages to convert policy making into a highly profitable enterprise. When public policy making is thus removed from legislatures, so too is political accountability and public participation in the process."[36] This is a key reason, in his view, for reining in plaintiffs' lawyers.

Shaping the Law: Going Rates

In addition to shaping the law formally through new or novel legal arguments adopted by appellate courts as general rules, lawyers also help to shape the law

35. *Id.*
36. Brickman, *supra* note 3, at 12–13.

in a second way. They shape the law informally—the law in practice rather than the law on the books—in given jurisdictions. While perhaps more mundane and less visible generally, this role is no less important. It has always been the case that most civil matters are settled rather than actually tried before a jury or a judge. By choosing which cases to take to trial, plaintiffs' lawyers help to set the "going rates" used to settle the vast majority of cases in any jurisdiction. "Going rates" are set, in the first instance, by the verdicts lawyers obtain for particular kinds of cases in a locale and then refined and reinforced by subsequent settlements made in similar cases.[37]

Although the idea has been around for some time,[38] it is usually associated with Marc Galanter's metaphor of the "radiating effects of courts."[39] He argues that even though jury verdicts resolve only a small proportion of all civil disputes, they have a symbolic value and impact that extends well beyond their frequency. They transmit signals about cases that contribute "a background of norms and procedures against which negotiations and regulation in both private and governmental settings take place . . . not only the rules that would govern adjudication of the dispute, but also remedies and estimates of the difficulty, certainty, and costs of securing particular outcomes."[40]

As Galanter's argument presumes, the participants in the civil litigation process—plaintiffs' lawyers, defense lawyers, and insurance companies—look to jury verdicts to help identify the going rates used to settle the vast majority

---

37. See H. Laurence Ross, *Settled out of Court: The Social Process of Insurance Claims Adjustment*, 2nd ed. (Chicago: Aldine, 1980), 144–149, for an account dealing with auto accident cases; see Herbert Kritzer, *Let's Make a Deal: Understanding the Negotiating Process in Ordinary Litigation* (Madison: University of Wisconsin Press, 1991), 64–66, for an account dealing with personal injury cases more generally.

38. The idea of "going rates" appeared in the early 1950s, for example, in a series of national magazine advertisements by an insurance company aimed at influencing potential jurors in personal injury cases. *See Bill Set Me Straight on Jury Awards*, Saturday Evening Post, Mar. 28, 1953, at 155; *A True Verdict Render According to the LAW and the EVIDENCE*, Saturday Evening Post, Feb. 14, 1953, at 118; *Me? I'm Paying for Excessive Jury Awards?* Life, Mar. 9, 1953, at 157; *YOUR Insurance Premium Is Being Determined Now*, Life, Jan. 26, 1953, at 91. All four advertisements were the work of one insurance company: American-Associated Insurance Companies.

39. Marc Galanter, "The Radiating Effects of Courts," in *Empirical Theories about Courts*, eds. Keith Boyum & Lynn Mather (New York: Longman's, 1983).

40. *Id.* at 121.

of matters that do not go all the way to trial.[41] For instance, one Texas plaintiffs' lawyer shared the following regarding soft tissue injuries: "I read them [verdict reporters] all the time... juries are so .... Most of them [plaintiffs] are getting zero verdicts. So, yeah, I hear about them in the trial reports. That's why I don't really want to go to trial on a soft tissue case." During our research, information on local verdicts was available to lawyers in Austin, East Texas, Dallas, Fort Worth, Houston, and San Antonio in locally produced verdict reporters, some of which also include verdicts from elsewhere in Texas.

Galanter and Luban also see a connection between the going rates and the potential exit of elite lawyers from the plaintiffs' arena because of tort reform. The most skilled plaintiffs' lawyers tend to get not only the best verdicts but also the best settlements. They get the best settlements "because defendants do not want to confront them in jury trials . . . and information about the size of settlements is often disseminated among both the plaintiffs' and defense bars." This, in turn, will influence not only future trials but future settlements as well. Using the radiating effects metaphor, they said, "If too many good lawyers exit the plaintiffs' bar, the shadow [of past settlements] shortens, and defendants will be able to bargain harder for lower settlements."[42] In other words, the "going rate" may change to the advantage of the interests on the defense side—change the law *in practice*—if the best players significantly alter their practices or leave the field altogether.

SOME CONTEXT FOR TORT REFORM

It's Ultimately Political

In the Preface, we noted that one longtime observer of tort reform in Texas admonished us about using the term "reform" without placing it in quotation marks. His point is that what is called "tort reform" has little or nothing to do with reform as that term is commonly understood—as a change for the better,

---

41. In our 2000 survey of Texas plaintiffs' lawyers, 61 percent said that they regularly read a local verdict reporter, as did 49 percent of the respondents in the 2006 survey. *See also* Ross, *supra* note 37, at 112, 189–191, on the use of verdict reporters by insurance adjustors.

42. Galanter & Luban, *supra* note 34, at 1453–1454.

a meaningful upgrade to a current state of affairs in dire need of improvement. Such improvements are portrayed not as favoring a narrow set of interests but rather as a needed step forward toward some more ideal or superior state of affairs benefiting the common good. The advocates for certain changes in the tort system, and more generally in the cultural environment surrounding the civil justice system, have skillfully and strategically used the term "reform" to characterize their efforts and take advantage of its symbolic value.

Our informant is not alone in reminding us to look under the hood, kick the tires, and not be fooled by the shiny new paint job. Thirty years ago Kenneth Jost, then the editor of the *Los Angeles Daily Journal* (a legal newspaper), wrote at the end of a series on tort reform, "The current tort reform movement seeks not neutral efficiency-enhancing procedural changes, but substantive legal revision to rewrite rules more in their [the reformers'] favor."[43] Jost's conclusion about tort reform in the middle 1980s still resonates today. More recently, Haltom and McCann observe that "the tort reform movement . . . developed to challenge, roll back, and otherwise reconstruct this expanded liability regime of tort law."[44] Their reference to an expanded regime refers to numerous changes in the twentieth century, especially in the last third of the century. Legal historian Lawrence Friedman summarizes those twentieth-century changes in the following way: "The old tort system [that generally favored defendants] was completely dismantled; the courts and the legislatures limited or removed the obstacles that stood in the way of plaintiffs."[45]

Leading the reform effort, Haltom and McCann point out, are "corporate defendants and those who feared they would soon be civil defendants."[46] In Thomas Burke's assessment, the politics of tort reform are relatively straightforward. "Groups aligned with plaintiffs fight groups aligned with the defendants. . . . [The] battles are thus highly partisan, with most Republicans on the anti-litigation side and most Democrats lined up with the plaintiffs. These are struggles over distributional justice—who gets what."[47] The patterns Burke and Haltom and McCann see at the national level are found in Texas as well, as the next chapter will show. It is no coincidence that the increasing success

43. Kenneth Jost, *Polemics Won't Solve Insurance Crisis*, Los Angeles Daily Journal, Dec. 9, 1985, at 2.
44. Haltom & McCann, *supra* note 15, at 38.
45. Friedman, *supra* note 22, at 349.
46. Haltom & McCann, *supra* note 15, at 38.
47. Burke, *supra* note 2, at 27.

of tort reformers in Texas mirrored the ascendancy of the Republican Party in the state.

Most commentators date the beginning of the current tort reform movement to the early 1970s, with most successes being at the state rather than the federal level. Writing in 2002, Burke saw three waves or rounds of tort reform in the states. The impetus for the first round in the 1970s was medical malpractice. He found that "between 1975 and 1978, fourteen states passed laws encouraging arbitration, twenty-nine created screening panels for lawsuits, twenty limited attorney contingency fees, fourteen put monetary caps on damages, and nineteen restricted the collateral source rule."[48]

A second wave of tort reform began in the mid-1980s, and Burke noted that this round covered more than just medical malpractice cases. "Between 1985 and 1988 sixteen states capped 'pain and suffering' damages, twenty-eight limited punitive damages, twenty restricted the collateral source rule, and thirty modified their joint and several liability rules. In 1986 alone, forty-one of the forty-six legislatures that met passed some type of tort reform."[49]

The third wave came in the mid-1990s, again involving a broad range of reforms. "In 1995 eighteen states passed tort reforms, including extensive reform packages in Oklahoma, Illinois, Indiana, and Texas. Between 1995 and 1997 fourteen states limited punitive damages, thirteen modified their joint and several liability rules, and eight made significant changes in products liability law."[50] Another wave of reform efforts came in the early to mid-2000s, with the emphasis again on medical malpractice. Among the states with major medical malpractice reforms were Texas, Illinois, and Florida. A key provision of these reforms was a stringent cap on damages.[51]

48. *Id.* at 31–32.

49. *Id.* at 32.

50. *Id.*

51. These legislative successes have not gone unchallenged in the courts. There have been a number of challenges, some successful, in the state courts based on state constitutional provisions. Perhaps the most active player in these challenges has been the Center for Constitutional Litigation, a national public interest law firm whose mission is "serving trial lawyers, challenging laws that impede justice." The center has had a number of notable successes, including decisions striking damage caps in medical malpractice cases in Florida and Illinois (respectively, *Estate of McCall v. United States*, 134 So.3d 894 [Fla. 2014]; *Lebron v. Gottlieb Memorial Hospital*, 930 N.E.2d 895 [Ill. 2010]). *See* Center for Constitutional Litigation, *Our Work: Constitutional Challenges to Laws Restricting Access to Justice*, www.cclfirm.com/our-work/#sthash.OLkVVLan.dpuf.

The second and subsequent waves of reform coincided with the Reagan Revolution and the resurgence of the Republican Party at both the national and state levels. Especially important were the Reagan administration's focus on tort reform and its 1986 Report of the Tort Policy Working Group on the Causes, Extent and Policy Implications of the Current Crisis in Insurance Availability and Affordability. This focus continued into the George H. W. Bush administration, with its Council on Competitiveness headed by Vice President Dan Quayle. Building on these sources and others, reform advocates justified their efforts for broad changes with claims about serious and deleterious effects on American society and economy caused by a civil justice system run amok. Among these effects were the lack of physicians willing to practice in some geographic areas, the shortage of physicians in some specialty areas (like obstetrician/gynecologists),[52] the diminished willingness of industry to innovate, and the loss of competitiveness in the global economy and the concomitant loss of jobs.[53]

Such claims are not going unchallenged. A recent study of the medical malpractice reforms enacted in Texas in 2003 (primarily a cap on noneconomic damages) provides an excellent example. Using data from the Texas Department of Insurance on closed medical malpractice claims in conjunction with Medicare data on costs, Myungho Paik and colleagues examine the impact of those reforms on the cost of medical care in Texas. More specifically, their interest is in whether or not costs declined as the reform advocates have claimed. Costs did not decline, and they state, "No matter how we slice the data, we find no evidence that the Texas 2003 tort reforms 'bent the cost curve' downward, and some evidence of higher post-reform spending by Texas physicians who practice in high-risk counties."[54] Placing their findings in the context of other studies beyond Texas, they conclude that the "accumulation of recent evidence finding zero or small effects suggests that it is time for policymakers to abandon the hope that tort reform can be a major element in health-care cost control."[55]

---

52. *See* Governor Rick Perry, *Tort Reform Has Done the Job It Was Designed to Do,* Office of the Governor, July 2, 2012, http://governor.state.tx.us/news/editorial/17549/.

53. *See* Richard J. Mahoney & Stephen E. Littlejohn, *Innovation on Trial: Punitive Damages Versus New Products,* 246 Science 1395 (1989).

54. Myungho Paik, Bernard S. Black, David A. Hyman & Charles Silver, *Will Tort Reform Bend the Cost Curve? Evidence from Texas,* 9 J. Empirical Legal Stud. 173, 175 (2012).

55. *Id.* at 175–176.

Texas Governor Rick Perry made much of the 2003 malpractice reforms in his unsuccessful 2012 bid for the Republican presidential nomination. Not surprisingly, his office responded to this study in a sharply worded editorial piece. The editorial attacks the research as nothing but the work of the "trial lawyer lobby"—which, of course, is cast as a key part of the problem the 2003 changes were to solve. The governor dismisses the analyses as nothing more than "a mix of smoke and mirrors and statistical sleight-of-hand, specifically designed to obscure the success story of tort reform in Texas."[56] The governor then goes on to repeat the claims made before about the success of tort reform in Texas.

A 2011 *Huffington Post* story also takes issue with Governor Perry's claims that "his tort reform plan proved the wisdom of his business-friendly policies by expanding health care across the state." Citing data from the Texas Department of State Health Services, the story notes that, contrary to Perry's claims, tort reform did little to solve the problem of physician shortages in rural areas—especially for obstetrician/gynecologists —or a supposed shortage of and exodus of physicians from Texas generally.[57] A 2014 study by the same team of researchers attacked by Governor Perry shows "no evidence that the number of active Texas physicians per capita is larger than it would have been without tort reform. Any effect of tort reform is too small for us to measure, against the background of other, larger forces affecting physician supply, both in Texas and nationally."[58] More specifically, that team finds no evidence of increase for "three high-malpractice risk specialties highlighted by tort reform advocates—neurosurgeons, orthopedic surgeons, and ob-gynecologists [*sic*]."[59] Nor do they find an "increase in primary care physicians, nor in rural physicians."[60]

As political scientist John Kingdon observes in his study of agenda setting in Congress, "people generate and debate solutions because they have some self-interest in doing so . . . not because the solutions are generated in response

---

56. Perry, *supra* note 52.

57. Paul J. Weber, *Rick Perry Malpractice Reforms Did Not Expand Health Care Despite Candidate's Claims*, Huffington Post, Nov. 7, 2011, www.huffingtonpost.com /2011/11/07/rick-perry-tort-reform-health-care_n_1080044.html.

58. David A. Hyman, Charles Silver, Bernard S. Black & Myungho Paik, *Does Tort Reform Affect Physician Supply? Evidence from Texas*, Northwestern University Law School, Law and Economics Research Paper No. 12-11, Feb. 2014, at 3, http://ssrn.com/ abstract=2047433.

59. *Id.*

60. *Id.*

to a problem."[61] And this is true of tort reform—like any other policy arena, it is about the interests of those who will benefit by the changes. The veracity of the claims made in furtherance of those interests is not the measuring standard—political success is. This is why Governor Perry can dismiss the empirical research with gusto and with little fear of consequence.

The Politics of Ideas: Shaping the Public Mind

Like the Paik et al. study, much of the discussion of tort reform understandably focuses on the specific legislative changes offered by the reformers and whether those measures solve the problems used to justify them. As we noted in the Preface, however, tort reform as a political movement has always had broader goals than just changing the law on the books. Reform interests have invested heavily in shaping the public mind and altering the cultural environment in which civil litigation takes place. Some commentators—ourselves included—argue that the reformers may have been more successful in achieving this goal.[62] Burke, for instance, says, "Tort reformers have helped to reshape public discourse about litigation, undermining the heroic view of lawyers and lawsuits that has always competed in the American mind with more unsavory images of the legal profession."[63]

Shaping the public mind and the cultural environment surrounding civil litigation and litigiousness generally is important for three key reasons. First, and most immediately, is getting the favored formal changes on the public policy agenda. As Kingdon's study of agenda setting shows, "[at] any time, important people in and around government could attend to a long list of problems. . . . Obviously, they pay attention to some potential problems and ignore others . . . problems are not . . . entirely self-evident."[64] Consequently, those

---

61. John Kingdon, *Agendas, Alternatives, and Public Policies*, 2nd ed. (New York: HarperCollins, 1995), 91.

62. *See* Stephen Daniels & Joanne Martin, *The Impact That It Has Had Is between People's Ears: Tort Reform, Mass Culture, and Plaintiffs' Lawyers*, 50 DePaul L. Rev. 453 (2000) and Stephen Daniels & Joanne Martin, *The Strange Success of Tort Reform*, 53 Emory L.J. 1225 (2004).

63. Burke, *supra* note 2, at 30.

64. Kingdon, *supra* note 61, at 90.

wanting to get their issues and ideas on the agenda for governmental action must invest great effort and substantial resources in getting the attention of the public and important people in and around government, including key elites and the media. Successfully placing an issue on the policy agenda, in Kingdon's view, "requires changing the way people think about that issue."[65] The process of gaining a place on the agenda and eventually moving a favored change to enactment is essentially, in Deborah Stone's words, "a struggle to control which images of the world govern policy."[66] David Ricci, in his study of the rise of "think tanks," characterizes such a struggle as the "politics of ideas"—the aggressive marketing of ideas and images for political purposes.[67]

Second, shaping the public mind is important for a reason unique to this policy arena. Doing so is a means to a broader political end than just legislative or electoral gain—and one we heard Texas plaintiffs' lawyers talk about constantly and with dismay. Our letter writer's comments about "propaganda" provide an excellent example—lobbying the pool of people who may eventually serve on a civil jury. This is a unique policy arena because there is another official decision maker involved—the jury. Perhaps the best illustration of this is found in the words of a defense lawyer speaking to the jury in a 1999 trial in Houston: "What used to be the American Dream has turned into the American Scheme. . . . The best tort reform is the 12 of you."[68] The lawyer was representing basketball star Charles Barkley as the defendant in a personal injury suit. It is the possible effect on jurors that provides a crucial key to the impact of tort reform public relations campaigns on plaintiffs' lawyers.

Third, shaping the public mind is important more generally if it can influence what is perceived as an injury, whether to assign blame and to whom if there is an injury, and eventually what to do about it. To the extent these efforts are successful, fewer people may be willing to use the remedies the legal system provides. It is worth repeating a short excerpt from the mission statement of

---

65. Kingdon, *supra* note 61, at 114–115.

66. Deborah Stone, *Policy Paradox and Political Reason* (New York: W. W. Norton, 1988), 309.

67. David Ricci, *The Transformation of American Politics: The New Washington and the Rise of Think Tanks* (New Haven, CT: Yale University Press, 1993), 182–207.

68. Quoted in Ron Nissimov, *Plaintiff's Motives Attacked as Trial in Barkley Suit Begins*, Houston Chronicle, Aug. 4, 1999; see Daniels & Martin, *Between People's Ears*, *supra* note 62, at 472, n. 77, for full reference.

the American Tort Reform Association that we used at the beginning of this chapter: "ATRA's goal is not just to pass laws. We work to change the way people think about personal responsibility and civil litigation."

Tort reform advocates have been deeply engaged in trying to shape the image of the civil justice system that will govern policy for many years and in a variety of ways. Their message is a consistent one with two main themes. The first states the problem: an all-too-familiar vision of a system gone terribly and dangerously wrong. The vision's basic or unifying theme is a system run amok for which "we all pay the price"—an idea going back sixty years, at least. For instance, a full-page advertisement titled "Me? I'm Paying for Excessive Jury Awards?" appeared in the February 14, 1953, issue of the *Saturday Evening Post* (a mass-circulation magazine). It shows a woman standing at a grocery store checkout, about to take money out of her purse to pay for her purchase. The surprised look on the woman's face reflects the question in the ad's title, which is a reminder that the prices paid for goods and services depend on the decisions civil juries make. This ad was part of a series of ads that appeared in the *Saturday Evening Post* and *Life* magazine in 1953.[69]

Elizabeth Loftus refers to a public relations campaign that appeared in the mid-1970s: "One ad of the St. Paul Insurance Company begins, 'You really think it's the insurance company that's paying for all those large jury awards?' and goes on to answer that question, 'We all do.'"[70] The same theme appears again quite explicitly in a 1986 national public relations campaign by the Insurance Information Institute (a trade group) titled "We All Pay the Price: An Industry Effort to Reform Civil Justice." Its purpose—echoing Kingdon—is to present the industry's reform effort "to the broad general public. We must gain the widest possible awareness and support before we can expect political leaders to improve the legal system."[71] Built around the idea of the "Lawsuit Crisis," the campaign employs a series of eye-catching, dramatic graphics with titles including "The Lawsuit Crisis Is Bad for Babies," "The Lawsuit Crisis Is Penalizing School Sports," and "Even the Clergy Can't Escape the Lawsuit Crisis."[72]

---

69. *See supra* note 38 and accompanying text.

70. Elizabeth Loftus, *Insurance Advertising and Jury Awards*, 65 A.B.A. J. 69 (1979).

71. *We All Pay the Price: An Industry Effort to Reform Civil Justice*, Insurance Review, 1986, at 58.

72. *Id.* at 59.

The use of the theme continues. For instance, in April 2013, the organizational description on the website of Texans Against Lawsuit Abuse opens with the following: "Lawsuit abuse affects us all by reducing access to health care, driving up the cost of consumer goods, and limiting job creation. . . . When it comes to lawsuit abuse, we all pay—and we all lose."[73] ATRA's description of its mission provides an excellent summary of the preferred picture of the civil justice system: "These lawsuits are bad for business; they are also bad for society. They compromise access to affordable health care, punish consumers by raising the cost of goods and services, chill innovation, and undermine the notion of personal responsibility."[74] The key message, of course, is that tort reform is not about the self-interest of those advocating for change—it is about the public interest.

The second theme identifies the problem's causes, and plaintiffs' lawyers are at the top of that list. Again, we turn to ATRA's description of its mission: "Aggressive personal injury lawyers target certain professions, industries, and individual companies as profit centers. . . . The personal injury lawyers who benefit from the status quo use their fees to perpetuate the cycle of lawsuit abuse. They have reinvested millions of dollars into the political process and in more litigation that acts as a drag on our economy."[75] The quote from ATRA's president we used at the beginning of this chapter provides the concise combination of both themes: "There is clearly broad support for tort reform as a means to rein in greedy personal injury lawyers that are manipulating our legal system for personal financial gain at the expense of the average consumer."[76] ATRA is not alone in forcefully targeting plaintiffs' lawyers. The Manhattan Institute is particularly hostile to plaintiffs' lawyers—especially class action and mass tort lawyers. Manhattan, however, goes even farther in defining what "we all pay the price" means. It asserts that the political power and influence of the plaintiffs' bar is so great that it may even be a threat to the rule of law and to democracy itself. This idea is at the heart of Walter Olson's 2003 book written during his tenure at the institute: *The Rule of Lawyers: How the New Litigation Elite Threatens America's Rule of Law.*

---

73. Texans Against Lawsuit Abuse (TALA), *About TALA: Fighting Lawsuit Abuse Matters*, www.tala.com/about.

74. ATRA, *supra* note 4.

75. *Id.*

76. *Id.* at 7.

In many respects, it is a sequel to his 1991 book, *The Litigation Explosion: What Happened When America Unleashed the Lawsuit,* also written during his tenure at Manhattan. The plaintiffs' bar, and the contingency fee on which it is built, are identified as the problem in this book as well.

> Although contingency fee lawyers face many temptations to exploit their clients, the worst dangers of the fee do not rest primarily on that ground. ... The case against the contingency fee has always rested on the danger it poses not to the one who pays it but to the opponent and more widely to justice itself. As other nations recognize, it can yoke together lawyer and client in a perfectly harmonious and efficient assault on the general public.[77]

In his later book, Olson argues that the plaintiffs' bar has effectively become a fourth branch of government—bypassing the real branches of government and making broad-ranging policies through litigation. "The new rule of lawyers brings us many evils, but perhaps the greatest is the way it robs the American people of the right to find its own future and own destiny. . . . However uncertain the results of democracy . . . it is a better course than agreeing to turn over our rights of self-government to a new class of unaccountable lawyers."[78] The same anti-lawyer theme appears in Brickman's *Lawyer Barons*.[79]

The Politics of Ideas: Infrastructure

Successfully shaping the public mind and mobilizing it, as Haltom and McCann argue, requires not just the right message but leadership and funding as well.[80] As our discussion suggests, much has been invested in the effort to shape the public mind. Some of that investment comes from individual corporations in the form of their own public relations campaigns. Aetna Insurance, for example, conducted a major campaign in the mid-1980s called "Speaking Out

---

77. Walter Olson, *The Litigation Explosion: What Happened When America Unleashed the Lawsuit* (New York: St. Martin's Press, 1991), 44–45.

78. Olson, *supra* note 3, at 313–314.

79. Brickman, *supra* note 3.

80. Haltom & McCann, *supra* note 15, at 33–52.

for Civil Justice Reform." It involves an eight-part series of advertisements that appeared in a number of widely circulated national publications along with a direct mail campaign to various opinion leaders.[81] Some of the investment comes from trade groups like the multimillion-dollar campaign financed by the Insurance Information Institute.

Perhaps more important are the advocacy organizations specifically created to foster tort reform, prime among them being the American Tort Reform Association. Founded in 1986, ATRA describes itself as "a nonpartisan, nonprofit organization with affiliated coalitions in more than 40 states."[82] Haltom and McCann describe ATRA as a primary agent of tort reform and they provide an excellent overview:

> [ATRA] has coordinated more than three hundred corporate and trade groups and about forty state reform organizations. ATRA's conventional, "inside" politicking includes lobbying (e.g., assisting legislators with arguments, briefs, formulated legislation, credible witnesses, and speeches and speakers); strategizing (e.g., advising legislative and electoral leaders concerning tactics, phrasings, polls, and agenda items); coordinating (e.g., planning conferences, building coalitions, mobilizing corporate, trade, and interest groups); and facilitating (e.g., providing a clearinghouse for reform ideas and information for and among groups associated with tort reform or civil justice). . . .
>
> Crucial as such conventional politicking is, ATRA's most central role may be to formulate and reformulate "common sense" regarding torts in particular and civil justice in general. . . . Its mastery of the arts of perception and persuasion has augmented ATRA's success at conventional politicking by publicizing and popularizing tort reform messages.[83]

To change the way people think in the court of public opinion, ATRA has conducted an ongoing series of public relations campaigns on its own and in conjunction with other tort reform groups. Such campaigns can involve everything from roadside billboards to television and radio spots, from lobbying

81. *See* Stephen Daniels, *The Question of Jury Competence and the Politics of Tort Reform*, 52 Law & Contemp. Probs. 269 (1989).

82. ATRA, *About ATRA*, www.atra.org/about.

83. Haltom & McCann, *supra* note 15, at 43–44.

the media with press releases and other materials to direct mail to opinion leaders and individuals, and so on.

Especially important are the state-level coalitions and groups (some even more localized within a state) that ATRA has helped to create and fund—and often largely direct.[84] They provide a local presence for ATRA's message and foster the perception that their members' agenda is the result of grassroots interests and activity. According to ATRA, "One of ATRA's greatest assets is its network of tort reform advocates (state coalitions) that advance ATRA's agenda in state capitals. Their work is bolstered by an 'army' of more than 135,000 citizen supporters who have joined together in state and local grassroots groups. Together, the state coalitions and grassroots activists are an effective one-two punch in the fight for state tort reform."[85]

A number of these so-called CALAs (Citizens Against Lawsuit Abuse groups) were formed in Texas and elsewhere, starting in the 1990s, with ties to ATRA. According to ATRA critics Carl Deal and Joanne Doroshow, "Throughout the 1990s, CALAs have targeted public opinion and community leaders—and potential jurors—through expensive public relations campaigns that deliver carefully packaged messages over the airwaves, in newspapers, on billboards and in shopping malls and living rooms. As a result, CALA groups have helped make the supposed need for tort law changes a major political issue across the country."[86] Among these groups is Texans Against Lawsuit Abuse, which describes itself as "a non-profit, statewide grassroots coalition dedicated to educating the public about the cost and consequences of lawsuit abuse, challenging those who abuse our legal system, and returning common sense and fairness to our courts."[87]

---

84. *See* Carl Deal & Joanne Doroshow, *The CALA Files: The Secret Campaign by Big Tobacco and Other Major Industries to Take Away Your Rights* (New York: Center for Democracy and Justice, 2000), http://centerjd.org/content/cala-files-secret-campaign-big-tobacco-and-other-major-industries-take-away-your-rights.

85. ATRA, *supra* note 4.

86. Deal & Doroshow, *supra* note 84, at 6.

87. TALA, *supra* note 73.

*The Politics of Ideas: The Broader Conservative
Legal Movement*

The efforts of ATRA and the Manhattan Institute to shape the public mind point to a broader context for such activities and the infrastructure supporting them. It is evident in the title of political scientist Steven M. Teles's 2008 book, *The Rise of the Conservative Legal Movement: The Battle for Control of the Law.* Teles explains quite well that this legal movement is a consciously designed strategy in service of a broader conservative political movement, one favoring a more business-friendly, limited government that fosters a free enterprise ideology.[88] Teles's book does not address tort reform or plaintiffs' lawyers specifically—his interest is in tracing the intellectual and institutional development of the conservative legal movement, its core ideas as a part of that larger political movement, identifying the major actors, and analyzing their motivations and actions. Nonetheless, Teles's work reminds us that the more immediate interests our book explores take place in the context of much broader intellectual and political developments.

Although tort reform is not some wholly owned subsidiary of the conservative legal movement Teles describes, there have always been overlapping sets of actors and especially patrons—including groups like the Federalist Society; key individual players like Michael Horowitz or Professor George Priest; and patrons like the John M. Olin Foundation, the Sarah Scaife Foundation, the Smith-Richardson Foundation, and the Bradley Foundation—and a set of shared interests.[89] It is likely that those shared interests include curtailing tort litigation and would be consistent with Professor Brickman's view that tort reform would lessen access to the courts. They would probably also agree with his view of plaintiffs' lawyers.

88. Steven M. Teles, *The Rise of the Conservative Legal Movement: The Battle for Control of the Law* (Princeton, NJ: Princeton University Press, 2008).

89. These actors and patrons played key roles in Teles's story and also played key roles in the tort reform movement. Priest is well known; Horowitz worked on civil justice reform at the Manhattan Institute and the Hudson Institute and played a key role in the Reagan administration's Tort Policy Working Group; and the foundations noted provided important funding for the tort reform movement. *See* Stephen Daniels & Joanne Martin, *Civil Juries and the Politics of Reform* (Evanston, IL: Northwestern University Press, 1995), 252–256; Haltom & McCann, *supra* note 15, at 45–49.

A CONCLUDING ILLUSTRATION

Perhaps the best way to summarize our discussion in this chapter is showing what the targeting of plaintiffs' lawyers means in practice. The work of political strategist Frank Luntz in the late 1990s demonstrates quite dramatically how this negative view of plaintiffs' lawyers can be used in furtherance of tort reform and other political goals. In his 1997 how-to book for conservative Republican activists—*Language for the 21st Century*—Luntz includes a chapter titled "Legal Reform" (he used this term, he said, rather than "tort reform" because the public responds better to it).[90] In it he states, "When discussing changes to the legal system, Americans are more likely to believe business groups than trial lawyers by a healthy 2 to 1 margin. In fact, lawyers are about the least credible spokespeople when it comes to the legal system."[91]

This chapter in Luntz's book even includes a section labeled "The Villain." It opens with the following: "Unlike most complex issues, the problems in our civil justice system come with a ready made villain: the lawyer. Few classes of Americans are more reviled by the general public than attorneys, and you should tap into people's anger and frustration with practitioners of the law."[92] Luntz continues, "*It's almost impossible to go too far when it comes to demonizing lawyers. . . . Make the lawyer your villain by contrasting him with the 'little guy,' the innocent, hard-working American who he takes to the cleaners.* Describe the plight of the poor accident victim exploited by the ambulance-chasers and the charlatans—the individuals who live off the misfortunes of others" (emphasis in the original).[93]

Not content with merely demonizing plaintiffs' lawyers, Luntz advises the conservative activist to use humor and ridicule in attacking plaintiffs' lawyers: "Don't hesitate to resort to ridicule them to make your points. . . . Take a lesson from Rush Limbaugh and P. J. O'Rourke by making fun of the trial lawyers. . . . Make fun of them mercilessly. . . . They are truly one group in American society that you can attack with near impunity."[94] Of course, Luntz wants to do more than simply tap into what he thinks are pre-existing public attitudes.

90. Luntz, *supra* note 1, at 127.
91. *Id.*
92. *Id.* at 128.
93. *Id.*
94. *Id.* at 129.

He wants to reinforce and strengthen them. While it is one thing to have a generally negative view about all or some kinds of lawyers, it is another thing to mobilize people around those views—hence the need to demonize lawyers. In addition, by appealing to the popularity of someone like the radio personality Rush Limbaugh, Luntz wants to tell people it is all right to demonize lawyers—to almost dehumanize them. Such an appeal to opinion leaders like Limbaugh may also be an effort to shape the views of those who may not have an opinion on lawyers one way or the other.

Luntz's ideas on tort reform and attacking plaintiffs' lawyers were included almost verbatim on the GOPAC website in 1997 as an issue for Republican activists.[95] This time, however, they were under the heading "Tort Reform."[96] Not coincidentally, on December 11, 1997, *Roll Call* ran a story titled "Trial Lawyers New GOP 'Villain' for 1998 Elections."[97] In outlining how Luntz's strategy was likely to be used in the 1998 elections, the story quotes a GOP source as saying, "We'll unleash an attack on the trial lawyers never seen before."[98] The story also highlighted a tie-in to an aggressive US Chamber of Commerce plan for the 1998 elections that targeted lawyers. A Chamber source is quoted as saying that Tom Donohue, the Chamber's president, "wants to take on the trial lawyers. . . . It's a major initiative on our part to bring an end to the egregious behavior of the trial lawyers."[99] The chamber, of course, has been and continues to be a major player in the tort reform movement.[100]

Texas has not escaped the attention of tort reformers. There have been ongoing efforts and notable successes in changing the law on the books and in shaping the public mind. Chapter 2 provides a basic overview of tort reform in Texas and the politics surrounding it. It also begins the discussion of how tort

95. Founded in 1978, GOPAC describes itself as dedicated to "educating and electing a new generation of Republican leaders," www.gopac.org.

96. Copy on file with the authors.

97. Juliet Elperin & Jim Vande Hei, *Trial Lawyers New GOP "Villain" for 1998 Elections*, Roll Call, Dec. 11, 1997, at 1.

98. *Id.* at 2.

99. *Id.*

100. *See* US Chamber of Commerce, "Legal Reform," www.uschamber.com/legal reform; US Chamber of Commerce, US Chamber Institute for Legal Reform, www .instituteforlegalreform.com; and US Chamber of Commerce, National Chamber Litigation Center, www.uschamber.com/legal-reform.

reform is affecting plaintiffs' lawyers and ultimately access. In considering the next chapter, we ask readers to keep two things in mind: first, the idea of plaintiffs' lawyers as gatekeepers holding an important key to access, and second, the shared message of Professor Brickman's revealing views on the purpose of tort reform and the plight of our letter writer from the Preface.

2. "They Grabbed the Pendulum . . . and Nailed It to the Wall!"
Highlights of Tort Reform, Texas Style

THE PIT AND THE PENDULUM

"They grabbed the pendulum . . . they grabbed it and nailed it to the wall!" This is how one experienced East Texas plaintiffs' lawyer describes the legal environment in light of the 2003 tort reforms passed by the Texas Legislature. Most of his peers would agree. The pendulum metaphor has long been used by plaintiffs' lawyers and commentators to characterize shifts in tort law. The traditional idea is that tort law does not change in a neat, incremental, and linear fashion but rather changes as the result of swings from one side to the other—the plaintiffs' side versus the defendants' side, or the ideological left to the ideological right.

Whatever may have been the case in the past, the more recent trend belies the traditional metaphor. Plaintiffs' lawyers in Texas—and elsewhere—have seen a host of changes making it much harder for them to pursue their chosen specialty profitably. They have seen a Texas Legislature pass a series of increasingly stringent tort reform measures. They have watched a Texas Supreme Court change ideologically and shift to a far more conservative, defendant-oriented approach. In addition, they have experienced an ongoing, aggressive public relations campaign waged by tort reform interests that they believe has "poisoned" the jury pool—or at least shifted public attitudes, along with jury verdicts, in a more pro-defendant direction. These three factors are not independent of each other. They are fronts in a multifaceted and successful battle plan on the reformers' part that coincides neatly with the conservative Republican ascendancy in Texas.

It is probably not too strong a statement to say that the change in political dynamics is the key element in the reformers' success. It provides what political scientist John Kingdon says any policy entrepreneur needs to succeed—a window of opportunity.[1] Certainly plaintiffs' lawyers see it this way, but so do

---

1. John Kingdon, *Agendas, Alternatives, and Public Policies*, 2nd ed. (New York: HarperCollins, 1995), 165–195.

reform proponents. According to the Republican sponsors of some of the 1995 reforms in Texas, "a combination of factors, including the election of a Republican governor, a more conservative Texas Senate, and a more conservative approach to government nationwide, all contributed to an atmosphere that was conducive to the consideration of tort reform legislation."[2]

These developments have led some—like that East Texas lawyer quoted earlier—to conclude that the law will not swing back as the traditional metaphor predicts. One Texas commentator, writing in the late 1990s, reconsidered the pendulum metaphor and added an interesting and all-too-appropriate twist. Rather than the traditional notion of a simple pendulum moving back and forth in a somewhat balanced political space, Timothy Howell's reference point is Edgar Allan Poe's short story "The Pit and the Pendulum." Specifically, he focuses on the reaction of the story's main character—a prisoner sentenced to death by the Spanish Inquisition—as the character faced his doom. It is worth quoting Howell at length. The prisoner

> finds himself trapped in a dark, rat-infested dungeon that offers two apparently inescapable avenues to a horrible demise. Crawling to one side of the dungeon, the prisoner stumbles upon a seemingly bottomless pit awaiting his fatal misstep. Looking upward, the prisoner discerns the sweep of a large pendulum gaining in momentum and slowly descending toward him. . . . The prisoner's initial feelings of "wonder" [in watching the pendulum] turn to sheer horror, as he realizes that the pendulum is not only gaining in speed but is also "formed of a crescent of glittering steel, about a foot in length from horn to horn; the horns upward, and the under edge evidently as keen as that of a razor."[3]

Howell continues, "Much like the doomed prisoner in Poe's short story feared the pendulum as the harbinger of his impending death, tort plaintiffs and their attorneys today are watching with horror as conservative courts and leg-

---

2. Teel Bivins et al., *The 1995 Revisions to the DTPA: Altering the Landscape*, 27 Tex. Tech L. Rev. 1441, 1442 (1996).

3. Timothy D. Howell, *So Long "Sweetheart"*—State Farm Fire & Casualty Co. v. Gandy *Swings the Pendulum further to the Right as the Latest in a Line of Setbacks for Texas Plaintiffs*, 29 St. Mary's L J. 47, 48–49 (1997).

islatures propel the pendulum of tort reform perilously close to the livelihood of their claims and remedies."[4]

In this chapter, we look at each of those three fronts in the context of the Republican ascendancy that helped reform happen. As the chapter's subtitle notes, the idea is to highlight the key matters. The history of tort reform in Texas is a fascinating and politically significant story, and systematically telling it would take much more than a chapter or even two. In discussing the highlights, we will occasionally draw from the interviews we did in Texas and our surveys to show how some things may, or perhaps may not, affect plaintiffs' lawyers'—the gatekeepers'—practices. This discussion will help set the stage for later chapters.

THE SHIFTS IN THE FORMAL LAW: LEGISLATION

Pre-reform

All commentators agree that by the 1970s, the pendulum began shifting.[5] In summarizing the literature, Howell notes more specifically, "The metaphorical pendulum of tort law reached a leftward apex sometime during the 1970s to mid-1980s."[6] Before this, the law favored defendants more than plaintiffs. In 1973, the situation in Texas began to change as the Texas Legislature changed the negligence standard and replaced the traditional and long-standing contributory negligence idea with modified comparative negligence.[7] This change was especially important for two reasons. First, the new standard meant a very broad change, cutting across a wide variety of injury situations. Second, as a result, it allowed plaintiffs to win more often. The same case that was an automatic loss before the change became a win after. As a Fort Worth lawyer explained it in one of our interviews, "When I started practicing in 1970, contributory negligence was a complete bar to any recovery. I tried an intersection

4. *Id.* at 51–52.
5. *Id.* at n. 11 and n. 12.
6. *Id.* at 51.
7. For a summary of those initial changes, *see Special Project: Texas Tort Law in Transition,* 57 Tex. L. Rev. 381 (1979).

case in which my opponent's client ran a red light. He argued, well, it may have been 95 percent his guy's fault, but it was 5 percent the other guy's [the Fort Worth lawyer's client] fault. The jury put $10,000 of damage and found fault with both of them: we got nothing." With comparative negligence, the Fort Worth lawyer's client would win but would receive 95 percent of the award—5 percent deducted because of the plaintiff's fault.

The changes continued. As Howell summarizes it, "By the 1980s, a string of consumer-related legislation and rulings had created a favorable climate for Texas plaintiffs."[8] Among the changes Howell highlights are "the passage of the Texas Deceptive Trade Practices Act, the recognition of new and more expansive amounts of damages, the adoption of strict liability, the abrogation of contributory and similar defenses, the abolition of common-law immunities, and the expansion of common-law duties."[9] As the retired appellate judge whose remarks we discussed in Chapter 1 explained, some of these changes were the result of Texas Supreme Court decisions in cases brought by the more proficient members of the plaintiffs' bar. Of course, such changes offered greater opportunities for Texas plaintiffs' lawyers, and times were rather good for them compared to the past.

1987: Tort Reform

The timing of tort reform in Texas generally resembles the waves Thomas Burke saw that we noted in Chapter 1. The first reforms were modest, narrow in focus, and did not stop the plaintiff-oriented momentum. Dealing primarily with medical malpractice, they were passed in 1977. The most prominent part of the legislation was a cap on damages, a change especially favored by reformers eventually struck down by the Texas Supreme Court. This decision, in turn, was overruled by a 2003 voter-approved constitutional amendment as a part of a later wave of reform.[10] The 1987 measures mark the beginning of

8. Howell, *supra* note 3, at 52.

9. *Id.* at 53–55.

10. *Lucas v. United States*, 757 S.W. 2d 687 (Tex. 1988). The cap was struck down as a violation of Article 1, Section 13 of the Texas Constitution: "All courts shall be open, and every person for an injury done to him, in his lands, goods, person or reputation, shall have remedy by due course of law."

the swing back to the defense side because they reflect a changing landscape for tort reform. That changing landscape eventually provides the evidence for why Howell's choice of "The Pit and the Pendulum" is the more appropriate metaphor.

Perhaps most importantly, the 1987 legislation was a broad, omnibus reform package. A law review article coauthored by John Montford and Will Barber (the former, a pro-business Democrat, was one of the key legislative leaders for tort reform) characterizes it as "the most significant legislation ever enacted in Texas with respect to civil actions for personal injury, death, and property damage."[11] The package covers sixteen main areas, among them frivolous pleadings, venue, joint and several liability, punitive damages, vaccines and drugs, immunities or special rules for charities, public officials, and governmental functions.[12]

With the passage of the 1987 legislation, in the words of academic observers Joseph Sanders and Craig Joyce, "Texas thereby joined the great majority of states, which enacted tort reform legislation between 1985 and 1988."[13] The package itself, along with the politics surrounding it, illustrates the connection to a developing national and state Republican ascendancy. It also illustrates the related importance of the developing network of national and state tort reform advocacy organizations and the accompanying public relations campaigns that—among other things—demonized plaintiffs' lawyers.

Montford and Barber explicitly place the Texas legislation in the broader national context. In explaining the need for the measures passed in 1987, they rely prominently on the Reagan administration's position on tort reform as the solution to a problem defined as an "insurance crisis." They also note the key role played by the administration's Tort Policy Working Group and its 1986 report, saying the report's "analysis parallels—and markedly so—not only various findings and conclusions in the Majority Report of the Texas House/Senate Joint Committee on Liability Insurance and Tort Law and Procedure, but

11. John Montford & Will Barber, *1987 Texas Tort Reform: The Quest for a Fairer and More Predictable Texas Civil Justice System*, 25 Houston L. Rev. 59, 68 (1988). This article lays out the reasoning for the changes as well as outlining the legislative debate itself. Montford is also one of the coauthors for Bivins et al., *supra* note 2.

12. *Id.* at 66–67.

13. Joseph Sanders & Craig Joyce, *Off to the Races: The 1980s Tort Crisis and the Law Reform Process*, 27 Houston L. Rev. 207, 207 (1990).

also the multipurpose rationale and legislative history of the 1987 Texas Tort Reform Laws."[14] A key cause of the problem in Texas, the reformers argued, was an overly pro-plaintiff Texas Supreme Court and the lawyers who take advantage of the opportunities provided by the Court.

Montford and Barber give special mention to the Texas Civil Justice League, an increasingly influential tort reform organization with national ties. "The League was the prime mover of tort reform legislation. Its strong point continued to be an extraordinary grassroots organization." The Civil Justice League also engaged in a variety of "public education" efforts (and continues to do so; it can be followed on Facebook and Twitter).[15] Mention also goes to the Texas Trial Lawyers Association (TTLA)—the prime tort reform opponent (which can also be followed on Facebook and Twitter).[16] According to Montford and Barber, the tort reform advocates "had for the past several years been out-funded and out-lobbied by the Trial Lawyers."[17] Although they described TTLA as the "most powerful and best-financed lobbying arm at the capitol," the plaintiffs' bar could not stop tort reform. Whatever the strength of tort reform advocates and their associated organizations at the time, they quickly became dominant players.

A Democratic filibuster killed the reform package at the end of the regular legislative session. It passed in a special session called by Governor William Clements—a Republican—at the request of reform advocates. What passed was a compromise bill negotiated by teams that included members of both legislative chambers and representatives of interest groups on both the plaintiffs' and defendants' sides. The final package, Montford and Barber concede, was "not as much tort reform as the proponents sought; it is more than opponents wanted to see passed. Approximately half of the smorgasbord of tort reform recommendations . . . passed as modified versions of those proposals."[18]

The reform package passed in a matter of hours in the special session. The hasty, interest-group-driven, compromise nature of the complex piece of legislation was severely criticized by Sanders and Joyce (neither of whom were involved in the 1987 process). In their view, the package "represents a series of

14. Montford & Barber, *supra* note 11, at 62.
15. Texas Civil Justice League, http://tcjl.com/about/.
16. Texas Trial Lawyers Association, https://www.ttla.com.
17. Montford & Barber, *supra* note 11, at 83.
18. *Id.* at 65–66.

political compromises relatively uninformed by facts, that likely will produce unfortunate outcomes."[19] Bemoaning the bill as a "reform-by-crisis methodology," Sanders and Joyce argue for the creation of a permanent law revision commission to bring more rationality to the process. As the political fortunes of the interested parties changed, the need for political compromise disappeared. But as our discussion of the 2003 reforms will show, this did not mean a more rational process. In 2003, bald self-interest prevailed—a conclusion reached even by some who were originally reform supporters.

We know little of what effect the 1987 legislation had on plaintiffs' lawyers' practices. Our research did not begin until the middle 1990s, but our first round of interviews asked lawyers about tort reform generally and its effects on their own practices. One lawyer ended his involvement in cigarette litigation after a change in products liability law that ended pure comparative negligence and introduced a rule saying the plaintiff could be no more than 60 percent at fault. The lawyer said, "What killed cigarette litigation, and I did nothing else but cigarette litigation in 1986—in '87, the legislative session came in and tobacco companies and the tort reform groups passed legislation which did away with pure comparative in all products cases. And it brought it to . . . 60 percent. . . . The thought at that time was that it would be very difficult to have a jury put anything less than 70 percent fault on a deceased smoker." After 1987, this lawyer moved on to handling other kinds of complex personal injury suits, predominantly products liability.

With most lawyers, however, little was said about the 1987 package beyond acknowledging that it existed. It may be, as one lawyer's comments suggested, that by itself 1987 was not seen as a major problem—"We had a bit of tort reform then; not much passed." Still, not all were so sanguine. One lawyer—more prescient than most—told us that he and his then partners in a well-established plaintiffs' firm decided to dissolve their practice. Not so much because of the 1987 legislation itself, he said, but because of what they thought it was saying about the future. "We decided to do that . . . simply because there were a lot of uncertainties about tort reform. . . . There was more tort reform on the horizon." And, of course, he was right.

Instead of hearing a lot about the 1987 changes themselves, we heard much about declining settlement values caused by changes involving juries because

19. Sanders & Joyce, *supra* note 13, at 212.

of the tort reform public relations campaigns. As one lawyer put it, "Just all of the propaganda that the insurance industry and big business has put out about the need for tort reform—and how the public, the people that end up on juries, have bought the propaganda and how it has affected them on their jury verdicts." As we noted in Chapter 1, a number of major national public relations campaigns ramped up in the mid-1980s and into the early 1990s, as did the efforts of reform organizations like the Texas Civil Justice League and those emerging in the early to mid-1990s, like Texans for Lawsuit Reform (TLR) and the various Citizens Against Lawsuit Abuse chapters (CALAs) across the state.

We heard about the increasingly conservative bent of the state supreme court and "the election of certain insurance and big business minded jurists of the Texas Supreme Court. . . . Their attitude [insurance and big business] . . . if you want that kind of money, if you think you can get that kind of money from a jury in this case, go ahead and try your case; the 'high nine' will take it away from you." That change started in 1987, with Governor Clements's appointment of Thomas Philips as chief justice to fill a vacancy that can be traced to the aftereffects of the scandals surrounding substantial plaintiffs' lawyers' contributions to Texas Supreme Court elections in the 1980s and allegations of favoritism (as we will see later in the chapter, producing a window of opportunity fully exploited). Relatedly, we heard about the Republican ascendancy. One lawyer spoke for almost everyone in saying, "It's hard for me to separate out tort reform from what's been happening in Texas in the Republican shift. . . . There's so much hand in hand, absolutely."

1991: Workers' Compensation

Most importantly, we heard a great deal about a different piece of legislation in our interviews. The Texas Workers' Compensation Act was passed by the Texas Legislature in 1989 and took effect on January 1, 1991. All agree that this law had a profoundly negative effect on Texas plaintiffs' lawyers, their practices, and their clients.

Changes involving workers' compensation may be overlooked in discussions of tort reform. It is, after all, a system created to operate outside of tort law. Nonetheless, the "insurance crisis" idea driving tort reform in the 1980s encompassed workers' compensation, too, as rates paid by employers for workers' compensation insurance increased substantially, along with rates for liability insurance more generally. Changes in workers' compensation fit nicely into the broader notion of tort reform as a political movement, with many of the same players on both sides involved. Like formal tort reform legislation, calls for change in workers' compensation involve questions about the rules and processes governing certain kinds of activities; responsibility for the consequences of activity; and recompense for those consequences, as well as the role of lawyers in that process.

The changes in the Texas workers' compensation system were substantial. A law review article explaining them opened by saying, "Sweeping changes went into effect on January 1, 1991, in almost every area of the workers' compensation law." The changes ended the previous process, which allowed for a "pre-hearing-award-trial-de novo-system. . . . In its place stands a new administrative system of dispute resolution with limited court access."[20] Prior to those changes, workers' compensation cases were a major part of the dockets of Texas district courts, with over 10,000 filings a year in the late 1980s. Afterward, once the pre-1991 cases cleared the courts, workers' compensation cases virtually disappeared from the dockets, dropping to near 1,000 by the mid-1990s.

Among the changes were the rules affecting the representation of injured workers. While lawyers could still represent claimants, under the new rules the amount they could bill for their services was severely limited. There were specific time limits on the number of hours for which a lawyer could bill for certain activities, such as the number of hours for client conferences per month. All fees had to be approved by the Texas Workers' Compensation Commission (or the court if a matter got that far) and could not exceed 25 percent of the recovery. In addition, the way in which awards were to be calculated was changed, functionally lowering them in many situations. Finally, the lawyer's fee would come out of the claimant's check.[21]

Because of the unique place of workers' compensation matters in the world of plaintiffs' practice, the 1991 changes had a profoundly negative effect. To a large extent, as Chapter 3 will argue, the plaintiffs' bar in Texas was built on workers' compensation and other statutory schemes for handling work injuries that did away with many traditional defendant-oriented rules. Until

20. Tony Korioth, *Workers' Compensation Law*, 45 S.W. L.J. 697, 697 (1991).
21. *Id.* at 708–709.

the early 1990s, many plaintiffs' lawyers—especially the bread-and-butter lawyers with modest practices for whom the value of their typical case was below the median case value for all respondents in our two surveys—handled some amount of workers' compensation.[22] These were typically simple matters that could be handled inexpensively and relatively quickly. The fees generated paid overhead and generated a steady cash flow—and everything else was built on this foundation.

The limitations on fees all but ended workers' compensation as a profitable area of business, and few continued to handle such matters. In one lawyer's words, "I think everybody who did any sort of plaintiffs' work . . . was hurt. I've heard attorneys communicate that it's roughly at least, probably low end, 15 to 20 percent of their practice, and that part of their income just went bye-bye." He could have been talking about an Austin-area lawyer who said, "We lost, even though we had a small practice in comp . . . about $50,000 a year in comp off our balance sheet." More specifically, a Fort Worth lawyer described the impact on his practice:

> The big difference was that I had at any given time 25 to 35 workers' comp cases. That's the main difference between my practice now and before. I never had hundreds of workers' comp cases, but I'd have 25 or 35 of them. If you have that, several of those are going to be operated disc cases. After you work them up and get the doctor's evaluation, most of those will settle for around $35,000 or $40,000. You make 25 percent [the pre-1991 fee] on it. You pay your office overhead, and that funds the rest of your practice. That is the difference. I don't have that now.

He couldn't replace the lost business and closed his practice shortly after we interviewed him.

Workers' compensation cases were equally important because of their role in building a base of satisfied clients who would recommend the lawyer to friends, family, fellow church members, and so on. A lawyer in a firm that had about 50 percent of its caseload (and 30 percent of its fees) in workers' compensation explained:

---

22. We call those with a typical case value above the median "heavy hitters." More details can be found in Chapter 5's discussion of the plaintiffs' bar's structure.

We had 200 a year we were representing on workers' compensation cases. . . . We're very client-friendly. . . . The best advertisement for ourselves was a satisfied client going back to the union. . . . Just because someone was hurt, we represented them on a comp case, got them a settlement, shook their hand good-bye, and wished them Godspeed didn't mean they stopped being a client. When anyone in their family gets in a car wreck or whatever . . . they were zealots about it. They want you to go see *their* lawyer.

The loss of this source was especially important because client referrals are a significant source of new business, far more than advertising, and building a client-referral base can take years. Lawyers like this one and those quoted earlier lost twice: the loss of steady cash flow and the loss of a major source of future clients. Some never recovered.

There is an additional reason why the effects of the 1991 changes were so negative, and it deals with a second referral system—one moving cases among lawyers. This system benefits the bread-and-butter lawyers who refer cases to other lawyers for a fee. The referral fee for even one higher-value case that is successful could make the difference between a break-even year and a profitable one for such a lawyer. This system is especially important for heavy hitting lawyers handling complex matters, paid referrals being a primary source of business for many (see Chapter 6). The process also benefits clients by getting their case to the lawyers best equipped to handle them. Pre-1991, workers' compensation matters provided third party suits—especially products liability suits—that were referred for a fee to heavy hitters. Reducing the attractiveness of workers' compensation matters had a serious ripple effect on the plaintiffs' bar generally because of its impact on this process. In the words of one such heavy hitter, "It's all a food chain."

A lawyer whose very successful firm did primarily high-value personal injury cases and relied heavily on referrals from lawyers handling workers' compensation cases for third party suits explained the importance of the pre-1991 system for practices like his:

[They] pretty much destroyed the workers' comp system back in '91. Back before that, virtually every on-the-job accident in Texas was reviewed by a lawyer. . . . Looking at all these accidents and looking for third party suits, products liability, clients who were using dangerous equipment, negligence of other contractors, things of that sort . . . we took lawyers out of the system . . . you took the vast majority of industrial accidents off the plate for legal review. So I think that, in large part, destroyed the old referral system in Texas. And it cut the number of personal injury cases, especially products cases, we were seeing as lawyers who depended upon referrals.

With the demise of that old system—and the source of most of his business—this lawyer dissolved his partnership and reoriented his practice to handling commercial litigation on a contingency fee basis. In Chapter 1, we noted the argument of Marc Galanter and David Luban that certain kinds of legislative changes may drive the more proficient plaintiffs' lawyers to other areas of litigation. This lawyer's story is an example.

1995: Another Round of Reform

Following the national pattern, another round of broad tort reform came during the Texas Legislature's 1995 session. According to one summary, "Changes to both procedural and substantive law are evidenced in several major areas: medical malpractice, exemplary damages, joint and several liability, venue, and the Deceptive Trade Practices Act."[23]

One might notice that the 1995 legislation covered some of the same ground as the 1987 legislation. This reflects the unfinished and compromised nature of the 1987 package. As Montford and Barber concede, for political reasons the reformers were unable to achieve all they wanted in 1987. More could be achieved in 1995 because the political tides were shifting in a fundamental way. Tort reform was a key element, as a *Texas Monthly* editor noted, in "accelerat[ing the] trend towards Republicanism."[24] It was a major part of Karl Rove's strategy for George W. Bush's successful 1994 gubernatorial campaign, in which Bush defeated Democrat Ann Richards. Richards was strongly supported by the plaintiffs' bar. The 1994 election cycle also saw a substantial

---

23. Frank Branson, *Personal Torts*, 49 SMU L. Rev. 1221, 1241 (1996).
24. *See Frontline*, "Tort Reform in Texas: Rove's Genius at Work," www.pbs.org/wgbh /pages/frontline/shows/architect/texas/tort.html, posted Apr. 12, 2005.

growth in tort reform advocacy groups with national ties, like local CALAs and Texans for Lawsuit Reform. TLR would quickly become a major political force not just for tort reform but also for pro-business and conservatives' issues more generally.

Unlike the situation for the 1987 legislation, we do have some idea of how the 1995 changes affected plaintiffs' lawyers. Interestingly, those effects were quite varied, and those variations reflect the structure of the plaintiffs' bar. A few examples are worth examining here, with more details to come later. One change with a differential effect was the additional tightening of the rules for venue (where a case can be filed). High on the reformers' priority list, it affected the heavier-hitting lawyers handling complex, high-value cases more than the bread-and-butter lawyers. An experienced Houston attorney who had a substantial statewide practice of higher-value cases said,

> Where a case is filed is of critical importance. . . . That was changed [in 1995] in such a way that it's going to drastically affect my business. It takes me out of counties that I've practiced in now for 26 years, that I know the judges, I know the lawyers—and it's going to change that. . . . It's something that I think will affect, at least for a period of time, the value of our cases, and therefore will affect our income.

Still, his firm continued to be successful, though with a somewhat different mix of cases.

Our 2000 survey clearly showed the differential effect. The largest percentage of respondents—48 percent—said the change was having a negative effect on their practices. However, an almost equal percentage—44 percent—said the change was having no effect. As with the lawyer quoted above, the key factor here appears to be the geographic scope of a lawyer's practice. Generally speaking, the broader the scope of a lawyer's practice, the more complex and valuable the matters handled and the more likely that venue changes were seen as having a negative effect. Of those respondents describing their practices as local, meaning that most cases come from the county in which the practice's principal office is located or adjacent counties, 39 percent said the venue changes had a negative effect (14 percent strongly negative) and 57 percent indicated no effect. For those describing their practices as regional, meaning a substantial amount of business comes from one or more Texas counties not adjacent to the principal office site, 61 percent said the effect was negative (22 percent strongly), and 34 percent said there had been no effect. Finally, like the lawyer quoted above, for those describing their practices as statewide, meaning a substantial amount of business from all over Texas, 73 percent said the effect was negative (36 percent strongly), and 27 percent reported no effect. The relationship between scope of practice and effect of the negative venue changes is statistically significant.[25]

Another change—dealing with joint and several liability—appears to have had a more generally negative effect while still hitting some lawyers a bit harder.[26] The rule was changed so that a co-defendant was severally liable only if greater than 50 percent at fault. Sixty-nine percent of all respondents to our survey reported those changes as having a negative effect (31 percent strongly), while only 26 percent said no effect. For the bread-and-butter lawyers, 65 percent reported a negative effect (27 percent strongly), and 31 percent reported no effect. For the heavy hitters, 74 percent indicated a negative effect (35 percent strongly), and 20 percent said there had been no effect. The difference between the two groups of lawyers is statistically significant but small.[27]

In contrast, at least one of the 1995 changes may have had little or no effect at all on lawyers' practices. The sanctions included in the legislation to punish and deter frivolous litigation appear to have been almost beside the point, despite the constant refrain of reformers about the vast numbers of frivolous lawsuits. The vast majority of all respondents to our survey said those changes had no effect—82 percent.

Unlike the examples above, the medical malpractice changes were narrower, focusing on a particular kind of case. The package imposed stricter filing requirements for medical malpractice cases, including a $5,000 bond for each defendant named, along with new qualifications for experts. Interestingly, while we might expect the medical malpractice specialists to be the target, the comments of one heavy hitter point in the other direction—to bread-and-

---

25. Spearman's rho = .258, significance = .000.

26. Joint and several liability means: "When two or more parties are jointly and severally liable for a tortious act, each party is independently liable for the full extent of the injuries stemming from the tortious act. Thus, if a plaintiff wins a money judgment against the parties collectively, the plaintiff may collect the full value of the judgment from any one of them. That party may then seek contribution from the other wrong-doers." Legal Information Institute, Cornell University Law School, www.law .cornell.edu/wex/joint_and_several_liability.

27. Spearman's rho = .094, significance = .02.

butter lawyers as the ones most likely to face a negative effect. Familiar with the negotiations that produced the measure that passed, he said,

> They [reformers, especially doctors] were saying that we need to get the workers' comp lawyer out of the medical malpractice business. . . . We [the malpractice specialists in the plaintiffs' bar] assisted in writing that provision. . . . The reality is, the firms that specialize in this business, either they're successful or they go out of business. So the ones that have been longtime malpractice specialists don't mind the $5,000 per head [bond for each named defendant]. . . . I think it has kept the workers' comp lawyer out of the business.

At first glance, this might appear to be market protection as much as tort reform. Regardless, the malpractice changes did not have an obvious differential effect. The pattern for bread-and-butter lawyers was not significantly different than that for the heavy hitters—43 percent said they had experienced a negative effect (16 percent strongly), and 50 percent reported no effect. For the heavy hitters, the figures are 41 percent negative (13 percent strongly) and 53 percent no effect. Since most plaintiffs' lawyers handle little or no medical malpractice, the "no effect" responses are not surprising, but the consistent level of "negative effect" should have pleased the reformers.

The real importance of that lawyer's comments lies in what they say about the process. Even though the political tides were turning, the plaintiffs' bar and its Democratic allies were not dead quite yet. Negotiation among interested parties still played an important role. As Mimi Swartz wrote in *Texas Monthly*, "There were enough Democrats in high places that TLR didn't get everything it wanted. Lieutenant Governor Bob Bullock, who presided over the Senate, forced TLR and other tort reform groups to sit down with the trial lawyers and negotiate a compromise, which they did, near the end of the 1995 session."[28]

In the view of someone on the reformers' side with direct knowledge of the 1995 process, there was a "pretty high-level debate" among the interested parties. He told us, "It was a negotiated process among fairly knowledgeable negotiators. A bit different than essentially just taking the TLR stuff and saying, 'Well, we got 80 or 90 votes, and so it's gonna pass.'" These comments were

---

28. Mimi Swartz, *Hurt? Injured? Need a Lawyer? Too Bad!* Tex. Monthly, Nov. 2005, www.texasmonthly.com/content/hurt-injured-need-lawyer-too-bad.

made to contrast this source's knowledge of the 1995 process with what he saw in 2003.

2003: "Well, They Just Had the Power at That Point"

Political Context

Major changes came in 2003, and they started with the 2002 elections. Governor Perry easily won the election in his own right (as lieutenant governor, he had taken over when George W. Bush resigned after winning the 2000 presidential election). The 2002 elections also saw the Republicans gaining control of both chambers of the Texas Legislature for the first time since Reconstruction. Tort reform (and tort reform advocacy groups) played a prominent role in the 2002 elections and was at the top of the agenda for the 2003 legislative session. Governor Perry made medical malpractice reform a major policy goal for the session, and it was one of two emergency issues for his agenda, the other being insurance reform.

According to a *Texas Lawyer* overview of that agenda, a Perry spokesman said, "The governor believes med mal reform is the key to reducing skyrocketing insurance rates for medical doctors . . . [and] also says that frivolous litigation is the reason for the premium increases."[29] The overview also notes the politics involved, saying the governor's agenda "takes aim at the plaintiffs' lawyers—a group that will assuredly take plenty of hits from the Republican-controlled, tort reform minded Texas Legislature."[30] And plaintiffs' lawyers did take plenty of hits with the passage of another omnibus tort reform package with medical malpractice as a key component.

"Modestly titled 'An Act relating to reform of certain procedures and remedies in civil actions,' House Bill 4 (commonly called HB4) passed by the 78th Legislature in 2003 is among the most sweeping statutes the Legislature has ever enacted."[31] This is how Texas Supreme Court Justice Nathan Hecht, a Republican, described the legislation. He went on to say that HB4 affected a number of important parts of the Texas civil justice system, "including

29. *The 2003 Legislative Wish List*, Tex. Lawyer, Jan. 13, 2003, www.texaslawyer.com/id=900005379491.

30. *Id.*

31. Justice Nathan Hecht, *Foreword: Symposium on House Bill 4*, 46 S. Tex. L. Rev. 729, 729 (2005).

products liability, medical malpractice, class actions, multi-district litigation, multi-party litigation, venue, forum non conveniens, offers of settlement, pro-portionate responsibility, damage caps, pre- and post-judgment interest, jury charges, and interlocutory appeals. And this is but a partial list."[32] The key provision, however, and the most controversial one, was a $250,000 cap on noneconomic damages in malpractice cases.

What happened in 2003 was not just more of the same; it marked an im-portant turning point in the consolidation of Republican control. Even earlier supporters of tort reform—including some prominent Republicans—saw this and began to question what was being done under the symbolic umbrella of "reform." Most visible was the reformers' successful voter-approved constitu-tional amendment—known as Proposition 12—that allowed the aforemen-tioned cap to pass muster under the Texas Constitution. The Texas Supreme Court had struck down an earlier damage cap as a violation of the Texas Consti-tution's open courts guarantee as laid out in the Bill of Rights, Article 1, Section 13: "All courts shall be open, and every person for an injury done to him, in his lands, goods, person or reputation, shall have a remedy by due course of law."[33] That amendment specifically authorizes the legislature to impose limits on non-economic damages, "notwithstanding any other provision in this constitution."[34]

Perhaps the most important Republican opponent of the amendment was Deborah Hankinson, a former Texas Supreme Court justice originally ap-pointed to the Court by Governor George W. Bush. Although an earlier sup-porter of tort reform, she became a key fund-raiser (as well as treasurer) and spokesperson for the major opposition group, Save Texas Courts. Another for-mer Bush Texas Supreme Court appointee—Republican James A. Baker—also joined the opposition.

Hankinson was troubled by the process, saying that the tort reform package and the authorization for the amendment's special election "went through the Texas Legislature with very little comment." She found the date for the election especially troubling—"the first Saturday after Labor Day in September, which is a very unusual date to have an election." Because it was a special election, she noted, turnout was likely to be low compared to that for the already sched-uled November election, in which "there were going to be some significant

32. *Id.*
33. *Lucas v. United States,* 757 S.W. 2d 687 (Tex. 1988).
34. Texas Constitution, Article 13, Section 66(b).

local elections in places like Houston that would've very much affected voter turnout." In addition, the special election turnout would be affected because, as she pointed out, "you know, Texas is a very big football state, and Saturday afternoons are college football times."[35]

More important for Hankinson was the amendment's substance. Her concern was about access to the courts (the purpose of Article 1, section 13 of the Texas Constitution). The proposed amendment and the legislation it would allow "would be closing the doors to a great many citizens." In 2005, Hankinson told a journalist, "This amendment . . . wasn't designed to cut-off bad—that is frivolous—lawsuits; it was designed to cut-off lawsuits by people with legitimate claims by restricting access to the courthouse. . . . This tort reform went too far . . . I view this as something that deprives people of their constitutional rights."[36] Former Justice Baker agreed, arguing that the reformers had gone too far in allowing the legislature to limit damages. Such limits would undermine the rights the framers of the Texas Constitution provided to citizens to have their disputes fully heard by the courts.[37]

While HB4, Proposition 12, and medical malpractice dominated the discussion of the politics of tort reform in 2003, another former reform supporter—the lawyer quoted at the end of the previous section—pointed to a different measure passed in 2003 to illustrate his concerns. Unlike in 1995, he said there were no negotiations in 2003 among the relevant parties. He questioned the existence of the "problems" or "crises" used to justify the need for certain "reforms" passed in 2003, which he believed were anything but. He ruefully summarized 2003 in these words: "Well, they just had the power at that point." His illustration of what tort reform in Texas had become was the Texas Residential Construction Commission Act (HB730), also passed in 2003.[38]

---

35. For all quotations in this paragraph, see Katharine Hannaford, *The Fellows CLE Seminar—The Juice Isn't Worth the Squeeze: The Impact of Tort Reform on Plaintiffs' Lawyers and Access to Justice*, Researching L. 7 (Spring 2013).

36. Swartz, *supra* note 28.

37. *See* Mary Alice Robbins, *Big Names, Big Change*, Tex. Lawyer, July 7, 2003, www.law.com/jsp/tx/PubArticleTX.jsp?id=900005389832&Big_Names_Big_ Change.

38. Title 16. Texas Residential Construction Commission Act; *also see* Swartz, *supra* note 28, and Dave Mann, *Capitol Offense: The Agency That Bob Perry Built*, Tex. Observer, Feb. 4, 2005, www.texasobserver.org/1869-capitol-offense-the-agency-that-bob -perry-built.

In his view, HB730 was nothing more than the agenda of powerful interests who had the votes to ramrod a change through with no debate or real discussion. He said, "Nobody ever suggested we had a crisis among homebuilders . . . yet they stepped up and passed a bill to create a new commission which . . . basically just removed the common law right to sue over those kinds of things. . . . I mean, there's no crisis, it's just purely a power play to assist a particular group of business people. . . . It was just a law and a set of protections for an industry that needed no protection."

HB730: *Texas Residential Construction Commission Act*

HB730 created the now defunct Texas Residential Construction Commission (TRCC) to handle complaints against home builders and remodelers. In doing so, it removed those matters altogether from the courts and from coverage under the state's consumer protection and deceptive trade practices laws. This meant such matters would be handled quite differently. Unlike consumer protection laws, this legislation did not provide for the payment of attorney's fees or other fees if the consumer were successful. Nor did it, like those laws, provide for multiplying damages in successful cases. In addition, consumers could no longer file a lawsuit without going to the TRCC first, making the costs to the consumer even greater. Even if the consumer prevailed in appealing to the trial court, the costs expended at the TRCC were not automatically recoverable.

A San Antonio lawyer who handled home-buyer suits explained the consequences of this change: "When I can't recover fees, I can't advance fees for those people." He continued, "It's dramatically curtailed my practice. I will tell you . . . it's also hurt the consumer pretty badly." Most people simply cannot afford the costs involved. He used one of his recent cases as an illustration—a case involving a more affluent client. "The expenses in the case, it had $10,000 worth of deposition expense, it had $9,800 worth of expert expense, and another, I don't know, three grand or so of miscellaneous expense, and the average Bexar County individual cannot afford to dump 22 Gs into a case. . . . So it's really denying the lower socioeconomic folks access to their rights. They just—a lot of 'em just hafta take it."

The process for handling residential construction disputes also changed dramatically. As one lawyer familiar with the TRCC process noted, with some frustration, "It's fairly draconian." He elaborated, saying that "the plaintiff has to give the builder all of their expert reports, documents, or they can't use 'em in any subsequent legal proceeding. . . . The builder has to give the plaintiffs nothing." In addition, the TRCC (comprised of industry-friendly people) would have its own inspectors examine the property in advance of a hearing. In addition, said the lawyer, "if the inspector determines that you don't have a defect . . . then there's a presumption that there's no defect going in that you have to overcome."

In 2006, a formal review of the TRCC's impact on Texas homeowners and the Texas economy was requested by State Representative Todd Smith, the Republican chairman of the Texas House Committee on Appropriations and its Subcommittee on Government Efficiency and Operations. The Office of the Texas Comptroller of Public Accounts conducted the review. The elected comptroller was Republican Carole Keeton Strayhorn. Her review states, "After reviewing TRCC and its enabling statute, it is clear that the agency functions as a builder protection agency. It is doubtful TRCC will significantly impact the Texas economy. But the economic impact on the homeowner with a defective home can be devastating."[39]

HB730 is prime evidence for the argument that much of tort reform really isn't about reform in the sense of improving the public good. It reflects not just the importance of the Republican ascendancy in changing the Texas civil justice system but also the success of certain interests in taking advantage of that ascendancy to achieve even their narrowest, most obviously self-interested goals. Investigative reporter Mimi Swartz saw the 2003 changes as a one-sided rebalancing of the scales of justice. In her words, "The Texas Constitution plainly states, 'all courts shall be open' and that every injured person 'shall have remedy by due course of law.' But through the efforts of a small group of wealthy and politically influential businessmen and a legislature slavishly devoted to the organization they founded, Texans for Lawsuit Reform (TLR), those days are gone."[40] HB730 passed, she said, because "during the tort reform frenzy of 2003 that TLR helped stir up, the Legislature, after intense lobbying

---

39. Carole Keeton Strayhorn, letter to Rep. Todd Smith regarding the Texas Residential Construction Commission, Jan. 23, 2006, http://www.window.state.tx.us/trcc/trcc.pdf. Strayhorn challenged Governor Perry in the 2006 Republican primary and was soundly defeated.

40. Swartz, *supra* note 28.

and millions of dollars in contributions from homebuilder Bob Perry, created the Texas Residential Construction Commission (TRCC)."[41]

The TRCC closed on September 1, 2010, after failing to get the necessary reauthorization under the Texas Sunset Act. All laws creating an entity are subject to a mandatory sunset provision. TRCC's stated that it "is subject to Chapter 325, Government Code. Unless continued in existence as provided by that chapter, the commission is abolished and this title expires September 1, 2009."[42] In its review of the TRCC, the Texas Sunset Commission staff recommended that the TRCC not be reauthorized saying,

> The Texas Residential Construction Commission was never meant to be a true regulatory agency with a clear mission of protecting the public. It has elements of a regulatory agency in its registration of homebuilders, but this program is not designed to ensure that only qualified persons can enter the field—the way true regulatory agencies work—and so does not work to prevent problems from occurring. . . . Because homeowners must submit to this process before they may seek remedies in court, those who fail to satisfy its requirements either out of confusion or frustration lose their access to court. No other regulatory agency has a program with such a potentially devastating effect on consumers' ability to seek their own remedies.[43]

The TRCC itself was not prepared to accept the Sunset Commission staff's recommendation to close the TRCC, and it recommended that the Texas Legislature make changes and reauthorize the TRCC anyway. While the needed legislation passed the House during the 81st Legislative Session in 2009, it died in the Senate.

HB4 and Medical Malpractice
As we noted, HB4 included a host of changes. Most prominent are those dealing with medical malpractice, but there are others. The various changes

41. Swartz, *supra* note 28.

42. Property Code, Title 16. Texas Residential Construction Commission Act, § 401.006. Sunset Provision.

43. *Sunset Commission Final Report: Texas Residential Construction Commission,* July 2009, at 1 https://www.sunset.texas.gov/public/uploads/files/reports/Residential%20 Construction%20Commission%20Final%20Report%202009%2081st%20Leg.pdf.

had mixed effects on plaintiffs' lawyers, and even a few unexpected effects. Some of this appears to be the result of "Well, they just had the power at that point" and pushing favored reforms with little or no concern for practicality. The changes with regard to offer and settlement and fee shifting provide an excellent example. They were long a major priority for the tort reformers in Texas and elsewhere. In the words of one law review commentator, HB4 "provides for shifting of certain 'litigation costs' when an offer to settle is rejected and the ultimate judgment is less favorable to the offeree by a twenty percent or greater margin. The litigation expenses to be shifted and imposed on the party who 'unreasonably' rejected an offer (even though that party may win the case), include post-rejection costs, reasonable attorney's fees, and fees for two expert witnesses."[44] Just over one-half of the responding lawyers in our 2006 survey (56 percent), however, indicated that this provision had no effect on their practices. Although 39 percent said it was having a negative effect, only 14 percent said the effect was strongly negative. There was no significant difference between the bread-and-butter lawyers and the heavy hitters.

The less-than-overwhelmingly negative effect makes sense in light of the story we have been telling about the politics of 2003. The remarks of that disgruntled former reformer familiar with both the 1995 and 2003 processes with regard to the offer and settlement provision are again worth quoting. He said,

> Some of the leadership in TLR had always wanted to have it, and they just said, this has got to—we just have to have a deal where if the plaintiff loses a case, he has to pay the defendant's attorney fees, and that would really deter a lot of suits. . . . But you know, the plaintiff doesn't have any money most of the time . . . so they fiddled around with it and fiddled around with it and fiddled around with it and came up with some complicated plans . . . but it was so complicated and so dreamed up in the minds of guys who were not day-to-day practitioners that it's almost never been used.

He went on to say that when this provision has been used, it has worked "the exact opposite of what they were trying to put together." It has allowed the

44. Elaine Carlson, *The New Texas Offer-of-Settlement Practice: The Newest Step in the Tort Reform Dance*, 46 S. Tex. L. Rev. 733, 735 (2005).

plaintiff to recover attorney's fees from the defendant. More colorfully, he concluded with the following: "As they say down here, it winds up kicking harder than it shoots."

One key part of the 2003 package has had a very real effect on plaintiffs' lawyers' practices, especially the medical malpractice specialists—the $250,000 cap on noneconomic damages in health care cases. As we will see in Chapter 7's detailed analysis of the impact of the cap on lawyers' practices, plaintiffs' lawyers are handling fewer health care cases. The reason is financial—the cap makes it much harder to handle these cases profitably. As one medical malpractice specialist put it, because of the cap on noneconomic damages "there are many cases we cannot take that are legitimate cases, but they're not economically viable because you're going to spend more working up the case than you can hope to get under the caps, or the amount coming to the client would be so small that it doesn't make economic sense." His firm has significantly cut back on health care cases—"For a while there, it was probably 90 percent of our practice. . . . We'd rather be at 50 percent of our docket instead of the 90 percent."

The damage cap has an additional and unintended effect. It is not just that medical malpractice cases have become less attractive; it is that cases involving certain clients are almost toxic. Few lawyers will take them on, and these are the clients some commentators call the "hidden victims" of tort reform.[45] In the words of a major specialist, "They essentially closed the courthouse door to the negligence that would kill a child, a housewife, or an elderly person." The reason: "There are no medical expenses, no loss of earning capacity, and unless it's drop-dead negligence that you can prosecute with one or two experts, that's just not a case that I think in Texas right now is a viable case."

Post-2003

The Texas Legislature passed additional changes in 2005, but they are more narrowly focused. HB4 in 2003 contained "provisions that specifically and directly address the management of mass-tort litigation, such as the statute creating MDL [multidistrict litigation] procedures for mass tort cases and the

45. *See* Lucinda M. Finley, *The Hidden Victims of Tort Reform: Women, Children, and the Elderly*, 53 Emory L.J. 1263 (2004).

statute amending rules governing class actions."[46] Senate Bill 15, passed in 2005, addresses these matters again. In the estimation of lawyers from one of Texas' major toxic tort plaintiffs' firms, this legislation represents "an overhaul of the common law rules for resolving claims for injuries caused by exposure to asbestos or silica. Under the common law in Texas (and in most states), a person could recover for any injury or abnormality caused by asbestos or silica, regardless of its severity."[47] With the change, those "seeking compensation for an injury caused by asbestos or silica must file a report from a board certified physician attesting to the presence of the disease and its relationship to the substance in question."[48]

In addition, certain provisions in the 2005 reforms dealing with multiparty litigation and multidistrict litigation also apply to asbestos and silica cases filed before the passage of the 2003 legislation. Perhaps most importantly —and causing the most harm—for those plaintiffs' lawyers who handled such cases, "the new law prohibits consolidation of asbestos and silica cases personal injury cases for trial; the case must be tried individually 'unless all parties agree otherwise.'"[49] Though narrowly focused, journalistic accounts suggest that these changes have been quite devastating to the plaintiffs' firms that handled large numbers of such cases, and some actually have gone under.

Tort reform in Texas did not end in 2005, although it is the last round of reform relevant to our research. In 2011, for instance, the legislature passed another key measure, long wanted by the reformers, directing the Texas Supreme Court to issue new rules allowing defendants to move for early dismissal of frivolous cases that allow for "loser pays" (the losing party paying the successful party's costs) in such matters. In summary, by the 2000s, that pendulum to which plaintiffs' lawyers refer had clearly swung to the defendants' side. Or, as that East Texas lawyer more strongly characterized the swing, "They grabbed the pendulum . . . they grabbed it and nailed it to the wall."

46. Brent M. Rosenthal, Misty Farris & Amanda Tyler, *Toxic Torts and Mass Torts*, 59 SMU L. Rev. 1579, 1580 (2006).

47. *Id.* at 1580.

48. *Id.* at 1581.

49. *Id.* at 1582.

THE TEXAS SUPREME COURT

Politics and the Texas Supreme Court's Shift to the Right

The Texas Supreme Court was the site of the reformers' first truly important victories—even more important than their initial legislative victories. In the words of two academic observers of Texas judicial politics, "by 1983, justices who had significant backing from the plaintiffs' bar had gained a majority on the Texas Supreme Court. And, with the election of a pro-plaintiffs' court came the movement of Texas tort law in a plaintiffs' direction."[50] A plaintiffs' lawyer we interviewed in the late 1990s described that time, saying, "Back in the '80s you had [people] on the Supreme Court that were pro-consumer, pro-worker. . . . You had a passionate Supreme Court, you had some good laws."[51] By the early 1990s, the Court dramatically shifted back to a pro-defense orientation, where it has securely remained. By the end of the 1990s, all nine members of the Court were pro-reform Republicans. Another lawyer told us in the late 1990s, "Right now, we see the Texas Supreme Court is just loaded with people that hate our guts, and you can see that in the opinions. . . . Now the pendulum is stuck." A third assessed the situation by saying, "There is no way I would appeal anything to the Texas Supreme Court right now." Just as a more pro-plaintiff court can enhance access, a more pro-defense one can diminish it.

Those victories also played a crucial role in building the Republican ascendancy in the state. In the view of most observers, the key actor was Republican strategist Karl Rove. He was, the *Texas Monthly*'s S. C. Gywnne says, "the driving force behind one of the great tectonic political shifts in American history: the Republicanization of Texas."[52] It was Rove who saw the political advantages

50. Kyle Cheek & Anthony Champagne, *Judicial Politics in Texas: Partisanship, Money, and Politics in State Courts* (New York: Peter Lang International Academic Publishers, 2004), 40.

51. As the retired appellate judge's example in Chapter 1 dealing with products liability suggests, the Texas Supreme Court's shift toward a more pro-plaintiff position began before the 1980s. Also *see* Howell, *supra* note 3, at 48–56, discussing changes in tort law in Texas and elsewhere starting before the 1980s.

52. S. C. Gywnne, *Genius*, Tex. Monthly, Mar. 2003, www.texasmonthly.com/story /genius.

of using tort reform as a political issue in building the Republican Party. He coupled tort reform, the Court's then pro-plaintiff orientation, and the demonization of plaintiffs' lawyers to organize and mobilize a set of political interests and contributors not only to elect favored judicial candidates but also to build the foundation for the shift to Republican political control in Texas. As one plaintiffs' lawyer ruefully put it, "I don't think the Supreme Court did anything other than take us to the left edge of the mainstream, but they did it in a real arrogant, obnoxious way. The plaintiffs' lawyers were in the paper all the time. There was a whole lot of real grotesque sort of publicity. So we set ourselves up. . . . The Republican Party figured out that trial lawyers were an enemy [and] . . . we were such easy targets."

Rove's running of Thomas Phillips's successful campaign for Texas chief justice in 1988, was, in Gwynne's words, "a watershed."[53] It was the test of the political valence of tort reform and the demonization of plaintiffs' lawyers. Phillips won, and Rove successfully ran the campaigns of six other Republican Supreme Court candidates using a similar strategy through the 1990s. Building on the success in judicial races, tort reform was also one of the key issues in the Rove-designed campaign for George W. Bush's successful gubernatorial run in 1994 (and the issue came with Rove and Bush to Washington, DC, after Bush won the presidency).

Timing and context were everything for Rove's strategy. A window of opportunity was opened in the mid-1980s by a major scandal surrounding allegations of favoritism in light of financial contributions to several justices. One involved a prominent and flamboyant plaintiffs' lawyer, his equally flamboyant client, justices to whom they both made substantial campaign contributions, and actions within the Court by one justice that made the then chief justice so angry that one witness said the chief "tore [Justice X] a new asshole, he was so mad."[54]

The scope of the scandal unfolded as tort reform was beginning to gain steam in Texas and nationally. As we have seen, the mid-1980s was a time during which tort reform legislation was being enacted in Texas and many other states. It was also the time in which tort reform advocacy organizations were being organized and, as noted earlier, a time during which there were a series of major tort reform public relations campaigns. In addition, there was

53. *Id.* Also *see Frontline, supra* note 24.
54. Ken Case, *Blind Justice,* Tex. Monthly, May 1987, at 137, 195.

intensive media coverage of the "insurance crisis" and the alleged failings of the civil justice system in the mid-1980s.[55] Coverage even reached deep into East Texas, with an editorial in the *Tyler Morning Telegraph* (Texas) in early 1986 worrying about the "crisis" and the city's increasing insurance costs.[56]

The precipitating events that helped open that window of opportunity occurred in 1985 and involved Justice C. L. Ray and prominent plaintiffs' attorney Pat Maloney Sr., a major contributor to Ray's campaign coffers and to those of another member of the Court.[57] Maloney asked Ray to transfer two cases involving Maloney clients from one appellate court to another (the Supreme Court can transfer cases from one appellate court to another as needed and appropriate). The chief judge of one of the affected courts questioned the propriety of the transfers. His objections attracted local media attention and eventually led to legislative committee hearings in 1986. The hearings, in turn, brought to light additional questionable activities involving the Texas Supreme Court and some of its members. The most damaging again involved Maloney and Ray and Ray's efforts to convince his colleagues to reverse an appellate ruling. That ruling involved Maloney client Clint Manges who, like Maloney, made substantial contributions to Ray's campaign and that of another member of the Court.

After intense debate and some intrigue within the Court, that appellate decision was reversed (during breaks in the conference discussing the case, Ray would be on the telephone with outsiders, and some were concerned that information about the discussions was on the street). But it was reversed only after a surprise move by Justice Ted Z. Robertson. During the consideration of the case, Robertson, also a recipient of Maloney's and Manges's contributions, decided that he should recuse himself. Another justice had recused himself because he had been involved in a lawsuit against Manges. With the recusals, the vote to reverse was 4 to 3, but when Chief Justice Jack Pope noted that a vote of 5 was needed to reverse an appellate decision, Robertson quickly changed his mind about the recusal and voted in Manges's favor. The decision seemed so contrary to established law that a request for a rehearing was made—a request

---

55. *See* Stephen Daniels, *The Question of Jury Competence and the Politics of Tort Reform*, 52 L. & Contemp. Probs. 269, 277–292 (1989).

56. *Liability Problem: Solutions Needed*, Tyler Morning Telegraph, Jan. 25, 1986, at 1.

57. The summary that follows is based on Case, *supra* note 54. This story has become the source for most subsequent descriptions of the scandal.

that included the stipulation that three justices recuse themselves. The Court reversed itself and upheld the original appellate court decision, with only Justice Ray dissenting.

The scandal attracted substantial media attention in both the general and the legal press, with two prominent stories being the most important. The story of the scandal's unfolding and the activities involved was described in brutal detail in a lengthy investigative article—"Blind Justice"—in the widely read *Texas Monthly* magazine in May of 1987.[58] The scandal also attracted national attention that year with a 1987 CBS *60 Minutes* segment titled "Justice for Sale." While thinner on the specifics than "Blind Justice," it shone a dramatic light on the seamy politics of the Texas judicial system.

In the view of nearly all commentators, as well as a number of the lawyers we interviewed, this national attention is what made the scandal a window of opportunity. In investigative journalist Stephanie Mencimer's words, "The broadcast caused a national stir and proved to be the opening salvo in the 1988 state judicial elections, which marked the beginning of Rove's campaign to create a long-term Republican majority in the state."[59] Some plaintiffs' lawyers we interviewed emphasized Maloney's help in opening that window. Said one, "Pat, for whatever reason and we've never discussed it and I don't know the answer, was involved in all of the events that led to *60 Minutes* coming down and taking a hard look at the Texas Supreme Court." Another more pointedly explained the changed court, saying, "Mainly thanks to Mr. Maloney, who did some stupid things that resulted in us getting the Republican Supreme Court."

The chief justice during those events, Jack Pope, retired in 1985. His replacement—Democrat John Hill—resigned in 1987, in the scandal's aftermath, to start a campaign for merit selection of judges in Texas. Governor William Clements appointed Republican Thomas Phillips to replace Hill. Justice Robert Campbell (a Democrat) resigned early in 1988 to fight Hill's merit-selection efforts, and Clements appointed another Republican as Campbell's replacement. A third justice retired in early 1988, with a Republican appointed to replace him.

These three Clements appointees were the first Republicans ever to serve on the Texas Supreme Court. All three (including new Chief Justice Phillips) had

58. Case, *supra* note 54.
59. Stephanie Mencimer, *Blocking the Courthouse Door* (Free Press, 2011), 95.

to face the voters in 1988, along with three seats on the court already scheduled for the ballot that year. With six seats in play, the Court's future was on the line. Karl Rove, as noted above, was deeply involved in Phillips's campaign, and Phillips led what were called the Clean Slate candidates, "who were opposed to the incumbent Democrats who were backed by the trial lawyers."[60] The slate "could campaign against the plaintiff-backed candidates on the grounds they were reformers who wished to bring integrity back to the Court."[61] Phillips, in an interview after he left the Court, said that the 1988 elections were "absolutely a chance to shape the whole Texas Supreme Court."[62]

That reshaping did not literally happen with the 1988 elections, but, in the words of political scientists Kyle Cheek and Anthony Champagne, that election was "the beginning of the end of the pro-plaintiff court of the 1980s."[63] Republicans captured three seats in 1988 (including the chief justiceship), and the Democrats won three seats. One of those Democrats, however, was pro-business and pro-reform (Justice Raul Gonzalez, who was reelected). After 1990, there was a one-vote Democratic majority, but with Gonzalez's stance, the reformers now had a one-vote majority. Cheek and Champagne cite the 1994 election as the one that functionally solidified the reformers' victory. The plaintiffs' bar tried unsuccessfully to defeat Gonzalez in the Democratic primary. With Gonzalez's primary victory, his Republican challenger withdrew from the race. After the 1996 elections, the Republicans had a 6-3 majority, and after the 1998 elections, "all nine Texas Supreme Court justices were Republicans. Rove had run the winning campaigns of seven justices."[64]

By all accounts, the reshaping of the Texas Supreme Court has been quite successful. A lawyer interviewed in 1997 said, "The worst thing that's going on right now is what's going on in the court system and the rulings on the cases [by the Supreme Court]. That has had much more of an impact on our practice than what the legislature's doing." In a 1998 law review article, Philip Hardberger (a former plaintiffs' lawyer and at the time a Texas appellate judge) expresses the view of most plaintiffs' lawyers at the time with regard to the Texas Supreme Court and its swing from the left to the right. In his view, "by

60. Cheek & Champagne, *supra* note 50, at 42.
61. *Id.*
62. *Frontline, supra* note 24.
63. Cheek & Champagne, *supra* note 50, at 43.
64. Gywnne, *supra* note 52.

the end of the 1980s, the expansion of rights and remedies in the Texas court system reached its apex."[65] By the mid-1990s, in Hardberger's view, the change was complete with almost the entire Court being conservative. The results and retrenchment were predictable.

> Those interests that were aggrieved by the expansive Court of the 1980s are now in total control; the victory is complete. For example, in the 1997–98 term of the Court, defendants won sixty-nine percent of the time; the term before, 1996–97, defendants won about three-fourths of the time. But with certain defendants, the results are even more one-sided. Either in whole or in part, insurance companies won almost all of their substantive cases in 1996 and 1997; physicians, hospitals and pharmaceutical companies won all seven of their cases; governmental entities won six out of seven of their cases.[66]

The other side, of course, offers a different characterization, one emphasizing a return to an older, "better," or "fairer" regime.

The Texas Supreme Court remains very much a conservative court. Governor Perry consistently appointed conservative, pro-reform Republicans to any vacancies that occur, and the voters just as consistently elected conservative, pro-reform candidates.

The Shift to the Right and the Rules Governing Referrals

In addition to the obvious importance of the Texas Supreme Court's decisions, there is also the less-obvious—at least to the outside observer—importance of the Court's other powers in two areas. The first involves the power to promulgate the rules of civil procedure,[67] and the second involves the rules governing attorneys. The latter power is important because it sets the disciplinary rules that attorneys are required to follow or risk punishment and even disbarment.[68] Both of these powers came into play from the late 1990s into the early 2000s

---

65. Philip Hardberger, *Juries under Siege*, 30 St. Mary's L.J. 1, 1 (1998).
66. *Id.* at 5–7.
67. Tex. Gov't Code, sec. 22.004.
68. Tex. Gov't Code, sec 81.024.

with the Court's attempts to fundamentally change the rules governing referral fees among attorneys. A special target was the pure referral, or forwarding, fee, when a lawyer refers a case to another lawyer and receives a fee for doing so regardless of whether that referring lawyer did any work on the case or shared responsibility. Changing these rules is important for our purposes because referrals are a key source of business for plaintiffs' lawyers, especially the heavy hitter specialists handling products liability or medical malpractice. Any changes are also important because referrals benefit clients by getting their cases to the lawyers best able to handle them, thereby enhancing access.

Despite the Court's denials,[69] the story surrounding those changes—and the timing of those changes—easily lends itself to a political interpretation with plaintiffs' lawyers as a target. The Court's efforts with regard to the referral system coincide with the rise of tort reform in Texas, the changes in the larger political context, and the Court's own shift to the right. It is difficult to separate those efforts from this environment. Referral fees are a key target for tort reformers, as are the lawyers who benefit from them. Referral fees, for example, were on the TLR agenda for the 2003 legislative session: "Bring Texas into the mainstream of American jurisprudence with respect to the rules governing referral fees."[70] Chapter 6 will show that the referral system in Texas is dominated by tort cases, with plaintiffs' lawyers as the primary participants. These lawyers, in addition, are seen as formidable political enemies and significant funders of the Democratic Party and its candidates—including judicial candidates.

Referral fees, especially pure forwarding fees, have long been a controversial and contested issue in the legal profession. The American Bar Association's (ABA's) current Model Rules of Professional Conduct (adopted in 1983), which most states follow, prohibit pure referral fees.[71] Regardless, there has never

69. Supreme Court of Texas, *Proposed Rule 8a of the Texas Rules of Civil Procedure*, 67 Tex. Bar J. 116, 121 (2004).

70. Texans for Lawsuit Reform, "Our Agenda for the 2003 Texas Legislative Session," at 6, www.tortreform.com/files/314.pdf.

71. Rule 1.5 Fees: allows a division of fees for attorneys not in the same firm "either on the basis of the proportion of services they render or if each lawyer assumes responsibility for the representation as a whole. In addition, the client must agree to the arrangement, including the share that each lawyer is to receive, and the agreement must be confirmed in writing." ABA Model Rules of Professional Conduct, Rule 1.5 Fees, Comment 7, Division of Fees.

been a real consensus on the propriety of referral fees, and lawyers across the country—especially plaintiffs' lawyers—have long used paid referrals.[72]

Reflecting that lack of consensus—until 2005—Texas took a different approach than the ABA and allowed pure forwarding fees. Before being amended in 2005, Rule 1.04(f) of the Texas Disciplinary Rules of Professional Conduct specifically allowed pure referral, or forwarding, fees. Writing in the *Texas Lawyer* in 2002, Fort Worth plaintiffs' lawyer Chuck Noteboom said, "Unlike most states, the Texas Disciplinary Rules of Professional Conduct specifically permit 'forwarding fees' among attorneys. . . . Referral fees are quite common in personal-injury law and in other areas to a lesser extent. . . . The practice is generally widespread, with many attorneys earning a significant portion of their income either referring or receiving cases."[73]

In October 2003, the Court announced a proposal that would fundamentally change the rule governing referrals—Proposed Rule 8a.[74] The story, however, begins in 1997, when the Court "asked the Texas Disciplinary Rules of Professional Conduct Committee of the State Bar of Texas for advice on whether Rule 1.04(f) of the Texas Rules of Disciplinary Conduct should be more restrictive of referral fees."[75] The apparent impetus for this appears to be nothing other than the fact that the Texas rule governing referral fees had always been more permissive than the ABA's rules, something the Court and others saw as a problem.

In 1998, that committee reported back to the Court. As the Court noted, the committee did not recommend the abolition of referral fees but suggested that some regulation was worth considering. The report also noted the very real differences within the bar with regard to referral fees and that the issue

72. *See* Glenn Greenwood & Robert Frederickson, *Specialization in the Medical and Legal Professions* (Chicago: Callaghan and Co., 1964), 137–138; F. B. MacKinnon, *Contingent Fees for Legal Services: A Study of Professional Economics and Responsibilities* (Chicago: Aldine, 1964), 181, 203; Thomas Hall & Joel Levy, *Intra-Attorney Fee Sharing Arrangements*, 11 Valparaiso U. L. Rev. 1 (1976); Stephen Spurr, *Referral Practices among Lawyers: A Theoretical and Empirical Analysis*, 13 L. & Soc. Inquiry 87 (1988); Luis Garicano & Tano Santos, "Referrals," Nat'l Bureau of Econ. Research, Working Paper No. 8367 (2001).

73. Chuck Noteboom, *Forwarding Fees in Texas Are Here to Stay*, Tex. Lawyer, Sept. 23, 2002, www.texaslawyer.com/id=900005372891.

74. Supreme Court of Texas, *supra* note 69.

75. *Id.* at 120.

involves more than just the ethical matters that are within the committee's purview. The committee said that a broader debate was needed—one including those who would be most affected by any change. Later in 1998, the "Court referred this report to the Board of Directors of the State Bar of Texas, and no further action was taken."[76]

Finding no support from the State Bar, the Court created its own task force in 2001 to look at referral fees and other issues: the Supreme Court Task Force on Civil Litigation Improvements.[77] In a late-2003 statement explaining some of the background for its efforts to change the rules governing referrals, the Court offered no specific reason for the new task force except the continuing general concern over referrals and a March 1999 article in the *Texas Lawyer* magazine. The article was titled "Referrals Get Rough around the Edges: Referral Fees Are Big Business for the Highest Bidder, But What about the Client?"[78] The Court did note that some of the prominent lawyers quoted in the article were plaintiffs' lawyers and that one particular complaint involved aggressive advertising lawyers who—allegedly—do nothing but collect clients and then refer their cases for the fee.[79]

In March 2003, the task force made its report to the Court, which included a recommendation to add to the Rules of Civil Procedure a set of rules governing referral fees. At the time, the rules governing fees were a part of the Texas Disciplinary Rules of Professional Conduct. Changes to the latter come only after a referendum of the State Bar membership; changes to the former do not involve such a vote. The Court transmitted the task force report to the Supreme Court Advisory Committee for its study and comment (this committee "assists the Supreme Court in the continuing study, review, and development of rules of administration and procedure for Texas courts"[80]). After its review "the Advisory Committee reviewed the referral-fee proposal on Aug. 22, it voted overwhelmingly to reject the rule by a 21-to-2 vote."[81]

76. *Id.*

77. Supreme Court of Texas, Misc. Docket No. 01-9149, Aug. 24, 2001.

78. Nathan Koppel, *Referrals Get Rough around the Edges: Referral Fees Are Big Business for the Highest Bidder, But What about the Client?*, Tex. Lawyer, Mar. 29, 1999, at 1.

79. Supreme Court of Texas, *supra* note 69, at 120.

80. Supreme Court of Texas, Supreme Court Advisory Committee, Misc. Docket No. 11-9259, Dec. 28, 2011, at 1.

81. John Council, *Supreme Court Proposes Capping Referral Fees*, Tex. Lawyer, Oct. 20, 2003, www.texaslawyer.com/id=900005395251.

On October 9, 2003, the Supreme Court issued an order, subject to public comment, adopting the rule proposed by the task force as a part of the Texas Rules of Civil Procedure, effective at the beginning of the new year (Proposed Rule 8a). Among other things, the proposed rule would prohibit pure referral fees and cap the referral fee at $50,000 or 15 percent of the winning attorney's fee, whichever is less.[82] Placing the new rule in the Texas Rules of Civil Procedure elicited a pointed and somewhat unexpected dissent from two members of the Court. Writing for herself and Justice Michael Schneider, Justice Harriet O'Neill states, "If such a rule is to be promulgated, it should be as a Rule of Professional Conduct, in accordance with section 81.025 of the Government Code, not as a Rule of Civil Procedure. . . . I encourage members of the bar and the public to offer comments on the procedure by which the Court has adopted this, as well as on the rule's substance."[83]

Justice O'Neill's suggestion got an immediate reaction. According to Richard Hile, the chair of the soon-to-be-created State Bar Referral Fee Task Force, "the Court ultimately received over 208 writings regarding Rule 8a, the overwhelming majority opposing such rule. Immediately after the proposed rule was published, members of the bar, various sections and special interest groups within the bar, and the State Bar leadership requested that the Court allow the bar to appoint a task force to review the issue of referral fees."[84] This task force would investigate the issue of referrals, hold public hearings across the state on the issue, and prepare a final report on its findings, including any proposed rule changes. The Court acceded to this request, and the Referral Fee Task Force was created and began work in early 2004, with Hile as its chair.[85]

The Referral Fee Task Force did offer a set of recommendations, but they were very different. And, unlike the Court's original proposal, the Referral Fee Task Force's recommendations were offered as an amendment to the Texas Disciplinary Rules of Professional Conduct rather than the Rules for Civil Procedure. This meant a vote of the State Bar membership, again something not

82. *Id. See also* Supreme Court of Texas, *supra* note 69.

83. Supreme Court of Texas, Amendments to the Texas Rules of Civil Procedure, Misc. Docket No. 03-9160, Oct. 9, 2003, at 4.

84. Richard Hile, *Background Leading Up to the Current Referral Fee Rules, in* Richard Pena, *The New Referral Fee Landscape in Texas,* State Bar of Texas, 3rd Annual Advanced Workers' Compensation Course, Aug. 24–25, 2006, Austin, TX. Pena was a member of the State Bar of Texas Referral Fee Task Force.

85. *Id.* One of us—Daniels—testified before the task force.

required for changes to the Rules of Civil Procedure. The Court accepted the recommendation, and the referendum was held. It ended on November 14, 2004, and the task force's recommendations were approved to be effective on March 1, 2005.[86]

The 2005 changes put the Texas rules much more in line with ABA's Model Rule of Professional Conduct, especially by adopting a shared work or joint responsibility standard that mirrors the ABA's standards. It requires full disclosure to the client of all lawyers involved and their fees as well as the client's consent to those arrangements. The rule also states that a fee may be shared in proportion to the work of each lawyer in the case, or alternatively, a fee may be shared if all lawyers involved in the case assume joint responsibility for the services provided.[87] There were also changes (effective June 1, 2005) in the rules governing lawyer advertising to deal with the issue of brokering—lawyers advertising heavily for cases they would not themselves handle but simply refer to other lawyers for a fee.[88]

SHAPING THE PUBLIC MIND

Tort reform as a political movement has always had broader goals than just changing the law on the books. Reform interests have invested heavily in shaping the public mind and altering the cultural environment in which civil litigation takes place. These efforts can, in the view of plaintiffs' lawyers, have a substantial effect because they are insidious, far-reaching, and long-term. Texas, the plight of our letter writer suggests, has not escaped the efforts at shaping the public mind. The two themes at the heart of the message, which we outlined in Chapter 1—the all-too-familiar vision of a system gone terribly and dangerously wrong for which we all pay the price and greedy plaintiffs' lawyers as a primary cause—are quite evident. By way of a telling example, in 1954, the Texas Trial Lawyers Association president needed to make a presen-

86. Supreme Court of Texas, "Order Promulgating Amendments to Rule 1.04 of the Texas Disciplinary Rules of Professional Conduct," Misc. Docket No. 05-9013 (2005).

87. *Id. See also Approval of Referendum on Proposed Changes in the Texas Disciplinary Rules of Professional Conduct*, 67 Tex. Bar J. 838 (2004) and Hile, *supra* note 84.

88. Supreme Court of Texas, Order Promulgating Amendments to Part VII of the Texas Disciplinary Rules of Professional Conduct, Misc. Docket No. 05-9013-QA, Feb. 7, 2005; *see also* Hile, *supra* note 84.

tation to the Tyler Lions Club in order to rebut a presentation by an insurance company official about jury verdicts causing increased insurance rates.[89]

Tort reform advocacy groups have been active in Texas since the 1980s. For instance, the Texas Civil Justice League was created in 1986 during a crucial time of national organizing efforts by the insurance industry and reform interests.[90] As we noted earlier in this chapter, one of the legislative sponsors of tort reform in 1987 said, "the League was the prime mover of tort reform legislation. Its strong point continued to be an extraordinary grassroots organization."[91] With regard to shaping the public mind, one of this group's organizers said in 1986, "The League presently uses direct mail, meetings, seminars, phone banks, and public relations efforts to get its message out. Its objective is to mobilize as many people as possible around the state."[92] Other groups—at the state level and the local level—were also created from the late 1980s into the 1990s. Primary among them are Texans Against Lawsuit Abuse (1990) and Texans for Lawsuit Reform (1993). These groups put out a steady stream of newsletters, reports, letters to the editor, and the like.[93] They bill themselves as grassroots organizations. The former states, "We work with Citizens Against Lawsuit Abuse (CALA) groups throughout the state. Launched in Texas's Rio Grande Valley in 1990, the CALA movement has spread across the country. In the Lone Star State alone, more than 25,000 Texans support CALA chapters in East Texas, Houston, Central Texas, Corpus Christi, and the Rio Grande Valley."[94] The CALA movement has strong ties to the American Tort Reform Association.[95]

One particular tactic that drew substantial attention in the 1990s and il-

89. John Laird, *A Short History of the Texas Trial Lawyers: Sixth Installment*, Trial Lawyers Forum, Mar.–Apr. 1968, at 14.

90. The league was discussed prominently in *When You Need a Coalition: How-to-Do-It Examples from Tort Reform*, J. Am. Insurance 1–3 (1st Quarter, 1986).

91. Montford & Barber, *supra* note 11, at 82.

92. *Coalition, supra* note 90, at 2.

93. For examples of letters to the editor in the late 1990s, *see* Stephen Daniels & Joanne Martin, *The Impact That It Has Had Is between People's Ears: Tort Reform, Mass Culture, and Plaintiffs' Lawyers*, 50 DePaul L. Rev. 453, 471, n. 75 (2000).

94. Texans Against Lawsuit Abuse, www.tala.com/about/.

95. "Fact Sheet: 'Citizens Against Lawsuit Abuse' Groups," The Center for Justice and Democracy, http://centerjd.org/content/fact-sheet-citizens-against-lawsuit-abuse-groups.

lustrates the efforts of the tort reform groups in shaping the public mind—it involves billboard advertising. A 1996 *Texas Lawyer* article reported that one Fort Worth lawyer interviewed for the piece complained about a "billboard by the tort reform group Citizens Against Lawsuit Abuse. The sign recently went up on Airport Freeway, right where potential jurors who live north of the city will see it when they drive to the Tarrant County Courthouse." The article continued, "It's the same story across the state. Tort reform groups like CALA and Texans for Lawsuit Reform have been spreading their message about lawsuit abuse in print, on the airwaves and on the highways."[96] In one of our interviews we learned that a plaintiffs' lawyer (not the one interviewed for the story) had paid for a competing billboard along the same highway, and it was closer to the courthouse.

A law professor at St. Mary's School of Law in San Antonio wrote in 2000, "In some metropolitan areas, it is virtually impossible for potential jurors to reach the courthouse for jury duty without driving past one or more huge signs intended to sway their attitudes about lawsuits. . . . One billboard advertisement that was ubiquitous in major Texas cities during the 1990s read: 'Lawsuit Abuse: We All Pay, We All Lose!' [It was] sponsored by a defense-oriented group styling itself as Citizens Against Lawsuit Abuse."[97] In the way of anecdotal evidence, he goes on to talk about a civil case in San Antonio, saying fifty prospective jurors were asked whether they had seen highway billboards complaining about lawsuit abuse, and forty-nine of the fifty persons reported that they had. In a footnote, he mentioned that he was one of those forty-nine prospective jurors.[98]

More recently, an October 5, 2011, press release by Texans Against Lawsuit Abuse touts the annual and officially proclaimed (by Governor Rick Perry) "Lawsuit Abuse Awareness Week" in Texas. It says in part:

"Texas was once known as the courtroom to the country, where personal injury lawyers would flock and brag about the huge verdicts they could win here," said Jon Smiley with Texans Against Lawsuit Abuse (TALA). "As a result of lawsuit abuse, doctors shuttered their practices, small towns

---

96. Joseph Calve, *Poured Out*, Tex. Lawyer, Dec. 16, 1996, at 5.
97. Vincent Johnson, *Tort Law in America at the Beginning of the 21st Century*, 1 Renmin U. China L. Rev. 237, 242 (2000).
98. *Id.* at n. 3.

went without medical specialists, and small businesses lived in fear that a single lawsuit would shut them down." . . . "Personal injury lawyers are relentless in their efforts to invent new ways to sue and to undermine reforms that are working for Texas," Smiley said. "Lawsuit Abuse Awareness Week is a good reminder to maintain a watchful eye on those who would abuse the legal system for greed. Our work to stop lawsuit abuse never stops."[99]

One can now follow Texans Against Lawsuit Abuse on Facebook and Twitter and follow Texans for Lawsuit Reform on Facebook.

A business leader interviewed as part of a 1998 Texas Department of Insurance study made the connection between such efforts and juries: "I think a big part of it is the education of the jurors. You know, I spoke about the movement, Citizens Against Lawsuit Abuse, I think that was. . . . My feeling is that that has helped educate jurors to where they can associate big awards to the price of their car insurance."[100] A San Antonio lawyer we interviewed also makes the direct connection between the public relations campaigns and jury verdicts: "There's an organization called Texans Against Lawsuit Abuse, which has been very, very proactive in regard to attacking the tort system. They have done a very effective job in doing that. . . . Many jurors have just bought the propaganda right now, the climate is such, at least in this community, that jurors are not enamored with personal injury plaintiffs or personal injury lawyers. So, verdicts are low."

The tort reform groups remain active, and their efforts at lobbying the public mind are ongoing. Texans for Lawsuit Reform now reports over 93,000 Facebook followers as of late 2014.[101] As these comments highlight, the effort to shape the public mind has, in the view of most plaintiffs' lawyers in Texas, helped to create and foster an environment that is extremely hostile to plaintiffs' lawyers, to their clients, and to the cases they bring to court.

99. Texans Against Lawsuit Abuse, "Lawsuit Awareness Week: A Reminder of the Need for Vigilance," copy on file with the authors.

100. Quotation from Texas Department of Insurance, *Selected Quotations from Focus Group Sessions*, 55 (1998), cited in Daniels & Martin, *Between People's Ears*, supra note 93 at fn. 79.

101. Texans for Lawsuit Reform, www.tortreform.com/about.

CONCLUSION

Life has become much more challenging for plaintiffs' lawyers in Texas—and access to justice more problematic as a result. The Texas Legislature has passed a broad series of tort reform measures; the Texas Supreme Court has shifted dramatically to the right; and tort reform advocacy groups have maintained an ongoing, aggressive public relations campaign that has demonized them and—they believe—"poisoned" the jury pool. These three factors are not independent of each other. They are fronts in a multifaceted and successful battle plan on the reformers' part that is inexorably linked to the Republican ascendancy in Texas. Unfortunately for the plaintiffs' bar, the exploits of some members provided the opening for a window of opportunity for tort reform and the "Republicanization" of Texas.

While this chapter has dealt with the recent past, there is a deeper past about which we need some appreciation if we are to fully understand contemporary plaintiffs' practice and its challenges. Chapter 3—the first of three focusing on the Texas plaintiffs' bar itself—explores the development of plaintiffs' practice in Texas along with the development of a professional infrastructure that permitted the growth of a well-organized plaintiffs' bar based on its own view of professional identity. This, in turn, allowed plaintiffs' lawyers in Texas to become well organized, influential, and powerful political and legal actors capable of an important, and continuing, role in maintaining and expanding their market—and supporting other political efforts as well. Of course, expanding that market also enhances access, as the next chapter will show.

3. A Glimpse of the Past and the Development of the Texas Plaintiffs' Bar

Then–Arkansas Bar Association president Ashley Cockrill got at least one thing right in his 1919 *Yale Law Journal* article, "The Shyster Lawyer," quoted in Chapter 1: plaintiffs' lawyers have been with us for a long time.[1] They have been working in Texas and viewed despairingly for a long time, too. Franklin Jones Sr.—an early president of the Texas Trial Lawyers Association (TTLA) in the 1950s and member of a three-generation family plaintiffs' firm in Marshall, Texas, that existed for a century—said, in describing his father, Solomon's, practice at the turn of the twentieth century, "Attorneys [like his father] who represented claimants against employers and members of the public in the early days were not regarded as being at the top of the social scale—in fact, they were called 'ambulance chasers.'"[2] Like Cockrill, an early-twentieth-century editorial in the *Houston Chronicle* characterized such a lawyer as "the shyster lawyer, who is a troublemaker and everything which a good lawyer ought not to be."[3]

It is hard to know how many lawyers like Solomon Jones practiced plaintiffs' law in the early twentieth century. Most likely not that many, but there were enough that dealing with them and the lawsuits they brought was a major concern of railroad law firms like Baker & Botts in Houston (currently known as Baker Botts, LLP).[4] Franklin Sr. joined his father's firm in 1926 (Franklin Jr. joined the firm in 1953), and in a profile of him and the firm, Joseph Goulden recounted what people in Marshall, Texas, said about Franklin Sr.: "People joked about Jones: 'Know the best way to improve the value of an old worn-out cow? Cross it with the Texas & Pacific Eagle (the T & P's fast, main east-

1. Ashley Cockrill, *The Shyster Lawyer*, 21 Yale L.J. 383 (1919).

2. Franklin Jones Sr., "Biographical Notes on S. P. Jones (1868–1953)," in *The Public and Private Letters of Franklin Jones, Sr., 1954–1974: Volume I, The Itch of Opinion*, ed. Ann Adams (Oak Harbor, WA: Packrat Press, 1984), 218.

3. Kenneth Lipartito & Joseph Pratt, *Baker & Botts in the Development of Modern Houston* (Austin: University of Texas Press, 1991), 23.

4. *Id.* at 11–31.

west train) and then hire Franklin Jones to bring your lawsuit."[5] Reflecting their outsider status, lawyers like the Joneses were not likely to be found in the membership of the professional legal organizations in Texas. At the time, the Texas State Bar Association—a voluntary organization until 1939—was dominated by railroad and defense firms like Baker & Botts. Eventually, lawyers like the Joneses created their own professional organizations.

The rise of the organized plaintiffs' bar in Texas and elsewhere, with its own unique professional identity, is a post–World War II phenomenon. It is also the result of a set of dynamics going back at least to the beginning of the twentieth century. Two factors appear to have been particularly important. First is the emergence of new legal markets for plaintiffs' lawyers that opened because of changes in the law. These changes were, in turn, reactions to changes in the socioeconomic environment and the rise of the administrative state.[6] Second is the subsequent development of a professional infrastructure that permitted the growth of a skilled, well-organized plaintiffs' bar with its own view of professional identity. This eventually allowed plaintiffs' lawyers in Texas to move from being political and professional outsiders to being influential and powerful political and legal actors capable of an important, continuing role in maintaining and expanding their market—and supporting other political efforts as well. To fully understand contemporary plaintiffs' practice, and the targeting of plaintiffs' lawyers as part of the tort reform effort, we need to have some understanding of that set of dynamics. We need some context.

With no existing written history of the Texas plaintiffs' bar to which we can turn, we hope to provide at least some of that context. Our discussion is divided into two main sections. The first explores some of the key factors underlying the evolution of the plaintiffs' bar in Texas. Specifically, it looks at the limited market for plaintiffs' lawyers in the past and the legal and other changes that allowed that market to expand. Rather than doing so through an abstract examination of the relevant legal changes, we will look to concrete examples of the practices and firms of some key actors who were instrumental in the development of the Texas plaintiffs' bar in the first half of the twentieth century. This section concludes with a short discussion of the broader, often

---

5. Joseph Goulden, *The Million Dollar Lawyers: A Behind the Scenes Look at America's Big Money Attorneys and How They Operate* (New York: G. P. Putman, 1977), 67.

6. *See* Lawrence Friedman, *American Law in the 20th Century* (New Haven, CT: Yale University Press, 2002), 349–375.

hostile, environment in which those lawyers worked and the plaintiffs' bar developed.

The chapter's second main section looks at the origins and purposes of the plaintiffs' bar's own professional organizations. For Texas plaintiffs' lawyers, these organizations are the most important in their professional lives. Of the respondents to our surveys, 60 percent belong to the American Justice Association (formerly known as the Association of Trial Lawyers of America), 68 percent belong to the TTLA, and 61 percent belong to a local plaintiffs' lawyers' organization. Only 36 percent belong to the American Bar Association.[7] This section also includes a brief exploration of the early professional development and continuing education efforts that were an important part of the growth of the organized plaintiffs' bar. These efforts helped to provide the infrastructure. This discussion will focus on the programs and classes offered by Dr. Hubert Winston Smith. Now an obscure figure, he was on the faculty of the University of Texas School of Law and director of the school's Law-Science Institute from 1952 until 1965 and was a key player in the development of those professional organizations.

Throughout this chapter, we will also begin to see the unique professional identity that undergirds the development of the plaintiffs' bar in Texas. (Chapter 4 will examine the plaintiffs' bar's current sense of professional identity in detail.) As we noted in Chapter 1, access is dependent on there being lawyers willing and able to work in this practice area. It is and has been their sense of professional identity—and a related political ideology—that leads some lawyers to continue working in this practice area despite its challenges. The plaintiffs' specialists of the first half of the twentieth century who are the examples in this chapter were "believers" motivated as much by a political perspective as by a desire to make money in their practice of the law.

Most were among the political progressives in Texas—and yes, they existed. Otto Mullinax's description of the ethos of his firm—the Mullinax, Wells firm, which was one of the most successful and influential plaintiffs'/labor firms in Texas during the mid–twentieth century—provides an example. The firm justified its existence by adhering to the following three simple objectives, and the normative content is quite evident:

7. These figures are based on the combined results of our 2000 survey and our 2006 survey.

First, to earn a good living for its members and staff;

Second, to make that living representing unions and working people, if possible; and,

Third, to use those resources, produced above the need to serve the first two objectives, in advancing liberal political processes in government and society.[8]

During the 1930s, many plaintiffs' lawyers, like Mullinax, were strong supporters of the New Deal (and of lawyer-politicians such as Maury Maverick Sr., a member of Congress in the 1930s and later mayor of San Antonio). In the 1950s and 1960s many were supporters of Senator Ralph Yarborough, a progressive icon in Texas. More recently, they were likely to have been supporters of Governor Ann Richards.[9] The TTLA now maintains its own political action committee (PAC), which contributes hundreds of thousands of dollars to candidates in Texas, independent of the contributions made by individual lawyers.

Not all plaintiffs' lawyers necessarily shared such political leanings, and not all do today. For instance, Houston's Mark Lanier, a well-known mass tort lawyer, regularly contributes substantially to Republican candidates and groups.[10] Most plaintiffs' lawyers, however, do not. Our surveys of Texas plaintiffs' lawyers show them to be more left of center than right or in the middle—two-thirds reported that they are Democrats, and 48 percent see themselves as liberal, while only 14 percent identify themselves as conservative.[11] At the very least, in the past there was always a critical core that did share the believers' perspective. They were important in the years after World War II in founding the TTLA, and some were also among the earliest members and officers of what is now called the American Association for Justice. Throughout this

8. Otto Mullinax, *Introducing the Honorable Oscar Mauzy as the Newly Elected Member of the Texas Supreme Court*, unpublished, Jan. 3, 1987, at 1 (on file with the authors).

9. *See* Chandler Davidson, *Race and Class in Texas Politics* (Princeton, NJ: Princeton University Press, 1990), on populist, progressive, and liberal politics in Texas in the twentieth century.

10. *See* Texas Ethics Commission, *Political Committees Sorted by Contributions Received during Calendar Year 2010*; www.ethics.state.tx.us/php/cesearchSimple.html. This URL allows you to search by name and by a date range.

11. These figures are based on the combined results of our 2000 survey and our 2006 survey.

chapter, we will draw from the extant literature, archival materials, and interviews.

THE EVOLUTION OF THE TEXAS PLAINTIFFS' BAR

The Law and a Limited Market

While plaintiffs' lawyers existed in the distant past in Texas and elsewhere, it is likely that the numbers were quite small. We have been unable to find anything that gives us a sense of the size of the plaintiffs' bar in Texas in the first half of the twentieth century. There is some evidence regarding the total number of lawyers in the state. In 1900, there were just over 4,600, and by 1939 (when Texas went to an integrated bar—meaning all lawyers licensed in the state had to be members of the State Bar), the number was approximately 7,500.[12] Lawyers may have handled a small amount of injury work, but only as part of a more general practice.

Evidence adduced by legal historians elsewhere in the United States suggests that the size of the plaintiffs' bar was indeed small. For instance, in his study of late nineteenth-century trial courts in Boston, Robert Silverman notes, "defense lawyers usually had the advantage of facing plaintiff's attorneys who did not specialize in negligence cases. Contrary to common belief, only a handful of lawyers concentrated on the filing of accident suits at the turn of the century, and they represented no more than one-fourth of the plaintiffs."[13] More specifically, he found that in his sample only five firms or solo practitioners appeared more than once in the court records during the period covered by his study. In contrast, Silverman found that most accident cases involved a skilled, experienced defense specialist on the other side.[14]

12. Texas State Historical Association, *State Bar of Texas*, www.tshaonline.org/hand book/online/articles/jos02.

13. Robert Silverman, *Law and Urban Growth: Civil Litigation in the Boston Trial Courts, 1880–1990* (Princeton, NJ: Princeton University Press, 1981), 117.

14. *Id.* at 115–118. A 1961 study of the economics of personal injury litigation in New York City, which also relied on trial court records, paints a picture similar to Silverman's: identifiable defense specialists and few plaintiffs' specialists. *See* Marc Franklin, Robert Chanin & Irving Mark, *Accidents, Money, and the Law: A Study of the Economics of Personal Injury Litigation*, 61 Columbia L. Rev. 1, 11–13 (1961).

Even if there were few plaintiffs' specialists in Texas, it appears that, as in Boston, there were defense specialists from the early part of the twentieth century onward. Much of the business of the Houston firm Baker & Botts, for instance, involved handling defense work for its railroad clients as well as insurance companies like the Travelers Insurance Company. In their history of the firm, Kenneth Lipartito and Joseph Pratt show that in the first third of the twentieth century, "most of the [Baker & Botts] lawyers spent some portion of their time in trial work. The firm's work for the Southern Pacific had always included a large number of damage suits, which required the lawyers to hone their courtroom skills. Similar skills were utilized in much of the work for the local street railway company and especially in the services provided after the 1910s for numerous insurance companies."[15] The firm was among the most influential in Texas at the time.

The small size of the plaintiffs' bar in the past was not because of a lack of injuries but because tort law strongly favored defendants rather than plaintiffs—and this severely limited access. Lawrence Friedman notes that in the United States, "nineteenth century tort law was a law of limitation: a law that set boundaries on the liability of enterprise; a law that made it difficult (especially for workers) to collect for personal injury."[16] Rather than favoring injured parties, "tort law favored enterprise, growth, a booming economy."[17] The picture in Texas was similar well into the twentieth century. Although Texas introduced workers' compensation (functionally a no-fault system) in 1913, the tough, traditional common law defenses in tort cases—such as contributory negligence or assumption of risk—were not fully eliminated until the 1970s, as explained in Chapter 2.[18]

As one older lawyer we interviewed told us:

Go back to the situation that those of us who've been practicing for a while faced . . . and the plaintiffs' situation was worse than it is now. We were facing total immunity for charities. We were facing total governmental immunity. We were facing, here in Texas, the slightest negligence was total—a total loss. You know, we didn't have comparative

---

15. Lipartito & Pratt, *supra* note 3, at 112.
16. Friedman, *supra* note 6, at 349.
17. *Id.* at 372.
18. *See Special Project: Texas Tort Law in Transition,* 57 Tex. L. Rev. 381 (1979).

sharing of fault. I mean, any contributory neglect, the plaintiff lost. We had no product liability defect law. We only had to prove that—we could only prove negligence against a manufacturer, which was almost impossible to do. And so, there were a lot of things. And there was the guest statute. We had a guest statute. You were riding with somebody and they were negligent as the dickens, you lost. I mean, you were a guest, you couldn't sue. We had the interfamily immunity—all those things. And some others that I'm not naming.

The traditional, harsher rules would suggest a more limited market for plaintiffs' lawyers, one that could support only a small number of lawyers relying primarily on the contingency fee.

Because it applies to cases across the board, changing the negligence system from contributory negligence to some form of comparative negligence may be the single most important change for broadening access and the market for plaintiffs' lawyers.[19] This is especially so for the more frequently occurring modest cases that provide a key ingredient of the foundation on which the plaintiffs' bar is built—like auto accident cases. These cases are the "bread-and-butter" business for many contemporary plaintiffs' lawyers, and they provide a steady—if not always spectacular—flow of income and profits.

As noted in Chapter 2, the Texas Legislature replaced contributory negligence with modified comparative negligence in 1973. With modified comparative negligence, the plaintiff cannot recover if his or her fault is more than a certain percentage—usually 49 or 50 percent. If the plaintiff's degree of fault is less than the limit, then the plaintiff can recover with the recovery reduced by the percentage of fault. Data on auto accident cases from Dallas County, Texas, for the 1970s show an increase in win rate after the legislative change. Once the legislature made the change, the Texas Supreme Court began eliminating other common law defenses throughout the 1970s,[20] and win rates remained higher than in the early 1970s: 36.1 percent from 1971 to 1974, 44.6 percent from 1975 to 1978, and 47.4 percent from 1979 to 1982.[21]

19. *See* Friedman, *supra* note 6, at 360.

20. For a summary, *see Special Project, supra* note 18.

21. Raw data obtained from Dallas County Trial Report Service. *See* Stephen Daniels & Joanne Martin, *Civil Juries and the Politics of Reform* (Evanston, IL: Northwestern University Press, 1995), 66–68, 91.

What makes the changes in win rates important is what we know about the way most tort matters, especially automobile accident cases, are handled. Most auto matters are not resolved in court but are settled far short of trial. Jury verdicts for the few that do go to trial help to set the "going rates" used to settle the vast majority of matters, so it is reasonable to assume that the informal processes disposing of most matters changed in favor of plaintiffs.[22] This would expand the plaintiffs' market of potentially profitable cases and allow for more lawyers to participate.

Plaintiffs' Lawyers' Practices in the Past

What draws us to the erosion of the common law defenses—like the fellow servant rule, contributory negligence, and assumption of risk—are the practices of attorneys in Texas who successfully worked as plaintiffs' lawyers in the first half of the twentieth century. Many built their practices around state and federal statutes that covered injured workers. What these statutory programs shared was the elimination or relaxation of a number of the traditional common law defenses, especially contributory negligence; the existence of some kind of insurance plan to pay compensation to injured workers; and a paying role for the injured worker's attorney.[23] In an oral history, Otto Mullinax summarized the advantage of taking cases under the state workers' compensation law or federal laws covering railroad workers or seamen. In talking about the National Maritime Act, he said it was "loaded in favor of the seaman," and for all such programs for workers, he added, "being a contributor of negligence is no defense."[24] Eventually, these programs and the firms that took advantage of them laid the foundation for the contemporary plaintiffs' bar.

Worker injury cases brought under one kind of statutory scheme or another were the foundation of the Jones firm. Like many lawyers at the time,

22. *See* Herbert Kritzer, *Let's Make a Deal: Understanding the Negotiation Process in Ordinary Litigation* (Madison: University of Wisconsin Press, 1991), 64–66; and H. Laurence Ross, *Settled Out of Court: The Social Process of Insurance Claims Adjustment,* 2nd ed. (Chicago: Aldine, 1980).

23. Friedman, *supra* note 6, at 355–356, 360.

24. Otto Mullinax, oral history conducted by Professor George Green on June 28, 1985, 49–50. University of Texas at Arlington Oral History Project, Texas Labor Archive, Collection 9 (9-3-12), Division of Special Collections, University of Texas at Arlington.

Solomon Jones did not attend law school; rather, he read law while working as a teacher.[25] Solomon's grandson—Franklin Jones Jr.—characterized Solomon's practice at the beginning as a "360-degree" practice: "He handled land titles, lawsuits, he read abstracts, he did wills, he was just a general, what I call a 360-degree lawyer. He was practicing at the time that the Federal Employers Liability Act [FELA] was passed."[26] The passage in 1908 of FELA, which covered railroad workers, was particularly important for the firm's development during the first half of the twentieth century. While not a no-fault plan like state workers' compensation plans, it allowed railroad workers to sue their employers for negligence and collect damages under a comparative negligence system. It was the foundation that allowed the Jones firm to prosper until the firm's long life ended with the death of Franklin Jr. in 2008. It also allowed other long-lived plaintiffs' firms like Houston's Helm, Pletcher to prosper (Shirley M. Helm, the firm's founder, was licensed in 1929); FELA cases remained a mainstay for this firm until it dissolved in the early 2000s.

What made FELA important for the Jones firm was a key factor in the economy of their hometown—Marshall, Texas. Sometime after 1900, the town became "a division point for the Texas & Pacific Railway Company and the location of its main shops. . . . It was to be expected that some of them would be injured in their work and need the services of a lawyer. So many of these cases came into [Jones's] office over the years."[27] Solomon Jones was one of the first lawyers in Texas to become proficient in representing injured workers under FELA. Once Texas enacted a workers' compensation statute in 1913, the firm moved into that arena as well. According to Franklin Jones Sr., "As time went on, his [Solomon's] overpowering instinct to take the side of the underdog caused him to accept more and more claims for personal injury and wrongful death."[28]

When Franklin Sr. joined his father in 1926, he too specialized in railroad and workers' compensation cases. He always saw himself as a plaintiffs' lawyer. In a 1981 letter, he referred to his "almost fifty years of active practice as

25. There were only two law schools in the state when Jones read: Baylor and the University of Texas. Both his son and his grandson were graduates of the University of Texas School of Law.

26. Interview with Franklin Jones Jr. at Marshall, TX, Aug. 30, 1995; we also spoke briefly with Franklin Jones Sr.

27. *Id.*

28. Jones Sr., *supra* note 2, at 218.

a 'damage suit lawyer.'"[29] His sense of himself as a lawyer can also be seen in a 1985 letter that talked about his law school experience at the University of Texas: "When I was in Law School Dean [Leon] Green was teaching Torts and Civil Procedure. I did not do well in Torts, for I always thought that in every case submitted the plaintiff should have prevailed. In Civil Procedure I was even worse. . . . I advised him [Green] that when I could make only 35 in a course teaching Civil Procedure, there must be something terribly wrong with the statutes and judicial precedent that created it."[30] Franklin Sr. was not only a trial litigator but also an appellate lawyer who tried to reshape the law by attacking traditional common law defenses like the "no duty rule."[31] Even after he ended his litigation practice in the mid-1960s, Franklin Sr. continued to work on appellate briefs for the firm.

The Jones firm also handled non-worker cases against railroad defendants, involving human injury as well as injury to livestock, as Goulden noted. An oral history interview with another Texas plaintiffs' lawyer gives a sense of the firm's practice in the late 1930s. The attorney is J. E. Smith, and he told sociologist Chandler Davidson about the first trial on which he ever worked. In February 1937, Smith was a young lawyer, and his first job after law school was working for the Jones firm. He described that first trial:

> That was a [railroad] crossing case where a man and his wife . . . had one of his daughters injured in a crossing accident there [Center, TX]. And we represented them in that crossing accident. . . . And I went down there with Jones and helped him try the case. And he was the lead lawyer, but I did some of the work and got to argue to the jury. . . . We won, I think, about $30,000, which was big money in those days.[32]

29. Jones Sr., letter to DeButts Saunders, May 27, 1981, in *The Public and Private Letters of Franklin Jones, Sr., 1981–1984: Volume III, Firestarter Files*, ed. Ann Adams (Oak Harbor, WA: Packrat Press, 1985), 86.

30. Jones Sr., letter to Ann Adams, Apr. 1, 1985, *id.* at 22–23.

31. The editor of Franklin Sr.'s letters included a footnote to the letter cited in note 30 explaining the reference to the "no duty rule." It says, in part, "That is, the doctrine of *volenti non fit injuria* (He who is willing cannot be injured). . . . For many years the Texas Supreme Court used this doctrine to prevent injured workers from collecting damages against employers whose workplaces were unsafe." Adams, ed., *id.* at 23.

32. J. E. Smith oral history, 11, conducted by Chandler Davidson, Dec. 1990, at 11, Rare Books and Special Collections, Tarlton Law Library, University of Texas at Austin.

Smith also gave a summary of the Jones firm's business in the late 1930s. It was, he said, "mostly damage suit law, workman's insurance law, and title cases—a lot of land litigation because of oil fields in the area. A lot of tort law. We represented the men injured in accidents and so forth. . . . We had a lot of workmen's insurance cases in those days."[33] Needless to say, this was work done on the plaintiffs' side. Smith described himself and the Joneses as being among "those of us who represented people as distinguished from a corporate clientele."[34] Franklin Jr. estimated that about 50 percent of his father's practice during the middle third of the twentieth century was injury work.

In the mid-1960s, Franklin Jr. and his cousin Scott Baldwin took over the firm as Franklin Sr. began winding down his litigation practice. Workers' compensation and FELA matters were still the mainstay of the business, but the amount started to decline. Gradually, through the 1960s and 1970s, the firm moved to a specialization in other kinds of injury work. They found themselves doing more third party suits arising out of work injury matters. Some of these were premises liability cases (workers injured on someone's property), and once the rules for products liability began to change in Texas during the mid-1960s, the firm moved into that area as well. The firm was well positioned to move into both of these markets and take advantage of new opportunities once the rules began to change.

In 1986, Baldwin started his own firm with his son in Marshall, Texas, with an office located right across the street from the Jones office, doing much the same type of business that the Jones firm was doing. By the 2000s, both firms began doing a small amount of commercial trial work on a contingency fee basis—another new area of opportunity for experienced litigators.[35] Finally, it is important to note that Franklin Sr. was among the founders of TTLA.

33. *Id.* at 10.

34. J. E. Smith, "Law Practice Then and Now," 2, Box M121, Folder 9, Rare Books and Special Collections, Tarlton Law Library, University of Texas at Austin at 2. After leaving the Jones firm, Smith started his own plaintiffs' practice in Houston, again one with a heavy reliance on work injury cases.

35. For example, the website for Baldwin & Baldwin emphasizes its traditional focus on personal injury: "At the firm of Baldwin & Baldwin, L.L.P., we represent victims in wrongful death and serious personal injury cases." But that page on the website also includes: "Note: We handle IP cases in addition to PI cases." *See* Baldwin & Baldwin, LLP, *About Our Firm*, www.baldwinlaw.com/aboutourfirm.php.

Franklin Sr., Franklin Jr., Smith, and Baldwin all served on the TTLA board, and all but Smith also served as TTLA president.

While the Jones firm, because of its longtime focus on work injuries, had regular contact with the unions to which its clients belonged, it was not a labor firm. Other firms focused on worker injuries and also represented unions to fill out their business, in contrast to the more general practice of the early Jones firm. Otto Mullinax and his firm provide an example. Mullinax earned his law degree in 1937 from the University of Texas School of Law, where he was a controversial political activist (he was a founder of a pro–New Deal student group—the Progressive Young Democrats). During a Red Scare Texas experienced in the mid-1930s, Mullinax was subpoenaed as a witness to appear before a Texas House of Representatives committee investigating communism on the University of Texas campus.[36]

After trying to start a practice in his hometown in East Texas, Mullinax took a job with a labor law firm (on the union side, of course) in Houston—the firm of Mandell and Combs, one of the first labor firms in Texas. The firm represented the National Maritime Union throughout the South and all of the Congress of Industrial Organizations (CIO) unions in the South. The firm also handled a substantial number of work injury cases for the members of the unions it represented (it handled all of the injuries in the South for National Maritime Union members). Much of this work was in Galveston, where there was a government-run hospital for seamen. These cases, Mullinax said in an oral history interview, were especially lucrative: "Oh, I'm telling you, Workers' Compensation and ordinary negligence in this state at that time was penny-ante compared to the kind of things you could get by suing for a seaman against a ship."[37]

The Mandell and Combs firm split up at the beginning of World War II, in part for ideological reasons and in part for monetary reasons. According to Mullinax, two of the four partners took most of the firm's American Federation of Labor (AFL) work, and the other two took the CIO work. Mullinax's explanation for the breakup gives us some idea of what these lawyers were doing:

36. *See* Mullinax oral history, *supra* note 24, at 31–45.
37. *Id.* at 49–50.

Chances are, it's my guess, there was more litigation coming out of the
CIO side of it than there was on the AFL side of it. And [there] probably
were some differences because Arthur Mandell [one of the partners]
would have been much more of a New Dealer and much more of a liberal
than Arthur Combs [another partner]. And Arthur Combs was getting
off into the plaintiff practice a good deal. And so I don't know how, but
it's my guess that Arthur Combs was money-oriented in looking for those
good plaintiff cases. Chris Dixie [another of the partners, who went with
Combs] was labor-oriented, just labor, but no real political philosophy.
Mandell and Herman Wright [the last of the partners, who went with
Mandell] would be more ideologically oriented to the left and even into
the socialist area, at least, the Marxist area. These things finally divided
them.[38]

Leaving aside the political dynamics of Mullinax's story, what is important is
that all of the lawyers involved were handling a substantial number of injury
cases, especially those involving workers. Two of these four partners (Combs
and Wright) were among the founders of TTLA, and three (Combs, Wright,
and Mandell) served on TTLA's board and each served as its president. Combs,
to whom we will return, and Mandell were also officeholders in the national
plaintiffs' lawyers' organization in the early 1950s—the National Association of
Claimants' Compensation Attorneys (NACCA).[39]

In 1947, after serving in World War II, Mullinax moved to Dallas and
formed his own firm with Sam Barbaria and Nile Ball. They were soon joined
by Nat Wells. Originally, it was a labor firm that also handled worker injury
claims and some other plaintiffs' work. Mullinax himself was especially interested in the more general market for plaintiffs' work. In his words, "I wanted
to be a personal injury lawyer. I came to Dallas to be a personal injury lawyer,
not a labor lawyer."[40] Still, the firm's regular source of business was labor work,
and it had a distinct left-of-center political perspective, as the quotation from
Mullinax at the beginning of the chapter reflects. By 1948, the firm had major

38. *Id.* at 76–77.
39. The National Association of Claimants' Compensation Attorneys is now known
as the American Association for Justice and until 2006 was the Association of Trial
Lawyers of America (ATLA).
40. Mullinax oral history, *supra* note 24, at 101.

retainer agreements with the AFL and the Teamsters to represent locals across the state (the first AFL retainer was for $25,000).[41] In addition, Barbaria and Ball handled a substantial amount of workers' compensation,[42] and Mullinax also had some personal injury cases.[43] A 2000 article in the *Texas Lawyer* noting the passing that year of Mullinax, Wells, and Oscar Mauzy (another partner, political activist, and Texas Supreme Court justice) included the following: "Willie Chapman, communications director for the Texas Trial Lawyers Association and a former labor activist in Dallas, says Mullinax represented plaintiffs in numerous personal injury cases during the early days of the firm. 'He was doing that to pay the bills while Nat [Wells] was building the labor law firm,' Chapman says."[44] The article characterized the firm as one that "earned its reputation in labor and civil rights litigation and as a hotbed for liberal Democratic activism."

The firm went through a number of personnel and name changes (it was Mullinax, Wells, Baab & Cloutman when it dissolved in 1990), but from 1952 onward, Mullinax and Wells were the key players. Mullinax retired in 1982, and by then the firm was no longer a labor firm but a plaintiffs' firm that still handled some labor work. The change occurred gradually as a greater and greater amount of its business and revenue came from non-labor matters. Some of those matters, however, arose out of its labor work, such as third party suits and products liability cases (like the Jones firm, this firm was well positioned to take advantage of the opportunities created by the changes in the law dealing with products liability).

The two key cases, according to Mullinax, occurred in the early 1970s. One was an asbestos case with more than 100 clients in Tyler, Texas. The firm represented the Oil Workers Union, and the union's members were the injured workers. Mullinax, Wells handled the workers' compensation and third-party asbestos cases. The Tyler asbestos case earned the firm a $1.8 million fee. The other case was non-labor and involved a damage suit by a Dallas dentist who had been beaten by a policeman. This brought the firm a $500,000 fee. Accord-

41. *Id.* at 87.
42. *Id.* at 90.
43. *Id.* at 102.
44. Mary Alice Robbins, *End of an Era: The Legacy of a Texas Legal Triumvirate*, Tex. Lawyer, Nov. 20, 2000, reproduced on the website of the Law Offices of Baab & Denison, LLP, in Dallas, TX, http://baabdenison.com/article.html.

ing to Mullinax, it was only during his last ten years in practice that the firm was not a labor law firm (from the 1970s onward).[45]

A lawyer we interviewed who worked for Arthur Combs and knew him well provided additional insight into Combs and his practice after the break-up Mullinax described. Combs, this lawyer said, had "a very clear conception of the world. You had good guys and bad guys, you know. Some people wore gray hats, but most people wore white hats or black hats. He was a self-avowed bleeding-heart liberal." In the late 1920s, Combs started his relationship with organized labor in Texas:

> Arthur joined the Lawyers Guild, was accused of being a communist. Had disbarment petitions filed against him. Was beaten up two or three times. Had a cross burned in his front yard. I mean, went through some shit, okay? I don't think he was a quote, communist, unquote if that means you are a member of the party. But he was probably, at that time in his life . . . he probably had leanings in that direction. . . . The labor unions actually developed a very successful practice for him.

One might wonder if the lawyer's comments about the treatment Combs received because of his clientele—being beaten up and having a cross burned in his yard—should be taken seriously. There is no way to verify such stories. Still, there are similar reports involving other lawyers in Texas who faced physical danger because of the clients they represented. In his biography of his left-leaning lawyer father, the late Judge George Edwards Jr. tells the story of his father's kidnapping in 1931 in Dallas, apparently by the Ku Klux Klan. Edwards Sr. was kidnapped because he was representing two radical speakers arrested by the Dallas police. Edwards Sr. was a volunteer American Civil Liberties Union attorney at the time.[46] Edwards Jr. said, "Dad's practice was a trial practice. He was a poor man's advocate—by choice [and among his clients were] persons injured in accidents that they believed were the result of somebody else's negligence. In the Depression years, which I remember best, the anteroom frequently looked like the waiting room of a big-city hospital

---

45. Mullinax oral history, *supra* note 24, at 102.

46. *See* George Edwards Jr., *Pioneer-at-Law* (New York: W. W. Norton, 1974), 107–121.

clinic."[47] Edwards Sr. never achieved the kind of success the Joneses, Mullinax, or Combs did, but he apparently shared their professional identity and view of the world.

Returning to Combs: a key part of his success, the lawyer who worked for him noted, were the personal injury cases and other business that came from union members. The "specialty was labor law and personal injury, and labor law obviously made all the rain for the personal injury practice." It was the labor work that drew the other cases to Combs, and those other cases would come to the firm only if the union member was treated right. Combs consciously courted this business through the way in which he treated his clients, hoping that they would recommend him to others. His approach was summarized as follows (in terms, the lawyer said, Combs himself would use):

> Look, if you come to work every morning and you start looking at these files and thinking of them as people, and you decide, I'm going to do every goddamn thing I can for this guy. Maybe it's a broken foot, but he turned his broken foot over to you. I'm going to do every goddamn thing I can for him, everything. Any problem, I'm going to resolve in his favor. If he's a shithead, I'm going to understand. Because you get to be a shithead, it's not against the law. And we're not seeing him under the best circumstances. He's got five kids at home, he's scared or whatever. If you do every damn thing you can for your client, it's impossible to practice law and not make a damn good living.

Regardless of Combs's political views, he did believe in providing the best service he could to his clients—his livelihood and future client referrals depended on it.

Even later in his career, Combs continued taking on young lawyers, like the one quoted above, and training them as plaintiffs' lawyers. A number passed through his firm over the years. The same was true for the Mullinax, Wells firm. Well into the 1970s, it was one of the prime training grounds for young plaintiffs' lawyers. Perhaps the best known of the plaintiffs' lawyers who started their careers at the Mullinax, Wells firm is the late Fred Baron. Other lawyers and firms also played this role. As the experience of J. E. Smith with the Jones

47. *Id.* at 85–86.

firm in the 1930s shows, this kind of apprenticeship has a long history. It not only provided hands-on training for new lawyers, it also socialized them into a very particular professional identity and in doing so helped build the foundation of the plaintiffs' bar in Texas.

The lawyers discussed so far worked for much of their careers within a system in which the traditional common law defenses, especially contributory negligence, applied to all cases not covered by a specific statutory/insurance scheme like workers' compensation. It was a narrow market, but, as noted in Chapter 2, the picture began to change in the early 1970s. As one Houston plaintiffs' lawyer put it in an interview, "There starts a more liberal, whatever you call it movement" in favor of plaintiffs and more opportunity for plaintiffs' lawyers.

The immediate impact of such changes in market opportunities can be seen in the remarks of a San Antonio lawyer. He told us how changes dealing with deceptive trade practices (consumer fraud) in the 1970s helped him to establish his practice:

> Not long before I got licensed, they [the state legislature] passed the Deceptive Trade Practices Act [DTPA]. . . . In the late '70s the Supreme Court decided that the trebling provision [trebling the damages in these cases] was automatic. What that meant was that you could take as a young lawyer, you could take a small deceptive trade practice case, small in terms of actual damages, and you'd get three times whatever the jury gave you [the jury was not told of the trebling] . . . and attorney fees. So I tried the shit out of those DTPA cases when I was a young lawyer.

Although numbers are not available, lawyers we interviewed in the late 1990s argued that the size of the plaintiffs' bar began to increase after the middle to late 1970s as changes in the law helped broaden the market for plaintiffs' lawyers. They also pointed to the 1977 US Supreme Court decision *Bates v. State Bar of Arizona*,[48] in which the Court ruled that lawyer advertising was constitutionally protected and could not be barred.

The two factors—changes that relaxed or eliminated traditional defenses and those allowing advertising—proved to be a potent combination. For in-

---

48. 433 U.S. 350 (1977).

stance, one lawyer described the situation in Austin as follows: "Well, there's a lot more of us. When I started in '76, this was a very small community. At that time I estimated there were twenty of us in town that did it [plaintiffs' work] exclusively, forty that did it regularly. . . . Now, like I said, there's probably 200 to 250 doing it more or less exclusively and probably another hundred doing it occasionally. . . . There's a lot more specialization."

Legal changes provided the potential for entrants into the market, and the relaxed rules on advertising provided a potential way to attract clients quickly for the lawyer without an established practice in this arena.

Another Factor in an Already Hostile Working Environment

Plaintiffs' lawyers in Texas faced other challenges in the first half of the twentieth century in addition to the limitations produced by the law. The environment in which these lawyers worked could be quite hostile, as the earlier examples of Alfred Combs and George Edwards Sr. show. Not all of the hostility was as blunt as that Combs and Edwards faced, but it existed nonetheless and provides additional context for the contemporary situation and access. This context is best seen by looking at the opposition plaintiffs' lawyers faced in the legal arena—opposition that was specialized, organized, and well financed. It also helps explain why forming their own professional organizations was so important for the development of the plaintiffs' bar.

As we noted earlier, defense litigation in injury cases was already an area of specialized practice, with a few firms, like Baker & Botts, handling large numbers of cases for railroads, streetcar companies, and others. Specialized defense lawyers were working not just in the larger cities but also in the smaller ones as part of a sophisticated strategy. For instance, in his correspondence, Franklin Jones Sr. talked about a lawyer named Quince Mehaffey: "By the time I entered the practice [1926], he was general counsel for railroads in Texarkana [in the northeast corner of Texas], but had been a 'plaintiffs' lawyer' in his youth."[49]

Lawyers like Mehaffey worked as part of a large organization. The work Baker & Botts did for its main railroad client, the Southern Pacific (SP), pro-

49. Jones Sr., *supra* note 29, at 86.

vides an excellent illustration of how specialized and well organized the defense side could be in the early part of the twentieth century. As Lipartito and Platt describe it in their history of the firm, Baker & Botts (and other firms working for other major railroads) worked as part of a four-tiered pyramid. At the top were the corporate decision makers in the railroad's headquarters who set legal policy. Baker & Botts was the second tier, with responsibility for implementing those policies in Texas. "A major part of this work involved organizing and managing the activities taking place on the two lower tiers, the division and the local attorneys throughout the state."[50]

The division attorneys were in well-established firms in the larger towns, with the firms "having strong reputations for railroad work in their area."[51] They handled much of the railroad's more important legal work in their area or division, including the larger tort cases (Mehaffey would probably fit in here). At the bottom of the pyramid were the numerous local attorneys in the smaller towns along the railroad's line. They "took care of the innumerable claims and damages suits that arose in the normal course of railroad operations."[52] These were typically younger attorneys just starting out, the kind of attorney who otherwise would be looking for contingency fee cases against the railroad. Little discretion was left to either the division or local attorneys in the handling of the railroad's business. For instance, there were policies on when and what kinds of cases were to be settled or tried and the range for settlements.[53]

Local attorneys had other responsibilities. Working with their division attorneys, they monitored juries and kept "track of citizens who were known to be antagonistic to the railroad . . . [and were to] get to know every person on the jury panels and 'bring every legitimate influence to bear to overcome any local prejudice which may exist against the railroad.'"[54] If need be, money would be provided for such efforts when a case was coming to trial.[55] In short, even if there were lawyers willing to bring a case against the railroad, it was going to be an uphill battle.

---

50. Lipartito & Platt, *supra* note 3, at 25.
51. *Id.*
52. *Id.*
53. *Id.*
54. Lipartito & Platt, *supra* note 3, at 28.
55. *Id.* at 25.

Division and local attorneys also had available one valuable form of what Lipartito and Pratt call "political currency." "With its network of division and local attorneys scattered along its right-of-way, the railroad had well-placed representatives capable of bringing influence to bear on public officials." Especially important for this effort were the railroad passes that these attorneys could give to public officials. "The passes served a variety of purposes. . . . But of course, it was their use to create a favorable political climate and to restrict legal challenges by buying off potential opposition."[56]

The retired appellate judge we discussed in Chapter 1 told us that prior to Texas's move to an integrated bar in early 1939, "the Bar Association was a volunteer association. The people who attended the annual convention were for the most part railroad lawyers." The judge continued,

> Now, the railroads had a lawyer in each one of the 254 counties of Texas with a free pass to go to any of these places. The county judge was always given a free pass. All the judges of Texas were given free passes on the railroad. Every district attorney was, most of the county officials had free passes on the railroad and that was the chief form of transportation. . . . Now, this I tell you by way of some general background so that you know that the railroad lawyers were a special group of people. . . . I think by the time I got out of law school [in the late 1930s], I was seeing the last vestige of that railroad-dominated bar. . . . Of course, the railroad lawyers were always representing the defense side of the docket, and the plaintiffs' lawyers were the outsiders who were suing the railroads.

Jones Sr. provided an illustration of some of the other tactics used to alter the litigation landscape in talking about his father's practice.

> At first the T&P [Texas and Pacific Railway Company] had its supplies furnished by a general commissary, until a new local counsel for the company hit upon a scheme to make it harder to get jury verdicts against the company in Marshall by bribing local businessmen. He made the raw offer to them of spreading the purchases of the company among them if they would in turn use their influence to discourage jury verdicts against

---

56. *Id.* at 42.

the railway. With a lot of new business allocated among them, that gallant group created and fostered the rumor that if jury verdicts against the railroad continued, the T&P would move its shops away from Marshall. Whether this canard had influence on jurors or not, it became noticeably more difficult to procure a judgment in Harrison County against the T&P.[57]

Working for the railroad or some other interest provided a steady source of income and influence for an attorney, but it also imposed limitations. For instance, the Southern Pacific had a policy on what other business a division or local attorney could handle. Lipartito and Platt note, "One ready source of income for attorneys in towns near railroads was the representation of suits against the roads for damages caused by their operations. Obviously, employment with the Southern Pacific foreclosed the acceptance of such cases. In fact, the corporate policies of the Southern Pacific—and other major lines—went a step further and forbade attorneys representing the Southern Pacific from taking suits against any other railroad."[58] The railroad even built such restrictions into its settlements and did so in a way that combined the restriction with an enticement. Lipartito and Platt's words:

in one case, for example, the railroad paid $8,000 (in 1904) to a plaintiff in an injury suit. In the bargain, however, it gained a valuable ally in the plaintiff's lawyer. As a part of the settlement, he agreed to keep the terms of the award confidential, and to refuse to take any more anti-railroad cases, and to provide information on certain cases still pending. His firm later became local attorneys themselves for the Southern Pacific in Hondo, a relationship that continued until 1967.[59]

Other railroads acted similarly.

Such enticements to switch sides, apparently, were not uncommon. With Baker & Botts, it was a systematic effort to limit the amount of high-quality legal talent working on the plaintiffs' side. Lipartito and Pratt describe in some detail the efforts by the firm in this regard. They note that for Baker & Botts, "it

57. Jones Sr., *supra* note 2, at 221.
58. Lipartito & Platt, *supra* note 3, at 29.
59. *Id.* at 28.

was a corporate decision aimed at limiting the number and quality of plaintiffs' lawyers available to sue the railroads."[60] Often the strategy was successful because "the remuneration offered by corporate giants such as the SP was simply too enticing for entrepreneurially minded attorneys to pass up."[61]

Jones Sr. provides still another example of the hostile environment from the early 1950s, when he was president of TTLA. It again has to deal with influencing potential jurors, this time through public relations. Among his activities as president in 1954 was giving a presentation to the Tyler Lions Club. It was a "rebuttal to one earlier given by the claims manager of an insurance company. It seems the good brother had earlier in the year regaled the Lions with stories of fraudulent insurance claims and the danger of higher insurance rates coming from so-called big verdicts."[62] In the early 1950s, TTLA leaders were complaining about other public relations efforts by their opponents. In particular, they were concerned with material in national publications they tied to "certain interest groups" and "a well-organized drive to influence prospective jurors against plaintiffs' attorneys and so-called 'big verdicts.'"[63] These were advertisements like those we mentioned in Chapter 1 that ran in *Life* and the *Saturday Evening Post.*

PROFESSIONAL ORGANIZATION

Origins and Purposes

The changes in the law that provided new opportunities for plaintiffs' lawyers were one key factor in the development of the plaintiffs' bar. Another was the creation of a professional infrastructure that fostered the growth of a *well-organized* plaintiffs' bar based on its own unique sense of professional identity. This, in turn, allowed plaintiffs' lawyers in Texas to move from being political and professional outsiders to being influential and powerful political and legal

60. *Id.* at 42–43.
61. *Id.* at 31.
62. Franklin Jones Sr. quoted in John Laird, *A Short History of the Texas Trial Lawyers: Sixth Installment,* Trial Lawyers Forum, Apr.–Mar. 1968, at 14.
63. John Laird, *A Short History of the Texas Trial Lawyers: Fourth Installment,* Trial Lawyers Forum, Nov.–Dec. 1967, at 24.

actors capable of an important—and continuing—role in maintaining and expanding their market.

What is now the Texas Trial Lawyers Association was formed in 1949, reflecting the development of the National Association of Claimants' Compensation Attorneys in 1946. NACCA, now the American Association for Justice (until 2006 the Association of Trial Lawyers of America [ATLA]), was founded by a group of plaintiffs' attorneys (including a number from Texas) involved in workers' compensation litigation and related areas. It was formed to further the common interest of lawyers who shared, more or less, a particular political perspective and professional ideology and who had similar practices. According to a 1952 NACCA brochure,

> NACCA is an association of leading attorneys throughout the United States who are primarily plaintiffs' lawyers; that is, those who specialize in workmen's compensation, railroad, admiralty, and allied personal injury (tort) law as attorney for the person injured. The purpose of the organization is to see that an injured person gets an adequate award which will justly compensate him for the injury he has received.[64]

In 1948, NACCA began its own journal, the *NACCA Law Journal*. The brochure also said that NACCA had an annual meeting "to bring together attorneys in the country who are doing the same type of work, to discuss mutual problems and to encourage legislation to improve the rights of injured persons."[65]

In addition, NACCA also began sponsoring or promoting seminars across the country—what we would now call continuing legal education—"where leaders in the medical and legal profession speak to enlighten its members as to the latest techniques in medicine, trial of case, presentation of evidence, argument to juries, and other phases of law which are helpful to the plaintiffs' attorney."[66] In 1950, lectures were held at Harvard, Cornell, Minnesota, Tulane,

---

64. Brochure for NACCA Southeastern Conference on Workmen's Compensation and Personal Injury Litigation, University of South Carolina Law School, Columbia, SC, Mar. 6–7, 1952, H. W. Smith Archives, Rare Books and Special Collections, Box M97, Folder 25, Tarlton Law Library, University of Texas at Austin.

65. Brochure for NACCA Southeastern Conference, Smith Archives, *id.*

66. *Id.*

and Arkansas law schools.[67] In addition, the NACCA president in 1950, Melvin Belli, conducted presentations across the country on the trial of personal injury cases and the adequate award.[68] Until this time, there were few if any such programs aimed at plaintiffs' lawyers. By 1950, NACCA had 1,300 members nationwide (it was estimated that there were approximately 2,500 plaintiffs' lawyers in the United States at the time and about 5,000 defense specialists).[69]

While the number of Texas members is unknown, Texas plaintiffs' lawyers were involved with the development of NACCA and in its early activities as officers or presenters at one of NACCA's meetings. For instance, among these Texas lawyers in 1952 were John Watts (NACCA president); Arthur Combs and Maury Maverick Sr. (NACCA vice presidents); and Gilbert Adams, Horace Brown, Shirley Helm, Bob Huff, Philip Kouri, Arthur Mandell, and Joe Tonahill (NACCA executive committee members). If we go back to 1951, we would add Nile Ball and Fred Parks as executive committee members along with Clyde Barnes, Russell Baker, Warren Burnett, Albert Jones, Harold Putman, and J. E. Smith as associate editors of the *NACCA Law Journal* and panel discussion leaders at the 1951 NACCA convention. Some of the lawyers listed in this paragraph, or their firms, have already been mentioned in this chapter: Combs, Maverick Sr., Helm, Mandell, Ball, and Smith.

In 1949, a group of plaintiffs' lawyers led by Joe Tonahill and Maury Maverick Sr. met at the Texas State Bar convention in Fort Worth and started a state plaintiffs' lawyers' organization. It was not a section of the State Bar, nor was it formally a branch or affiliate of NACCA. It was an independent organization originally named the Plaintiffs' Attorneys Association of Texas, which was changed to the Texas Association of Claimants' Attorneys (TACA) in 1949. In 1956, the name was changed to the Texas Association of Plaintiffs' Attorneys (TAPA), and by the 1960s it had been changed to its current name— the Texas Trial Lawyers Association. The new organization's membership was open to those "who did not regularly represent defendants in personal injury and workmen's compensation insurance cases."[70] Annual dues were set at

---

67. NACCA flier sent to members Nov. 16, 1950, Smith Archives, *id.*

68. Samuel Horowitz, "Important Notice to All NACCA Members," Jan. 1950, Smith Archives, *supra* note 64.

69. *Id.*

70. John Laird, *A Short History of the Texas Trial Lawyers Association, First Installment*, Trial Lawyers Forum, May–June 1967, at 30.

$10. There were also local affiliates in the larger cities—the one in Dallas was started in 1951.

Only a partial list of the names of those attending that 1949 meeting exists. Among those known to have attended are nine of the Texas lawyers listed above as being active in NACCA (Adams, Combs, Helm, Huff, Albert Jones, Kouri, Maverick Sr., Tonahill, and Watts). By the mid-1950s, all but Helm and Maverick Sr. would hold a leadership position in TTLA, and by the end of the 1950s, all of the lawyers noted in the earlier paragraph, with the exception of Ball and Barnes, held leadership positions. In addition, during the 1950s, both Franklin Jones Sr. and Franklin Jones Jr. served on the TTLA board, and Jones Sr. served as president. Scott Baldwin also served on the board and in the 1980s as president. Arthur Mandell and Herman Wright, mentioned earlier in the chapter, also served on the TTLA board and as president.

The organization's first goal, according to Tonahill, was to "defeat a bastard of a judge, I think it was in Dallas; that was going to be our first project. And we got together money from everywhere we could—ten here, twenty there—and pooled it into a campaign and got a guy elected and got rid of him."[71] More generally, a TTLA historian said, "for many years the attorneys in Texas who represented railroads, insurance companies, and other industrial groups had formed and operated their own association for the benefit of themselves and their clients. Not only were these attorneys organized, but their clients were also well-organized in various groups."[72] The first issue of the organization's *Bulletin* encouraged members to enlist new recruits and emphasized the importance of collective action: "Do not forget that if we expect to be able to impress the Legislature, State Departments and the Courts with the righteousness of our cause and the imperative need of the things which we expect to ask of them, we must have a strong and vigorous membership."[73] By April 1950, TTLA had a membership of 131; by 1956, the membership was 405; and by 1967, membership hit 1,000.[74]

71. Interview with Joe Tonahill at Jasper, TX, Aug. 29, 1995.

72. Laird, *supra* note 70, at 29.

73. *Id.* at 32.

74. For the 1950 figures, *see* Laird, *supra* note 70, at 32; and for the 1956 figure, *see* John Laird, *A Short History of the Texas Trial Lawyers Association, Eighth Installment*, Trial Lawyers Forum, July–Aug. 1968, at 24; and for the 1967 figure, *see* Laird, *supra* note 70, at 32.

The *Bulletin* was particularly important. When it started, it was just a mimeographed document circulated to TTLA members, but it included very useful information. It published material on recent appellate court cases of interest. Members were encouraged to submit reports on their successful verdicts, something the *NACCA Law Journal* also did. The *Bulletin* reported on matters of interest in the state legislature when it was in session, which was every other year, and on TTLA's activities with regard to the legislature. It also was a way for TTLA leadership to communicate with members—to tell them in some detail about the organization's plans and the legal changes for which it was lobbying at any given point in time. In 1950, TTLA began a "brief bank." Members were asked to send to the TTLA office in Austin copies of briefs filed with appellate courts, and the briefs could then be sent to other members requesting them.[75]

Continuing Education and Dr. Hubert Winston Smith

In the 1960s, TTLA began giving its own seminars and continuing legal education programs. Before that, the organization sponsored programs by others like Dr. Hubert Winston Smith, who spoke at a 1951 TTLA-sponsored seminar in Houston.[76] H. W. Smith was both a lawyer and a physician, and his talk in Houston was "on Medicolegal Aspects of Neuropsychiatric Disabilities with special reference to head injuries . . . including the fundamental principles involved in the various types of Traumatic Stimuli and the possible Neuropsychiatric consequences . . . [with emphasis] on head injuries."[77] Smith also was a presenter at a seminar held the next day in San Antonio that was attended by eighty lawyers.

Smith forged symbiotic relationships with plaintiffs' lawyers' organizations because, as he helped their members, the organizations provided him with a

75. John Laird, *A Short History of the Texas Trial Lawyers Association, Second Installment*, Trial Lawyers Forum, July–Aug. 1967, at 22.

76. John Laird, *A Short History of the Texas Trial Lawyers Association, Third Installment*, Trial Lawyers Forum, Sept.–Oct. 1967, at 15.

77. H. W. Smith, letter to Horace Brown, Nov. 20, 1951, Smith Archives, *supra* note 64. Brown was the TTLA lawyer organizing the Houston presentation, and Smith's letter outlined what he was going to do.

steady stream of paying students. In 1952, H. W. Smith offered his four-day "medicolegal" course at Tulane, and it was advertised in a NACCA flier for the organization's winter regional meetings across the country: "Again this year over 100 leaders of NACCA are expected to attend the Tulane Law-Science Short Course (either basic or advanced) directed by Prof. Hubert Winston Smith."[78] In March 1952, H. W. Smith wrote to Sam Horowitz—editor of the *NACCA Law Journal*—and asked him to publicize five more 1952 short courses in San Antonio, Chicago, San Francisco, Denver, and New York. Shortly thereafter, Horowitz responded that a notice would appear in the next issue of the *NACCA Law Journal.*[79] Smith and NACCA continued this mutually beneficial relationship throughout the 1950s and into the 1960s.

H. W. Smith was on the faculty of the Tulane Law School when he started his medicolegal short courses in 1949. With the start of the 1952 academic year, Smith moved to the University of Texas School of Law school and also had an appointment in the medical school. The university was interested in developing a presence in the area of continuing legal education, and it created the Law-Science Institute with Smith as its director, a position he held until 1965. He was to "teach courses in Evidence, Legal Medicine and related subjects and would conduct short courses for lawyers and doctors over the state."[80] Smith was also allowed to continue offering his own short course three times a year outside the Southwest, which was an additional source of income for him.

Smith's programs, and similar ones by others, along with his courses at the law school played an important part in the development of the plaintiffs' bar in Texas as well as in the development of the professional organizations. In a 1986 oral history, Texas Supreme Court Chief Justice Jack Pope characterized H. W. Smith as something of a game changer with regard to transformations in the Texas legal profession in the middle of the twentieth century.

78. Samuel Horowitz, letter to H. W. Smith (flier included with letter), Feb. 6, 1952, Smith Archives, *id.*

79. H. W. Smith, letter to Samuel Horowitz, Mar. 24, 1952, and Horowitz, letter to Smith, Apr. 1, 1952, Smith Archives, *id.*

80. Minutes of Advisory Committee Meeting, Office of the Chancellor, University of Texas at Austin, July 10, 1952, 1, Dean Page Keeton Archives, Rare Books and Special Collections, Box M77, Folder 9, Tarlton Law Library, University of Texas at Austin.

Following World War II there was a new concept that came into the practice of law. It came into practice, in my judgment, through the initiative of Hubert Winston Smith, and it was known as medico-legal practice. It was designed to bring into the legal profession learning and the technical knowledge and information from other disciplines. . . . Smith's ideas took fire all over the United States. . . . Lawyers were taught, and they learned, that the way to try a medical-legal case was to spend as much time in the medical library as in the law library, and began to take other professions by surprise when they discovered that a lawyer could sit there and could cross-examine a witness about the details of a technique, or about chemistry, or about diagnosis, and the lawyer could quarrel with him in an intelligent way. The lawyers became very well informed. As I say, this was a whole new ball game.[81]

Never before had this kind of practical, hands-on instruction been available, and plaintiffs' lawyers flocked to H. W. Smith's programs.

After going to the University of Texas, H. W. Smith offered his medicolegal short course at least once a year in Texas until he left the university in 1965. He also offered smaller versions for local bar groups across the state. He continued his symbiotic relationship with NACCA, which provided him with a steady stream of willing students for his short courses and provided NACCA with an excellent device for recruiting members. It also provided a unique networking opportunity for its members and very valuable litigation skills. Smith also worked with TTLA. The availability of these short courses in Texas on a regular basis provided an unparalleled opportunity for Texas lawyers, as did Smith's law school classes.

H. W. Smith's short courses were intense, four-day affairs—like a boot camp for trial lawyers. They went from 8 a.m. to 10 p.m. for three days and 8 a.m. to 6 p.m. on the fourth day, and the presenters were both physicians and lawyers (mostly physicians who were specialists). The course first taught lawyers about medicine and trauma, and then it taught them how to try a trauma case. As part of learning about trying the case, Smith used a very sophisticated

---

81. *A Texas Supreme Court Trilogy, Volume 3: Oral History Interview with the Honorable Jack Pope* (1998), 17, Jamail Center for Legal Research, University of Texas School of Law.

hypothetical case and had some of the very best plaintiffs' and defense litigators actually try the case before the attendees. For instance, he used Melvin Belli and his partner Lou Ashe as lawyers.

To provide an example, the topic headings for the February 1955 short course at the University of Texas, which focused on back injuries and head injuries, were:

Day 1:
- Trauma in Relation to Organ Systems
- Preparation of the Personal Injury Case for Trial
- Trial Tactics in Presenting the Personal Injury Case
- Problems of the Intervertebral Disc
- Trial of Case of Alleged Ruptured Intervertebral Disc

Day 2:
- Medicolegal Aspects of Back Conditions
- Portrait of a Law Suit: Life History of a Double Amputation Case, Problems of Preparation and Trial
- Medicolegal Aspects of Head Injuries: Foundation Concepts
- Head Injuries: Maxillo-Facial Injuries
- Life History of the Typical Head Injury Case
- Motion Pictures of Life Within the Human Brain Cell
- Craniocerebral Trauma: Possible Organic Injuries and Their Effects
- Value and Limitations of Clinical Psychology in Head Injury Cases

Day 3:
- Craniocerebral Trauma: Possible Organic Injuries and Their Effects—Detailed Consideration
- Craniocerebral Trauma: Psychological and Psychiatric Consequences
- Marshaling and Evaluating the Lines of Evidence in Head Injury Cases
- Trial of a Case of Alleged Organic Injury of the Brain
- Patterns of Proof and Special Tactics in Personal Injury Litigation

Day 4:
- Recent Developments in the Law of Torts of Interest to Personal Injury Lawyers
- Trial of a Case of Pre-Existing Brain Tumor Allegedly Aggravated by Trauma
- Vignettes of Medicolegal Trial Technique
- Evidence and Science of Proof in Supporting or Rebutting the Legally Recognized Heads of Damage in Personal Injury Cases

- Trial of a Case Involving Primarily Psychological Disability Following Head Trauma, with Minimal Evidence of Organic Injury to the Brain[82]

We interviewed a number of older plaintiffs' lawyers in Texas who took the legal medicine course at the law school, but the total number of lawyers who attended H. W. Smith's short courses in Texas is unknown, as is the number of law students who took his classes. In a 1955 grant proposal, Smith estimated that "close to 3,000 trial lawyers" attended his "more than 18" short courses in Texas and elsewhere in the country during the years 1950 to 1955.[83] We could find only two partial attendance lists for Texas short courses. One from 1953 with ninety-seven names; and the other from 1954, with sixty-three names. A 1957 letter to Smith noted that a recent short course "had over 200 registrants from 24 different states."[84] If we were to assume, conservatively, one short course per year in Texas for the years 1950 to 1960, with 100 Texas registrants per course, then over 1,000 Texas lawyers attended. We can then probably assume that half were plaintiffs' lawyers.

What information is available tells us that a number of prominent Texas plaintiffs' lawyers, including some names mentioned earlier in this chapter, attended or participated in H. W. Smith's short courses during the 1950s. Among them would be, in no particular order: Maury Maverick Sr., Ralph Yarborough, Don Yarborough, Bob Huff, Shirley Helm, Albert Jones, Franklin Jones Sr., Franklin Jones Jr., Joe Tonahill, Pat Maloney Sr., Tom Davis, Arthur Mandell, Fred Parks, Arthur Dormangue, Joe Spurlock, and Scott Baldwin.[85] Most of these men, as we have seen, held one kind of leadership position or another in TTLA, and they became very successful plaintiffs' lawyers.

---

82. Mid-Winter Law-Science Short Course, Feb. 2–5, 1955, Keeton Archives, Box 1, Folder 8, *supra* note 80.

83. H. W. Smith, Submission to National Institutes of Mental Health, July 9, 1955, Appendix II, 3, Keeton Archives, Box 1, Folder 7, *id.*

84. Harrison Rigdon, letter to H. W. Smith, Feb. 18, 1957, Keeton Archives, Box 1, Folder 7, *id.*

85. *See* "Checks Covering Full Registration of the Law-Science Short Course (1953)" and "Memo to Graves Landrum, Auditor," Feb. 18, 1954, Keeton Archives, Box 78, Folder 1, *id.*

Political Action

Thomas Burke notes that the national plaintiffs' lawyers' organization was not really active on a political level until the 1970s: "Until 1972 it didn't even have an office in Washington, D.C."[86] TTLA, in contrast, was deeply involved with legislative and electoral politics (including the elections of judges) from the very beginning, and, as noted in Chapter 2, TTLA's intense involvement continues. The earlier remarks from Joe Tonahill regarding the initial goal of replacing a judge in Dallas provide one illustration. John Laird's short history of TTLA provides another. In telling of the early years, he wrote, "During the regular session of the 52nd Legislature which convened in Austin in January of 1951, the first efforts were made by any organized group of lawyers in Texas to encourage the passage of legislation that would advance the cause of those who are damaged in person and property and must seek redress therefor at law."[87] While not particularly successful, Laird noted, "many members of the Association . . . went to Austin during the session and talked with their legislators at their homes on weekends in behalf of legislation for the benefit of the general public, their clients, and themselves."[88]

TTLA has always had its offices in Austin, the state capital. By 1967, TTLA's offices were moved to just west of the state capitol—across the street and literally a stone's throw from the capitol's west entrance—where they remain today. At the first annual meeting in 1950 after the organization's founding, a legislative committee was started, and it began to prepare for the next legislative session, which started in January 1951 (the first session after TTLA's founding). The monthly TTLA *Bulletin* "outlined the status of such legislation and from time to time special bulletins and letters were sent to the entire membership in regard to such status, naming the members of the [legislative] committees considering measures of interest" so that members could contact them.[89] A special leadership meeting was held in Austin on January 18, 1951: "At noon a luncheon was held. A number of senators and representatives were guests. All were introduced and some responded with brief talks. Mr. Watts [TTLA presi-

---

86. Thomas Burke, *Lawyers, Lawsuits, and Legal Rights* (Berkeley, CA: University of California Press, 2002), 47.
87. Laird, *supra* note 70, at 24.
88. *Id.* at 26.
89. *Id.* at 24.

dent] spoke briefly on the general purposes of the association and emphasized that its members represented a great mass of the citizenship of the state, which was not organized."[90]

TTLA has consistently been involved with the legislative process since then. It has had a positive agenda when the issues for which it pushes would expand its market or enhance existing opportunities. High on the positive agenda were measures expanding the market or enhancing existing opportunities. Chief among them were replacing contributory negligence with comparative negligence, increasing compensation benefits, replacing "blue ribbon" juries with a universal jury wheel, reforming the procedure surrounding "special issues" for juries, requiring a minimum amount of automobile insurance, and allowing nine-juror verdicts in civil cases. TTLA members were regularly apprised of legislative issues and where members of the legislature stood on those issues. Members were urged to contact legislators they knew.

TTLA has also had a negative agenda when the issues it wanted to stop potentially restricted or shrank its market. High on TTLA's negative agenda were countering the regular attempts to cut back on or change the way in which workers' compensation matters were handled. Texas was unlike most states in that matters not resolved at the compensation commission went to the court as a trial de novo, with a jury trial as an option. Eliminating the trial stage was a regular reform proposal, and as we have seen, workers' compensation was of crucial importance to plaintiffs' lawyers in Texas. It was one of the economic pillars of the market.

TTLA's lobbying extended beyond the legislature. For instance, in May 1952, "President Tonahill [convened a meeting] in Austin with representatives of the [Industrial Accident] Board to consider ways and means of obtaining quicker action on pending claims."[91] In June 1952, TTLA leaders attended a meeting of the State Bar Committee on Administration of Justice where the Missouri Plan for selecting judges was being considered. The TTLA representatives spoke vigorously in opposition to the plan, and among the speakers was Franklin Jones Sr.[92] TTLA members continued their attempts to reshape the law through appellate litigation.

---

90. *Id.*
91. Laird, *supra* note 75, at 16.
92. *Id.* at 16, 25.

By the mid-1960s, there is evidence of some internal discord as individual members, including influential leaders, disagreed on candidate choices and tactics used. Some of this discord was a function of a new, younger set of more politically pragmatic leaders emerging in TTLA, people who finished law school and joined the organization after its founding. The discord is evident in the following excerpt from a 1965 letter from Franklin Jones Sr. to David Copeland, a plaintiffs' lawyer in Waco: "The facts of life are that many of our cohorts among the Texas Trial Lawyers Association membership are political rightists. . . . The general stupidity of perhaps the majority of the membership gave us John Connally instead of Don Yarborough for Governor."[93] Connally was the conservative candidate, and Yarborough was a more progressive Democrat who was also a plaintiffs' lawyer and served on TTLA's board in the late 1950s and early 1960s. While it may have made practical sense to join Lyndon Johnson's political bandwagon, Connally was Johnson's man, and for those who fought the conservative elements within the Texas Democratic Party, the choice was clear. Franklin Sr.'s complaint suggests an organization maturing enough to move beyond the views and initial efforts of its founders.

One of the more interesting examples is a letter Franklin Sr. wrote to his old friend (and long-ago employee) J. E. Smith. Among other things, it concerned Franklin Sr.'s long-felt disagreement about actions taken in the 1960s regarding the Texas Supreme Court and whether to support the reelection of one of the justices. Franklin Sr., who chaired the TTLA committee reviewing candidates, was opposed to the justice, whereas the new leadership was not, and it appears that Franklin Sr. lost. In talking about the incident, he noted with some satisfaction that at least he "was able to kill a plan that would have had the association inviting all the members of the Supreme Court to a dinner. . . . As I recall this effort at toadyism, my argument was that the only thing any plaintiffs' organization owed the then Supreme Court was a dinner where Lucretia Borgia should be the caterer for the occasion, with instructions to go heavy on her poison sauces. Might not have been a bad idea, after all."[94] What Franklin Sr. saw as "toadyism" the newer leaders saw as a necessary change in strategy given what they saw as a lack of political success.

93. Jones Sr., letter to David Copeland, Nov. 23, 1965, *supra* note 2, at 100–101.
94. Jones Sr., letter to J. E. Smith, Apr. 22, 1986, in *The Public and Private Letters of Franklin Jones, Sr., 1985–1988: Volume IV, The Caddo-Hollywood Conflict,* ed. Ann Adams (Oak Harbor, WA: Packrat Press, 1988), 127–129.

Still one more example from Franklin Sr. is a 1986 letter to the lawyer heading the reelection campaign for a state appellate judge. It alludes to the scandals involving contributions to judicial campaigns noted in Chapter 2. Franklin Sr.'s letter was in response to a request for a monetary contribution to the judge's campaign. He made a small contribution and included his complaint with the check:

> I must say that I am bitterly disappointed at the developments
> concerning some of our plaintiffs' attorneys and their conduct toward
> the Texas Supreme Court. I remember back in the late forties when the
> late Congressman Maury Maverick, Sr. gathered a group of plaintiffs'
> attorneys together [at the State Bar meeting] and demanded that we
> form a State organization along the lines of NACCA. . . . For one of the
> members of the old organization to think about giving a Supreme Court
> Justice more than fifty dollars for his campaign expenditures would have
> been considered an ostentatious show of wealth. If you will forgive me, I
> repeat the corollary to Lord Acton's axiom that I can't get out of my mind:
> "Affluence corrupts, and greedy affluence corrupts completely."[95]

One wonders what he might say about TTLA having its own PAC or about the TTLA PAC receiving over $830,000 in contributions and having over $720,000 in political expenditures in 2010.[96]

Franklin Sr. most likely would disapprove of the contributions made by individual plaintiffs' lawyers to recent Texas judicial candidates at the maximum amount allowed. For instance, according to the Texas Ethics Commission, well-known Dallas plaintiffs' lawyer Frank Branson contributed $5,000 to each of five judicial candidates in Texas from 2009 to 2010. Well-known Houston plaintiffs' lawyer Mark Lanier contributed $5,000 to each of four judicial candidates and $7,500 to another from 2009 to 2010. And from 2009 to

95. Jones Sr., letter to Tom Ragland, April 21, 1986, *id.* at 127.

96. According to the Texas Ethics Commission, the TTLA PAC made contributions to no judicial candidates but to a large number of candidates—mostly incumbents—for the state legislature. See Texas Ethics Commission, *Political Committees Sorted by Contributions Received during Calendar Year 2010,* http://www.ethics.state.tx.us/dfs/c_elists.htm. This URL allows you to search campaign finance reports by year and by entity name.

2010 he contributed $5,000 each to two county Republican organizations and $50,000 to the David Dewhurst Committee.[97] Dewhurst was then the Republican lieutenant governor—the most powerful elected official in Texas—who lost a 2012 primary battle with now–U.S. Senator Ted Cruz. Franklin Sr. would not be surprised that from 2009 to 2010 the Baker Botts Amicus Fund contributed $1,000 or more to forty-seven judicial candidates, and seven of them received $5,000 or more.[98]

One need not speculate on what Franklin Sr. might say about Lanier, who is also a prominent leader of TTLA. In a 1986 letter to the editor in the *Marshall (TX) News Messenger* Franklin Sr. bluntly said,

> The profound conclusion . . . that I would vote against Jesus Christ if "He ran . . . on the Republican ticket" is eminently correct. In the first place, our Savior would not reject the example and teachings of His life and crucifixion by aligning himself with a political party whose spokesmen have proclaimed that the poor went "voluntarily" to soup kitchens "because the food is free," who have sought to deprive the poor and elderly citizens of legal counsel by abolishing the Legal Services Corporation, and who criticize the doctrine of presumed innocent by saying that if a person is innocent of a crime, he is not a suspect. . . . These are but some of the reasons that should the Republican Party inform me that their candidate is Jesus Christ, I would vote against him in the knowledge that the candidate is an imposter.[99]

This is not to say that Lanier's views mirror Franklin Sr.'s characterization, but Lanier is still in the minority.

CONCLUSION

In 1990, a legal journalist, speaking metaphorically, characterized the political battles of the 1980s over tort reform as the "hundred years' (tort) war."[100] From

97. *Id.*
98. *Id.*
99. Jones Sr., *To the Editor, Marshall News Messenger*, Aug. 27, 1986, *supra* note 94, at 155.
100. Andrew Blum, *The Hundred Years (Tort) War*, 1 Nat'l L.J. (Oct. 15, 1990).

the perspective of lawyers like Franklin Jones Sr. and his father, Solomon Jones, the journalist may have been right on target. But by the mid-1980s, both the political and legal landscapes had changed. The market for plaintiffs' lawyers' services had changed dramatically, providing a range of opportunities and expanding access to a level unknown at the beginning of the twentieth century or even in the late 1940s, when the plaintiffs' lawyers' organizations were founded. To use Lawrence Friedman's words about the tort system in the United States generally, the "tort system in general radically changed. . . . Defenses have eroded, and courts (and legislatures) have expanded liability to a point that in the 19th century would have been considered sheer, utter madness."[101]

Plaintiffs' lawyers became major political actors who could have a real influence on the outcome of elections and legislative debates. They had begun contributing heavily (individually and collectively) to see favored candidates elected. They were no longer the perpetual outsiders. And, perhaps more importantly, plaintiffs' lawyers had become successful enough to make substantial investments in political campaigns. Ironically, what Franklin Sr. seemed to be complaining about was, in part, the success of the plaintiffs' bar— something for which he and other lawyers like him had laid the foundation. We cannot say that the development of the Texas plaintiffs' bar as we know it today was inevitable, but without the infrastructure created by plaintiffs' lawyers of Jones's generation, the story would probably have turned out quite differently. So would the battle over access and the civil justice system.

Chapter 4 looks more closely at professional identity—the normative standards underlying plaintiffs' lawyers' sense of themselves as professionals. As we noted in the Preface, knowing something of professional identity helps understand how they navigate the challenges they face in building and maintaining a successful practice. If plaintiffs' lawyers were purely rational actors, we might legitimately wonder why they ever decided to enter this practice area and why—in the face of tort reform in Texas—anyone would stay in it. Again, access depends on there being lawyers willing and able to work in this practice area.

---

101. Friedman, *supra* note 6, at 355–356.

4. The Tension between Professional Norms and the Need to Generate Business

A Window into Professional Identity*

"As long as the phones are ringing, we're OK. If the phones stop ringing, I may as well turn out the lights." So said a plaintiffs' lawyer we interviewed in Texas in 2006. He was talking about the challenge facing *all* plaintiffs' lawyers—maintaining a steady stream of clients with injuries the legal system will compensate adequately. This means compensation sufficient for the client's needs; reimbursement for the costs incurred by the lawyer in representing the client; and the lawyer's fee, which must also cover the lawyer's overhead. Because plaintiffs' lawyers rely on the contingency fee, meeting this challenge also includes an assessment of the risks involved in light of the costs—not just for a single client but for all those in a lawyer's book of business. They must to at least some degree, as Herbert Kritzer argues, be rational business actors.[1]

This challenge is one reason plaintiffs' practice is so precarious and as a result is important for access. If it is not met, the lawyer goes out of business. If it is met, the lawyer will stay in business and may even have a very profitable business. The challenge is also a reason why the means used to get clients can be so controversial. The common fear—and often the presumption—is that plaintiffs' lawyers will do almost anything to get clients and make money. One need only think of the idea of "greedy" plaintiffs' lawyers, the image of the "ambulance chaser," and one's least favorite television-advertising lawyer.

A 1995 *Texas Lawyer* article on Dallas plaintiffs' lawyer Hudson Henley provides an example. Henley was a brash and prolific advertiser at the time. The article noted that Henley had never tried a case and was a young, largely unknown attorney until he started an "advertising blitz" that resulted in one

---

* An earlier, somewhat different version of this chapter appeared in Stephen Daniels & Joanne Martin, "Plaintiffs' Lawyers and the Tension between Professional Norms and the Need to Generate Business," in *Lawyers in Practice: Ethical Decision-Making in Context*, eds. Leslie Levin & Lynn Mather (Chicago: The University of Chicago Press, 2012).

1. Herbert Kritzer, *Risks, Reputations, and Rewards: Contingency Fee Legal Practice in the United States* (Stanford, CA: Stanford University Press, 2004), 9–19.

of the "biggest automobile claims caseloads in Dallas."[2] His visibility changed "when he started calling himself 'Maximum Cash Henley' on billboards and commercials during morning drive time radio programs"—commercials read by national radio personality Howard Stern, repeatedly saying, "Call Hudson Henley for maximum cash."[3] The article opened by describing a Henley "client appreciation" function at a Dallas bar and grill: "Construction workers in jeans and secretaries in cowboy boots are the clients who eat Henley's food, drink his beer and applaud his work."[4]

Although they do exist, we found few ambulance chasers or their contemporary equivalents in Texas—and few like Henley. Instead, we found lawyers trying to meet that challenge (not always successfully) in a variety of ways that were largely consistent not only with the requirements of the formal rules of professional conduct, but also with their sense of themselves as professionals bound by a set of normative values wrapped up in their professional identity. At the other end of the spectrum, that *Texas Lawyer* article spoke of another lawyer, "John E. Collins, who has practiced personal injury law in Dallas since 1965 . . . who notes that his one-line listing in the Yellow Pages reads, 'Collins, John E.'"[5]

In Chapter 3, we argued that one of the crucial factors in the development of the plaintiffs' bar in Texas was a particular sense of professional identity among a set of key actors. This chapter looks further into that professional identity. Whether one likes that professional identity or not, it suggests that plaintiffs' lawyers cannot be understood simply as rational business actors or as greedy ambulance chasers. Still, business necessity is always there, and it often puts lawyers in a position where that necessity may conflict with the normative values underlying their professional identity. Importantly, this tension between necessity and normative values is not one that will ever be resolved; rather, it is a constant for all lawyers, with only occasional relief. The issue is how *these* lawyers negotiate the coexistence of values that may pull them in different directions. Exploration of this issue provides a revealing window into their sense of themselves as professionals, not in some abstract way but in a practical sense.

2. Bruce Vincent, *Hudson Henley: Spending Cash to Make Maximum Bucks*, Tex. Lawyer, Nov. 20, 1995, at 32.

3. *Id.*

4. *Id.*

5. *Id.* at 33. Collins served as President of TTLA in 1982–1983.

Knowing how plaintiffs' lawyers get clients has obvious importance. Knowing something of their professional identity is also important for at least three key reasons. First is simply showing that there actually is a professional identity that helps shape the plaintiffs' bar in Texas as a community of practice and not simply a practice area. Second is outlining the substance of that professional identity and elucidating what it means to be a plaintiffs' lawyer, including what makes a professional reputation and why that reputation is important. Third is providing needed context for understanding the impact of tort reform on plaintiffs' lawyers. As a practical matter, much of tort reform—formal changes in the law as well as efforts at lobbying the public mind—makes plaintiffs' practice less profitable and hence less attractive. What can seem surprising from a purely business perspective is why lawyers actually chose to specialize in such a precarious practice area and, in light of tort reform, that anyone would stay in that practice area. But they're still there, and professional identity may help us understand why. Once again, we ask the reader to keep in mind the idea of plaintiffs' lawyers as gatekeepers along with the shared message of Professor Brickman and our letter writer from the Preface.

Chapter 4 is divided into five sections. The first briefly explains what we mean by professional identity and how we went about exploring it. The second outlines the challenge plaintiffs' lawyers face in maintaining the steady stream of clients needed to stay in business in the face of professional norms—formal and informal—that could limit what can be done and how. It includes a brief examination of the methods used by Texas plaintiffs' lawyers to get clients. (Chapter 5 and Chapter 6 will have more to say about client acquisition.) The third section looks at whether plaintiffs' lawyers see that challenge as purely a business matter or whether professional norms play a role. As we will see, the norms work to enhance access, but in an interesting way, they could also dampen it. The fourth section addresses the substance of those norms, and the fifth section looks at the tension between those norms and business necessity. While those values are interpreted and adjusted pragmatically in the face of the hard realities of cost and necessity, they still have an important sway over what lawyers do.

THE IDEA OF PROFESSIONAL IDENTITY

Professional identity is a nebulous concept, one discussed and debated primarily by those concerned with training for the professions—including law. The issue for educators is whether professional identity can be taught. Many seem skeptical because it is an ongoing process of socialization into a professional role, involving interpretation and reinterpretation of that role in a dynamic context.[6] More basic is the issue of what to teach, and this means normative debate over competing ideas of what the content of professional identity should be.

Our interest, however, is not normative. We are not, for instance, taking a side in the long-standing controversy between professionalism and commercialism in the legal profession, with the former seen positively and the latter negatively.[7] We do not even want to use what in reality strikes us as a false dichotomy. Our interest is empirical. We describe as best we can the professional identity of a particular community of lawyers, starting with the very simple idea that professional identity can be "understood to include the constellation of beliefs, values, and motives by which people define themselves in a professional role."[8]

Included in this simple idea is the element of a shared set of beliefs, values, and motives defined not solely by the individual but in the context of a given community. Although they do not use the term *professional identity*, what we have in mind is something akin to what Lynn Mather and her colleagues, in looking at divorce lawyers, call a "community of practice," with the emphasis on community as being about things held in common. For them, it is about an identifiable set of lawyers with a shared practice area and a shared set of values

6. Marie Clarke, Abbey Hyde & Jonathan Drennan, "Professional Identity in Higher Education," in *The Academic Profession in Europe: New Tasks and New Challenges*, eds. B. M. Kehm & U. Teichier (London: Springer, 2013), 7–8.

7. *See* Jerold Auerbach, *Unequal Justice: Lawyers and Social Change in Modern America* (New York: Oxford University Press, 1976), 40–73, and Carroll Seron, *The Business of Practicing Law: The Work Lives of Solo and Small-Firm Attorneys* (Philadelphia, PA: Temple University Press, 1996), 1–18.

8. Kath Hall, Molly T. O'Brien & Stephen Tang, *Developing a Professional Identity in Law School: A View from Australia*, 4 Phoenix L. Rev. 21, 22 (2010).

or norms tied to that area.[9] Mather et al. focus on the ethics of legal practice in day-to-day practice and how lawyers "exert limited collegial control over one another and thus help to shape the day-to-day choices that constitute legal practice."[10]

The concern with legal ethics is clearly there among Texas plaintiffs' lawyers, but there is something more than just this and it involves the difference between professionalism and professional identity. Both are important. In the view of law professor David Thomson, "*Professionalism* relates to behaviors, such as timeliness, thoroughness, respect towards opposing counsel and judges, and responding to clients in a timely fashion"—the kinds of norms found in the various codes of professional responsibility.[11] Professional identity, in contrast, goes beyond the minimum standards for appropriate behavior. It goes to what it means to be a lawyer and to a more fundamental set of norms. In Thomson's words, "*Professional identity* relates to one's own decisions about those behaviors . . . as well as a sense of *duty* as an officer of the court and *responsibility* as part of a system in our society that is engaged in upholding the rule of law."[12] Larger normative concerns are important here.

Thomson's idea of professional identity is about ends and not just means, and is similar to an idea found in an earlier work by Francis Zemans and Victor Rosenblum on legal education and professionalization. Zemans and Rosenblum distinguished between two "moralities." First is a "morality of duty" as a minimal standard of behavior, which looks to codes of professional responsibility "below which none should fall and for which some form of sanction is likely to follow."[13] This is Thomson's idea of professionalism and the focus for Mather and her colleagues. Second is a "morality of aspiration" that speaks to upholding "standards above those enforceable through a code, standards that take cognizance of a lawyer's and the legal system's role in achieving jus-

9. Lynn Mather, Craig McEwen & Richard Maiman, *Divorce Lawyers at Work: Varieties of Professionalism in Practice* (New York: Oxford University Press, 2001), 4–13.

10. *Id.* at 6.

11. David Thomson, *"Teaching" Formation of Professional Identity*, University of Denver Sturm College of Law Legal Research Paper Series, Working Paper No. 12-45 (2012), http://ssrn.com/abstract=2171321, at 1.

12. *Id.* (emphasis in original).

13. Frances Zemans & Victor Rosenblum, *The Making of a Public Profession* (Chicago: American Bar Foundation, 1981), 169.

tice."[14] It is an idea of professional identity that reflects what we find in Texas, although we should note that neither Thompson nor Zemans and Rosenblum had in mind the particulars of what we find.

While not formally institutionalized, a sense of the professional identity we find in Texas is reflected in the Texas Trial Lawyers Association's rules for full membership. Membership is

> limited to all members of the State Bar of Texas and all duly licensed out-of-state lawyers not licensed by the State of Texas who do not regularly and consistently represent insurance companies, corporations, utility companies and/or defendants in actions filed by individuals who have been injured or damaged and who are not associated with a law firm that regularly and consistently represents such entities or individuals; provided, however, an employee of an executive branch agency of state or federal government shall not be eligible for membership in the association.[15]

It can also be seen in the way Otto Mullinax described the ethos of his firm, which we quoted in Chapter 3. It is worth repeating:

> First, to earn a good living for its members and staff;
> Second, to make that living representing unions and working people, if possible; and,
> Third, to use those resources, produced above the need to serve the first two objectives, in advancing liberal political processes in government and society.[16]

Clearly, not all lawyers will accept these objectives as their aspirational goals. The issue for access is how lawyers who accept these kinds of aspirational goals

14. *Id.* at 170. In making this distinction, Zemans and Rosenblum rely explicitly on Lon Fuller's *Morality of Law* (New Haven, CT: Yale University Press, 1969).

15. Article IV, Section 1A, Bylaws of the Texas Trial Lawyers Association, www.ttla.com/index.cfm?pg=ArticleIVSection1A.

16. Otto Mullinax, *Introducing the Honorable Oscar Mauzy as the Newly Elected Member of the Texas Supreme Court*, 1, unpublished, Jan. 3, 1986 (on file with the authors).

navigate the coexistence of goals that may pull in different directions—making a good living and serving those values.

Exploring professional identity posed a challenge because it was not clear in our minds that a set of abstract questions about professional identity would provide much useful information—assuming that the lawyers we would be interviewing even understood academia's ideas about professional identity. This presumes, of course, that academics have a clear idea. Instead, without even bringing up the idea of professional identity, we asked our interviewees about an issue we knew from our research to be one about which plaintiffs' lawyers, like many others, are very concerned—how some plaintiffs' lawyers actually or allegedly get clients.

Our typical entry point was to ask how the lawyer got clients. This usually led to a discussion of advertising and other techniques, and to the boundaries of acceptable behavior. Talking in concrete terms about getting clients—what was considered the good, the bad, and the ugly—proved to be a fascinating and useful way to learn about the everyday sense of professional identity and the plaintiffs' bar as a community of shared norms. One of the most important things we learned is the importance of reputation in reinforcing the professional norms at the heart of the plaintiffs' bar as a community of practice and not simply a practice area. Reputation will also be one of the focal points for Chapter 6 and the discussion of the referral process that moves cases among lawyers—especially to the specialists. The next section looks at how plaintiffs' lawyers try—not always successfully or appropriately—to meet that all-important challenge.

MEETING THE CHALLENGE: GETTING CLIENTS

Plaintiffs' lawyers are not unique. Getting clients is a challenge for all lawyers, especially those working in the personal services sector. The challenge is particularly acute for plaintiffs' lawyers because they have one-shot clients rather than ongoing client relationships, and their practices rely on contingency fees. If they are not successful in handling a case, they receive no fee for their professional services and no reimbursement for the costs incurred. These lawyers must stay in business—and hopefully make a profit—while not running afoul of the formal rules in the disciplinary code governing client acquisition or the informal norms within the plaintiffs' lawyers' practice community that help define that community's view of itself and its notions of acceptable behavior. Violating the formal rules can lead to various levels of sanctions by a governing professional board, including disbarment. Violating the informal rules carries additional sanctions, the most serious of which are the erosion of one's reputation and even being ostracized or functionally shunned within the community of plaintiffs' lawyers. Either could seriously hurt a plaintiffs' lawyer's ability to prosper.

This challenge has long concerned the legal profession because it is seen as a major ethical issue with the potential to undermine the legitimacy of the profession and the legal system itself in the eyes of the public. After the U.S. Supreme Court's decision in *Bates v. State Bar of Arizona* in 1977, that concern deepened because *Bates* struck down long-standing bans on lawyer advertising.[17] In commenting on the impact of *Bates*, William Hornsby (an American Bar Association staff counsel specializing in legal ethics) notes that the decision meant the "ethics rule governing the conduct of lawyers in every state became unconstitutional. In the blink of an eye, lawyers had the right to advertise their service—a right that had been suppressed for nearly seventy years. . . . [*Bates*] is no doubt the most significant milestone in the evolution of client development."[18]

Hornsby sees the decision in terms of a long-term struggle that goes to the very heart of the concern about professionalism and dignity. This ethical concern, perhaps more than any other, cuts to the core of the profession's sense of itself as something different than a business. Rather than a business, the legal profession is about public service. Says Hornsby,

> To understand how client development threatens professionalism and dignity, we must look to the work of Dean Roscoe Pound. In 1953, Dean Pound defined professionalism as "a group of men pursuing a learned art as a common calling in the spirit of public service." Providing legal services may result in financial compensation, but according to those advancing this notion of professionalism, that compensation cannot be the motivation for a lawyer to provide those services. That motivation must be the pursuit of public service.[19]

17. 433 U.S. 350 (1977).
18. William Hornsby, *Clashes of Class and Cash: Battles from the 150 Years War to Govern Client Development*, 37 Ariz. St. L.J. 255, 255 (2005).
19. *Id.* at 257.

Plaintiffs' lawyers and their client acquisition techniques have long been seen as one of the major threats to professionalism and lawyer dignity. The long tradition, noted in Chapter 1, of characterizing plaintiffs' lawyers as "ambulance chasers" provides an apt illustration. Advertising, in the eyes of its critics within the profession, "inherently changes the practice of law from 'a common calling in the spirit of public service' to a business endeavor that could undermine the public's confidence in our system of justice."[20]

Like most states, Texas has struggled to find an appropriate set of rules dealing with lawyer advertising, solicitation, and other forms of client acquisition that are acceptable to the legal community. Most of the relevant rules are found in Rule VII: Information about Legal Services in the Texas Disciplinary Rules of Professional Conduct (which, as Chapter 2 noted, was amended in 2005). Rule VII is the second-longest section of the rules (Rule I: Client-Lawyer Relationship is the longest), and it imposes a host of limitations on the means lawyers can use to get clients (including the Internet, websites, and social media). For instance, Rule 7.03(a) prohibits direct in-person, telephonic, or other electronic solicitation of potential clients with regard to a particular occurrence or series of occurrences if there is no family or past relationship with the attorney. Rule 7.03(b) prohibits a lawyer from paying or giving anything of value to nonlawyers (such as paid "runners") to solicit clients.[21] Rule VII also places numerous requirements and restrictions on the use of allowed means of obtaining clients. For instance, Rule 7.04(a) lays out the requirements and limitations for a lawyer claiming any particular expertise or specialization. Rule 7.04(g) prohibits actor portrayals of the lawyer in an advertisement. Rule 7.04(h) lays out the requirements for a lawyer advertising a willingness to work on a contingency fee basis.[22]

Rule VII also imposes filing requirements for any type of advertisement, any type of direct solicitation, and any type of digital solicitation (including websites).[23] All are required to be filed with the State Bar's Advertising Review

20. *Id.* at 258–259.

21. Rule 7.03(a) and Rule 7.03(b) Prohibited Solicitations and Payments, and Comments 1 and 2. We need to remind the reader that all of the Rules and Comments we reference are always subject to review and revision and may change after this writing.

22. Rule 7.04(a), Rule 7.04(g), and Rule 7.04(h) Advertisements in the Public Media, and Comments 2, 7, 8, 12, and 13.

23. Rule 7.07 Filing Requirements for Public Advertisements and Written, Recorded, Electronic, or Other Digital Solicitations.

Committee. Comment 2 to Rule 7.07 states: "Presumably, the Advertising Review Committee will report to the appropriate grievance committee any lawyer whom it finds from the reviewed products has disseminated an advertisement in the public media or solicitation communication that violates Rules 7.02, 7.03, 7.04, or 7.05, or, at a minimum, any lawyer whose violation raises a substantial question as to that lawyer's honesty, trustworthiness, or fitness as a lawyer in other respects."[24] Interestingly, we find that few lawyers are publicly sanctioned by the State Bar for violations of Rule VII's provisions, although the number privately sanctioned is unknown.[25]

The first rules for regulating advertisements were adopted in 1982, but "the biggest changes to the rules came in 1995, when the State Bar first began requiring lawyers to seek pre-approval for their ads."[26] Reflecting the disagreement within the bar over the regulation of lawyer advertising, the initial proposal failed to get the needed majority vote in a 1993 referendum of State Bar of Texas members, but a second vote in 1994 on the same measures received the needed majority and went into effect in 1995. The second referendum reflected a certain urgency because of legislation requiring that the new rules for lawyer advertising be adopted by June 1, 1994.[27] The key parts of the new rules survived a federal constitutional challenge brought by a group of major advertisers led by one of Texas's most prolific advertisers—plaintiffs' lawyer Jim Adler of Houston, to whom we referred in Chapter 1.[28]

But one shouldn't assume that the constitutional challenge reflected the view of all Texas plaintiffs' lawyers. The leadership of the Texas Trial Lawyers Association (TTLA) was in favor of the legislation noted above, and key members were involved in the lobbying for the law and in the final drafting of the bill. TTLA was among those pushing for the deadline in the legislation in or-

24. *Id.* at Comment 2.

25. Stephen Daniels & Joanne Martin, "Plaintiffs' Lawyers and the Tension between Professional Norms and the Need to Generate Business," in *Lawyers in Practice: Ethical Decision-Making in Context*, eds. Leslie Levin & Lynn Mather (Chicago: The University of Chicago Press, 2012), 114–116.

26. Mary Alice Robbins, *Hammer Time: The Age of Lawyer Advertising*, 26 Tex. Lawyer, June 28, 2010, at 1; www.texaslawyer.com/id=1202463011853/Hammer-Time%3A-The-Age-of-Lawyer- Advertising#ixzz2sN5tLhIj.

27. *Id.*

28. *Id.*

der to force the State Bar to move on the problems surrounding client solicitation (especially direct mail to accident victims and television advertising). Key TTLA members were also involved in both of the State Bar referenda. Those new rules, among other things, created the State Bar's Advertising Review Committee, and the first chair of the committee was Richard Hile, one of those TTLA leaders (the same Richard Hile who would become the chair of the State Bar Referral Fee Task Force in 2004, as we saw in Chapter 2).

Still, there were plaintiffs' lawyers who opposed the new regulations, and TTLA did lose some members as a result of its stance. According to someone familiar with the meetings within TTLA at the time, "It was controversial. I can remember those meetings: they were really extremely hot, emotionally high; some who were saying that you could not have any involvement whatsoever [with regard to the legislation and the new rules]. Others saying that you need to go the full deal and ban advertising in any respect." He said that the rules eventually adopted were the product of political compromise: "We generally got a consensus . . . even some of the advertisers. . . . We tried to work out the language that we could try to highlight the evil and then try to address that evil without being overly restrictive."

TABLE 4.1. *How Texas Lawyers Get Clients*

	Plaintiffs' Lawyers[a]	In-State Private Practice[b]
Top four sources of business for respondent's practice (% of business from each)	Lawyer referrals 38 Client referrals 27 Advertising 14 Other referrals 12	Client referrals 34 Other referrals 22 Lawyer referrals 18 Advertising 7
Those who advertise in any way (%)	67	40
Top four forms of advertising (% using each)	Yellow Pages 52 Direct mail to lawyers 13 Television 12 Newspaper 11	Yellow Pages 21 Newspaper 10 Television 4 Direct mail to lawyers 3 Radio 3
Those with firm website (%)	57 (2006 survey only)	18

[a] Pooled data from our 2000 and 2006 surveys of Texas plaintiffs' lawyers, 1,012 total respondents.
[b] Data from State Bar of Texas: Texas Referral Practices Survey (2004), 861 in-state respondents in private practice (data on file with the authors).

Although advertising and direct solicitation attract most of the attention, they are not the primary sources of clients for private practice lawyers in Texas —and this includes plaintiffs' lawyers. The predominant source of clients is some form of referral. Table 4.1 uses data from our two surveys of Texas plaintiffs' lawyers and from the Texas State Bar's 2004 Referral Practices Survey (done for the Referral Fee Task Force). It shows that for private practice lawyers generally, almost three-quarters of their clients, on average, come from some form of referral (adding the three referral types together). For plaintiffs' lawyers responding to our surveys, the figure is just over three-quarters. Lawyer referrals, however, are much more important for plaintiffs' lawyers than for lawyers generally. Client referrals are the most important source of clients for lawyers generally and the second most important for plaintiffs' lawyers. The importance of lawyer referrals for plaintiffs' lawyers reflects their status as specialists and their willingness to pay referral fees to the lawyers who refer cases to them. The Referral Practices Survey shows that personal injury cases are by far the most referred cases in which a fee is involved, with the most referred case type being a medical malpractice case followed by an automobile accident case.[29]

This is the reason why there was another big fight over the rules governing client acquisition in the early 2000s, and it is the one described in Chapter 2 surrounding the Texas Supreme Court's efforts at fundamentally changing the rule governing lawyer referrals. As that discussion showed, the Court's preferred changes were not enacted, but changes were made in the referral process and in the rules governing advertising. A major concern underlying the enacted changes proposed by the State Bar Referral Fee Task Force was the brokering of cases by major advertisers who would advertise for large numbers of cases with no intention of ever actually representing the client. Instead, the clients would be referred to another lawyer, with the advertiser collecting a fee for the referral if the case was successful.[30]

Table 4.1 shows that advertising, despite the controversy surrounding it as

29. Chapter 6 discusses the Referral Practices Survey's findings in detail. For that survey's methodology, *see* Department of Research and Analysis, State Bar of Texas, *Texas Referral Practices Survey Report* (2004), http://www.texasbar.com/AM/Template .cfm?Section=Archives&Template=/CM/ContentDisplay.cfm&ContentID=11493.

30. *See* Supreme Court of Texas, *Proposed Rule 8a of the Texas Rules of Civil Procedure,* 67 Tex. B. J. 116, 121 (2004).

an ethical issue, is not a substantial source of clients for plaintiffs' lawyers or for all lawyers. Only 10 percent of plaintiffs' lawyers get more than one-half of their business from all sources of advertising combined, and few have anything close to a systematic marketing plan. This may be one more reason why research has not found that advertising has led to price competition among lawyers and lower fees for clients.[31] Nonetheless, the small number of lawyers who do rely heavily on advertising make a substantial investment in sophisticated marketing strategies using outside professionals and constant tracking. One television advertiser, for instance, used an outside firm to provide research on viewer demographics for different television programs and different times of the day (the demographics of interest being related to the types of case in which the lawyer was interested). Advertising buys were then made based on that research, including buys on both English-language and Spanish-language stations. Different toll-free telephone numbers were used to allow for systematic tracking. We should note that although this lawyer would refer the most complex cases for a fee, he handled most of the cases himself, including actually trying the cases. This lawyer is a proficient and experienced litigator and is certified by the Texas Board of Legal Specialization in personal injury trial law.

The most frequently used forms of advertising are basically the same for both sets of lawyers. The Yellow Pages are the most often used, with a higher percentage of plaintiffs' lawyers using them. Although most lawyers do not invest in television advertising, a higher percentage of plaintiffs' lawyers do so (12 percent versus 4 percent). Reflecting the importance of lawyer referrals as a source of business, a higher percentage of plaintiffs' lawyers use direct mail to other lawyers than is the case for lawyers generally (13 percent versus 3 percent). Finally, plaintiffs' lawyers have a much more prominent presence on the Internet, with more than half of the respondents in our 2006 survey reporting that they have a firm website, compared to less than one-fifth of all lawyers (our earlier survey did not ask this question). Still, on average, firm websites account for just 3 percent of business for the 264 respondents who reported having a firm website (and for 62 percent of these respondents, the firm website generated no business).

---

31. Nora Freeman Engstrom, *Attorney Advertising and the Contingency Fee Paradox,* 65 Stanford L. Rev. 633 (2013).

MEETING THE CHALLENGE: IS IT JUST BUSINESS, OR DO NORMS MATTER?

Just Business?

How do plaintiffs' lawyers navigate the challenge of keeping a steady stream of clients, given the potential for ethical problems or for offending the community's own sense of propriety? As we noted, few lawyers in Texas are disciplined for violating the formal rules governing client acquisition, and this includes plaintiffs' lawyers.[32] Perhaps the reason few lawyers are formally disciplined for matters related to client acquisition is that getting clients is easy, and consequently there are few ethical issues to confront. Reality, of course, is quite different. Almost all plaintiffs' lawyers see their environment as a highly competitive one. For instance, 51 percent of respondents to our surveys said that the growing number of lawyers is having a negative effect on their practices. In the words of a successful Dallas lawyer, "It's a competitive business, and all those folks want your business. . . . You know, you have children and families, and I mean, I've been lucky. . . . But trust me, I wake up at 4:00 in the morning plenty of times, either worrying about my case or worrying about where my next one's coming from." Another bluntly said, "It's Darwinism—survival of the fittest."

In the face of a competitive environment, some lawyers we interviewed complained that disciplinary enforcement by the State Bar is not vigilant enough. These complaints focus on major television advertisers, direct-mail solicitors, and those using "runners"—non-lawyers who sign up accident victims as clients for lawyers. The implication is that there is much unethical behavior in this area that goes unchecked. Even if this is presumed to be true, few plaintiffs' lawyers we interviewed seem interested in joining the crowd of ethical scofflaws in light of lax enforcement. According to one San Antonio lawyer,

It just seems like the State Bar . . . when some of these guys [referring to the late John O'Quinn, who the State Bar twice tried, unsuccessfully, to disbar] have gotten so large and so powerful, that whenever the State Bar has tried to actually enforce the regulations and the rules, these attorneys

32. Daniels & Martin, *supra* note 25.

are able to outspend the State Bar. It upsets me, too, that because of the money involved, these attorneys are able to hire, which I thought were highly ethical, highly qualified attorneys to represent them. Usually the State Bar either backs down or accepts a lesser fine. You see so much blatant solicitation just going on, and nothing is being done about it.

When it came to the question of his own behavior, he said, "There is a large group of us that . . . I am always afraid. I know if I did something like that, they'd make an example of me." Regardless of the level of enforcement, most lawyers are not interested in crossing the formal ethical boundaries in their client acquisition practices.

Still, as these comments suggest, there are some plaintiffs' lawyers for whom the normative values embodied in the formal rules of professional conduct are of little concern. Their business model—whether successful or not—relies upon practices that are explicitly not allowed by the formal rules. Of course, no lawyer we interviewed admitted to currently using such practices. However, one lawyer offered the following:

When I started doing it [personal injury work], the comp [workers' compensation] was the thing that ran most personal injury businesses in Texas, and in order to have a big comp business you had to pay runners to bring the cases in to you. Now that's illegal and unethical, but no one ever got prosecuted for it. There would be rumblings about it, but no one ever did. So what you were supposed to have is a bunch of guys out there that would have a comp case, and then when they came in they would get $50.00 or $100.00 for bringing a guy in, and that sort of thing. Now, since I've had my own office, I didn't do that. But I will say that I am familiar with the practice, let's put it like that.

Today, auto accident cases are the foundation of many plaintiffs' practices, and a number of lawyers we interviewed complained of similar practices in their cities—like paying "independent contractors," tow-truck drivers, or emergency room personnel to steer clients to the lawyer; having paid employees (often described as "investigators") directly solicit accident victims for the lawyer; or sending direct-mail solicitations to accident victims. San Antonio, Houston, Corpus Christi, and Beaumont were mentioned most prominently as sites of such activity. One lawyer said, "Have a fender-bender and you get 17 letters from lawyers saying let me help you. . . . [Some] of them just find it very profitable to do it . . . even if it's not particularly legal."

Another group of plaintiffs' lawyers appears to view ethical rules as simply being boundaries on their business practices—ones they must operate within. For them, not operating within those boundaries places their business at risk. There is little concern with the normative side of professionalism and its ideals—it's just about business. One heavy advertiser with a high-volume business explained his view as follows:

> Sometimes I think I really would like to get into the courthouse and try a lot of cases, because I think I'd be pretty good at it. But then again, it's more important to me, to be perfectly frank with you, to make money. I don't mean to sound crass about it, but, you know, heck, if I've got an opportunity to be liquid for a few million dollars by the time I'm thirty-five or so . . . I'd rather do that than, you know, become Perry Mason.

He needs to pay attention to the rules, or he won't have a shot at making the money that he wants.

A similar view of the nature of the business is evident in the comments of a critic of aggressive advertising. He recounted an exchange he had at a professional meeting with an attorney who worked for one of the mass advertisers. It involved the advertiser's television spots, which some considered inappropriate (although the spots were well within the rules). The attorney who worked for the advertiser responded to the criticism rather bluntly: "I ain't a big proponent of these ads, but this is what X wants to do. It's an economic thing—we're going to do it; it works; it makes money for us."

Lawyers like that will do whatever the rules allow and will try any number of things that the rules do not explicitly prohibit. If the rules change, they adjust accordingly. A different heavy-advertising, high-volume lawyer said he had to pay attention to what his competitors—other high-volume practices—were doing to get clients. For instance, with regard to direct-mail solicitation he said, "I was looking at it, just because there were so many in it. . . . I've got like a brochure that I was just going to send them [auto accident victims]. I decided not to do it and they [State Bar of Texas] made it illegal anyways, and so I didn't do it." Still another said with regard to a form of direct-mail solicitation that was allowed at one time, "Frankly, they [a competitor] were making a fortune out of it. . . . Our feeling was that if anybody else was going to do it, they're taking cases away from us, and so what are we going to do? Are we going to let them take away from us and do nothing? So we did it too and it was very effective." When the disciplinary rules changed, he stopped using direct mail.[33]

Such lawyers are business people, and they approach things much as any other business would—it just happens that law is their business. They seem little interested in the professional aspects of lawyering or the normative values important to other plaintiffs' lawyers. For instance, when asked if he participated in the organized bar to any extent, the lawyer just quoted said, "No, no, not at all. I never go to the meetings."

Norms Do Matter

Unlike the lawyers just described, there is a substantial number of plaintiffs' lawyers for whom the normative aspects of professionalism are important. These values are also important for the plaintiffs' lawyers' professional organizations in Texas—the statewide organization, TTLA, and the local organizations as well. For these lawyers, three factors are important in their approach to how they get clients, and they reflect the basic balance, seen in Otto Mullinax's comments about his firm, between the economic aspect and the public service or professionalism aspect. They are (1) the professional community's normative values; (2) necessity; and (3) cost, or the bottom line. In our interviews, we found that issues involving normative standards and professionalism were intertwined with concerns about the realities of getting clients in a competitive environment, costs, and profitability.

As we have seen, many of the lawyers we interviewed expressed serious concerns about aggressive techniques for getting clients. In our surveys, one-

---

33. The rules to which this lawyer is referring—involving the timing and substance of direct-mail solicitation and other matters—changed in 1994. As noted earlier, the changes were challenged in federal court by a group of plaintiffs' lawyers led by Jim Adler of Houston (then and now a major television advertiser), and the key parts of the rules were upheld. See "Bar Gets the Power It Wants to Regulate Ads," Texas Lawyer, Apr. 10, 1995, at 1; *Texans Against Censorship, Inc. v. State Bar of Texas*, 888 F. Supp. 1328 (E.D. Tex. 1995), aff'd 100 F.3d 953 (5th Cir. 1996).

half of respondents said lawyer advertising is having a negative effect on their practices and their profession.[34] The comments we heard reflect their concern.

> "It detracts from, I think, the dignity of the bar."
>
> "I think it's unprofessional."
>
> "It makes me sick. It's horrible. . . . I mean, they're tasteless, horrible ads. . . . Advertising demeans a profession."
>
> "Oh, it's [direct mail] ridiculous. It's terribly undignified."
>
> "My father [a lawyer] always thought that it was, I don't want to say not dignified, but that it was bad for the profession . . . and that filtered down to me."
>
> "I probably have to admit that I have a deep and abiding prejudice against lawyer advertising."
>
> "I don't like TV advertising, I'll make no bones about. I think it's bad. I think it's bad for the profession, and I think it's bad for the system."
>
> "I think it's been demeaning, undignified, harmful, crass, grotesque. I hate it."
>
> "It ain't fittin', you know. I don't think it looks professional is all I can say. It's just an intuitive, sort of gut feeling."

Clearly, these lawyers believe aggressive techniques for getting clients violate their sense of professionalism.

There is also a practical side to that concern. Worse, in the eyes of many plaintiffs' lawyers, was the increasing use of advertising from the late 1980s into the early 1990s, which occurred as the tort reform debate in Texas was developing into a major political issue. As Chapter 2 explained, Texas experienced a series of intense political battles over tort reform with substantial reforms enacted in 1987, 1995, and 2003. Those reform efforts included an aggressive public relations campaign featuring allegations of frivolous lawsuits, runaway juries, greedy plaintiffs' lawyers, and the like. All too often, the image of plaintiffs' lawyers one could take away from many television advertisements or direct-mail solicitations fit neatly into the tort reformers' critique of the civil justice system.

---

34. In contrast, only 16 percent said the effect was positive, with the remainder saying no effect.

The strong language many plaintiffs' lawyers use to criticize those using aggressive techniques is very telling. It is meant to label them as miscreants or outsiders to be shunned, and it says much about this practice community's sense of itself as a profession. One lawyer recounted a heated discussion he had with another lawyer working for one of Texas's prolific advertisers:

> I was in a meeting with one of X's lawyers on this topic [aggressive television advertising]. . . . "Well," he said, "we're in the same business. I don't know why you're against us." I said, "No, we're not in the same business." I said, "I know every one of my clients. Most of the time, I've been to their home, I've met their children." I said, "If one of your clients walked in the door right now, would you know 'em?" I said, "Don't tell me we're in the same area of practice."

Another lawyer's characterization, although somewhat extreme, literally paints aggressive advertisers as outsiders. He said of aggressive advertisers, "I don't see them; I don't interact with them; I don't touch them; I don't fool with them—what I call the soliciting lawyers . . . very aggressive advertising lawyers. I know some of them send us cases [refer cases with the expectation of a fee] when I don't know they're aggressive advertisers. . . . If I find out, I send the case back. I just . . . there's something about that I find repulsive." It is almost as if those outsiders, and even their cases, are literally diseased and the community needs to protect itself from them. This elite lawyer's remarks also suggest, as Sara Parikh has argued, that referral relationships can function as an important means of social control within the plaintiffs' bar.[35]

Consistent with such views, some lawyers adamantly refuse to advertise or solicit business in any way, even though their practices suffer as a result. This was the case with a lawyer in Fort Worth and another in East Texas. Both are experienced and previously successful lawyers facing competition at the time of the interview from heavy television advertisers for cases, especially for small-to-modest auto accident cases—the bread-and-butter cases for the plaintiffs' bar. When asked why he did not try advertising or some other more aggressive approach to getting clients, the Fort Worth lawyer said, "I've resisted

---

35. Sara Parikh, *How the Spider Catches the Fly: Referral Networks in the Plaintiff's Personal Injury Bar*, 51 N.Y.L. Sch. L. Rev. 244, 260–261 (2006).

it to this point. . . . I have an aversion to it, honestly. I have an aversion to putting myself forward that much. I'm probably wrong to think like that—a lawyer should be willing to promote himself a little bit more, but it's kind of an ingrained feeling that it's unseemly." He had thought of trying some other kind of legal work, including working on the other side or for an industry, but he concluded, "I'm not sure I could do it, I mean work for industry. . . . [I'd] be working for principles that I really don't believe in, and that would be hard to do. I may have to, but it would be difficult. It might cause a terminal clinical depression." He closed his practice not long after our interview.

The East Texas lawyer has a similar view of himself as a professional. He said, "I'm a solo practitioner. I like the freedom of being solo. . . . I just want to help people on a one-on-one basis with car wreck and workers' comp and, you know, premises liability. And I enjoy doing that." He built his practice on lawyer referrals.

> Over the years I've tried to develop a good referral network of other lawyers who send business. . . . I have never been able to develop the reputation of being . . . of handling gigantic cases, so most of the cases that are referred to me are small and medium-sized cases, but there's been a very steady stream of them for fifteen, twenty years now, and that's . . . how my practice has grown. . . . It's just been word of mouth.

A previously successful lawyer, he is facing intense competition from heavy television advertisers for cases. As he put it, "My practice has collapsed. I made $23,000 last year."

Trying desperately to find ways of staying in business without resorting to advertising or other forms of direct solicitation for clients, the East Texas lawyer has depleted his retirement savings to keep his practice afloat. Nonetheless, he cannot bring himself to advertise. He finds it, especially television, abhorrent. As he put it, "A guy comes home from work, gets his beer, sits in front of the TV, and hears this lawyer, this smarmy-looking lawyer, telling him, 'If you get hurt, I'll make you rich.' . . . And I know how I personally respond to lawyer advertising in a very negative way. . . . You know, when somebody looks at that, the average person, they see graft. They see fraud. They see corruption."

Later in the interview, he added, "It's part of my ministry, I guess. I'm a Christian, and I feel like this is part of my ministry to help people." One should not dismiss this religious reference point. For at least some, their religious faith is a real part of what they do. Another father-son plaintiffs' team went to some length in our interview explaining how they teach an adult Sunday school class at the Baptist church the family has attended for generations—a class that addressed lawyers and ministry. We saw something similar in Franklin Jones Sr.'s views noted at the end of Chapter 2 regarding the idea of Jesus Christ as a Republican candidate.

Such lawyers reflect the community's values in their purest form—they are the true believers. Perhaps the starkest statement came from a lawyer who, after talking about the sense of professionalism he inherited from his father, said, "If that's what it takes to keep the business going, then we aren't willing to keep the business going."

While the dislike of aggressive techniques is widely shared, the approach of most lawyers to getting clients in a competitive environment is more pragmatic. Lawyers must balance their commitment to professionalism with necessity. Once a lawyer starts considering some form of advertising or other aggressive approach to getting clients, the first thing that enters into the equation is the reaction of one's peers. One plaintiffs' bar leader put it very simply: "Reputation is everything in this business." Here one can see the complex effect on access that the norms underlying professional identity could have— dampening it as well as enhancing it.

THE COMMUNITY'S BASIC NORMATIVE VALUES

Three elements appear from our interviews as important in understanding the community's normative values, and they surface most clearly in the criticisms of the "miscreants" in which much of the plaintiffs' community indulges. First is the commitment to public service or the public good—as the plaintiffs' lawyers define it. Related is the idea of actually trying cases. Last is the nature and substance of the solicitation techniques used and whether or not they are "tasteful."

Commitment to the Public Good and Helping People

In explaining what they find objectionable in the practices of the miscreants, lawyers often point to the goals of those they criticize in contrast to what they view as a more appropriate set of professional goals. The criticized lawyers are interested *only* in making money or building their practices—it's just a business. One lawyer neatly summarized this view: "You know, those characters are obviously making money. If you speak to them of the profession or the culture of the profession or the traditions, they would look at you like you're from Mars. They're in it for a buck." Such lawyers are not concerned with their clients' best interests. Their practices are derisively called "mills," and the lawyers themselves are referred to as "bottom-feeders" or "scumbags." One highly respected plaintiffs' lawyer simply said that the heavy television advertisers "are not competent to handle business. . . . They make a fee on it, [but] their client is not very well served. . . . I view those people as bottom-feeders." Another lawyer said, "They don't give a damn. They got into it for no worthy cause."[36]

What is missing in the practices of these "bottom-feeders" (allowing, of course, for making a decent living) are the kinds of values that should be the motivating factor. It's the "worthy cause" that's missing—the "worthy cause" that helps to define for the critics what lies at the heart of their profession. Earlier we discussed the lawyer who talked about helping people as part of a personal ministry. Similarly, a younger lawyer in San Antonio said, "I've always had a feeling or empathy for the underdog. In most cases that I saw [while working during law school in a lawyer's office] in the plaintiffs' side of personal injury, you're the underdog . . . and going to take on more powerful interests."

An Austin lawyer, whose "father was a construction worker all of his life," offered a similar story: "Each summer and each winter [Christmas break], I worked on a construction crew. . . . I was an ironworker basically and a laborer." Needing money during the academic year while in law school, he found a job in a plaintiffs' firm. "I immediately found that what these folks did was help folks just like my father. They did things for people who couldn't do things for themselves. I thought that must be the calling of a lawyer." He continued, "I had always heard about lawyers, you know—the biggest lawyer in [an East Texas town] was the lawyer who represented the big buck. All of a sudden I saw a different side that I never seen or heard of before. . . . So that's how I became

---

36. To better inform and protect potential clients of "mills," Nora Engstrom has argued for requiring contingency fee lawyers to submit closing statements for each case handled to the appropriate authority and that statistics from such statements be compiled and put on the Internet in a searchable database. *See* Nora Engstrom, *Sunlight and Settlement Mills*, 86 N.Y.U. L. Rev. 805 (2011), 856–868.

a personal injury lawyer . . . knowing that they were sure helping the kind of people back where I came from."

What these examples reflect is the sentiment underlying the second of the guiding principles for Otto Mullinax's firm. Not all plaintiffs' lawyers, as we have seen, could be considered true believers, but the sentiment is a legacy that still runs strong even among younger lawyers. As one of them said, "Guys like me, we can do the commercial litigation and make money. . . . If you're a true believer, then what's the point of that? So you make money and you're not doing something you believe in. You're not helping people."

Trying Cases

Actually trying cases is fundamentally important to plaintiffs' lawyers' sense of themselves as professionals. It is not that one must always be in the courtroom. Rather, it is whether you ever try cases, or at least want to. The heavy advertisers and others who are openly aggressive in getting clients are seen as never trying cases, and this helps in characterizing them as outsiders. As one Houston lawyer said, they spend "a lot of money not only in advertising but in added personnel to . . . try to get the billable cases that are coming in the door. Most of those people . . . have never seen the inside of a courtroom and don't intend to ever see the inside of a courtroom, consider it a complete waste of time." He later added, "They are not fulfilling a role as an attorney; they're doing nothing but adjusting claims from the plaintiffs' standpoint."

The idea is that a lawyer cannot be serving his clients well if the lawyer is not willing or able to litigate. In a sense, it is the difference between mere access and high-quality access. The clients will not get the settlement they deserve because the insurance companies will not pay an appropriate case value to a lawyer unwilling to litigate. In discussing some of the television advertisers, a Fort Worth lawyer remarked, "The ones I knew . . . never tried any cases. . . . My impression of [a local advertiser] was that he used to settle for whatever he could get. He told the client he had to take it." A compliment—of sorts—paid by a respected Houston lawyer to the heavy advertisers says much about their standing among plaintiffs' lawyers like the speaker: "They are probably some of the best businesspeople I know."

Over and over we heard the complaint that certain lawyers are never seen at the courthouse or that their names do not appear in the local jury verdict reporters. In short, the major advertisers have no professional reputation—they are not really seen as lawyers. A San Antonio lawyer simply said, "You get the reputation over at the courthouse." This can be seen in the comments of an established Austin lawyer about a younger lawyer whose firm was originally viewed with a jaundiced eye. He said, "They made their practice around chiropractic referrals. They've done a lot of aggressive marketing. . . . Two years ago, they were really just thought of as having a chiropractor running cases for them." However, some successful medical malpractice cases changed things. "On the other hand, [this lawyer] has had a couple of outstanding results. . . . His results have started to at least confer something of a reputation on him."

Though some lawyers complain that those who aggressively advertise and solicit clients never see the inside of the courtroom, the reality is that some actually do. Rare is the concession made by the older lawyer in Dallas who said, "I think one of the things that a lot of people complain about the law-factory lawyers, or settlers, is that they don't believe they do an adequate job with the client, and that is probably true, but there are some of them that do. They don't do as good a job as [an experienced Dallas lawyer] or I would do." Actually, some of them might do as good a job. There are heavy television advertisers who are certified by the Texas Board of Legal Specialization in personal injury trial law and/or civil trial law, and certification requires a proven track record as a litigator. Certified or not, there are heavy advertisers who regularly litigate cases and have litigation sections within their firms. They may not litigate high-stakes or complex cases like medical malpractice, but they do know their way around the courthouse.

The bottom line with regard to "seeing the inside of the courtroom" is reputation. Being a heavy advertiser or being seen as using frowned-upon (but still on the right side of the formal rules) techniques for getting clients can damage one's reputation or hamper the development of a reputation. The presumption—the automatic normative judgment—is that only certain kinds of lawyers use aggressive techniques. These lawyers are not real plaintiffs' lawyers—not members of the community—because they never try cases. They don't contribute to the profession. As one critic put it, "Those are the individuals that are not participating and not contributing and not doing a damn thing except ruining the profession's reputation." They advertise because they have no reputation—nothing to attract clients. This means a plaintiffs' lawyer who advertises heavily or aggressively in the eyes of others will have to take into consideration the potential consequences for his or her reputation. A Houston

lawyer said simply, "You know, I never have done any advertising, mostly because of the stigma that is attached to it."

Of course, the derogatory comments are meant to indicate the outsider
status of the heavy advertisers and those using aggressive techniques to get
clients. In so doing, such comments help define the boundaries of the plaintiffs' lawyers' own professional community. To repeat part of a statement we
quoted earlier in this chapter, one lawyer bluntly said, "I don't see them; I don't
interact with them; I don't touch them; I don't fool with them." They're like a
disease and the community needs to protect itself from them.

"Tastefulness" and the Nature of Client Acquisition Techniques

What is it about the nature and substance of advertising and direct solicitation that is so troubling? In terms of its nature, at the extreme, some activities
actually violate the formal rules, such as the rule against paying non-lawyer
runners. Needless to say, there is no tolerance in the community for a lawyer using techniques that violate the formal rules—even if the violator is a
prominent plaintiffs' lawyer. Perhaps *the* example is the late John O'Quinn
of Houston, a highly successful plaintiffs' lawyer with a formidable reputation as a litigator. The Texas Commission for Lawyer Discipline twice tried
to disbar O'Quinn, both times based upon allegations of case running in the
aftermath of airplane crashes. The first attempt in the 1980s eventually led
to only a public reprimand, a fine, and community service. In the second, in
1998, one of the most-respected members of the Texas plaintiffs' bar, Broadus
Spivey of Austin (serving as President of TTLA, 1981–1982; President of the
State Bar, 2001–2002; President of the International Academy of Trial Lawyers,
2002–2003), took a substantial amount of time out of his own practice to act as
the lead attorney for the commission in the disbarment proceedings. A lawyer
knowledgeable of disciplinary matters remarked that not even O'Quinn's level
of success meant a free pass. "You know, somebody's got to . . . if you think
something's not right, then you've got to go in there and take it to the mat. And
that's what Broadus did."

The criticism also extends to the substance of activities that are within
the formal rules. The critics share the legal profession's traditional dislike of
advertising and direct solicitation of recent accident victims or their families

because they believe such practices erode the profession's legitimacy. The constant complaint is that the activities are somehow tasteless or tacky or even cheesy. But there is more behind the criticism—the fact that much of the substance of the objectionable activities dovetails with the aggressive tort reform public relations. It is like a one-two punch.

Lawyers are quite specific in talking about the consequences of tasteless advertisements, even if they are within the formal rules. The most concrete indicator of the effects of advertising for plaintiffs' lawyers is what they see when they go to the courthouse and select a jury. A Fort Worth lawyer's comments are typical of what many others said:

> I think advertising is bad. It greatly contributed to the public cynicism towards lawyers and personal injury lawyers. I think it's been a very major factor. Every time I go down to the courthouse for a trial, I ask this because this is a question that will always get you a response—have they seen the ads for lawyers advertising for clients? At a minimum, two-thirds have seen them, usually more than that. Then if you say, "How many of you formed a bad impression about personal injury lawyer or personal injury cases because of those television ads?," the vast majority of them raise their hand. The case I tried in Dallas, there were eight jurors disqualified for cause on that issue alone.

A Houston lawyer said, "I think advertising has been an engine that helped drive tort reform. . . . So many attorneys, particularly the less experienced and less capable, did an overwhelming amount of poor taste advertising that just gave the appearance of the worst. . . . I think it gave people the impression that we are all a bunch of used car salesmen, and I hate that. Does that answer your question!?" In short, the advertisers have helped "poison" the jury pool. A San Antonio lawyer said, "There is so much solicitation going on, the public is getting such a bad taste in their mouth for personal injury litigation in general —it's reflected in the jury verdicts." Almost all plaintiffs' lawyers would agree with this assessment. In other words, the concern over aggressive techniques for getting clients is not merely a matter of traditional professionalism. There is also the pragmatic assessment that such activities are bad for business in the long run.

Despite the community's general dislike of advertising and solicitation, some lawyers who share that dislike still feel they must advertise to stay in business. Their situation offers additional insight into the decisions lawyers make in meeting the challenge of getting that steady stream of clients they need to survive. They must find ways of attracting clients without offending their peers, especially the established lawyers who are the opinion leaders and the influential members of the plaintiffs' lawyers' professional organizations. From them, we can get a better sense of how the community's normative values influence what they do when necessity looms.

NECESSITY AND COMMUNITY NORMS: THE TENSION

"Tastefulness"

There is recognition on the part of some, but not all, lawyers that a certain amount of advertising may be necessary—especially for younger lawyers trying to build their practices in a highly competitive environment. The competitiveness has intensified because of tort reform and its supporters' aggressive public relations campaigns and because of the aggressive advertisers who have siphoned off a significant portion of the auto accident market. These cases, especially the numerous smaller ones, are the bread-and-butter cases a younger lawyer can handle successfully, build a reputation on, and use to grow a client base for referrals of future business. Many younger lawyers say they must advertise in order to develop their practice, and some established lawyers recognize this. One such lawyer said, "There is a group like our firm that doesn't believe in it [advertising]. There are a lot of other younger lawyers who do. They say, 'How else am I going to get business? I'm not established, and I've got to do this.' I don't argue with that."

Reflecting this idea, a younger lawyer said, "I don't like lawyer advertising, but I think—I realize that it's a necessary evil, to some extent, in order to maintain your business." He is not alone. Another said, "I've been in the Yellow Pages for five years, just pretty much out of necessity." He emphasized the idea of advertising tastefully and that he doesn't even object to television "as long as it's done tastefully." Another younger lawyer defended his firm's Yellow Pages ad (its only advertising), saying, "I think ours is fairly innocuous. If you looked at ours versus other people's, I mean, we don't have any dogs foaming at the mouth. . . . Ours says that we're clearly in the personal injury business." He went on to say,

I don't think we're offending anybody with our ad. We may be. Some lawyers don't like any advertising. They say that it is unprofessional . . . but it is a necessary part of our practice, particularly for those of us trying to build a client base. We may not get the greatest cases in the world through our Yellow Pages ad, but if we get cases that we're able to take, eventually those will result in referrals from our former clients.

A younger lawyer in Houston, who had just aired his first television ad, talked about the problem of juries with regard to advertising. In a changing, competitive market, he was not getting enough cases by relying on lawyer referrals. He faced a dilemma because he tried cases and was beginning to get a reputation as someone who tries cases and wins. As he put it, his television ad "was the best that I could come up with to balance the need to get business and the need not to hurt my ability to represent my clients." He described his ad as follows:

People tell me that they really appreciated my ad because it's just me in a courtroom in a suit. I say, "My name is [omitted]. If you are injured by another's negligence, please contact me. I will fight for you." There's no lightning bolts, there's no car wrecks, there's no graphics. It's just me saying, "If you're hurt, I will fight for you. I will try to do the right thing. Come hire me." . . . The people that were producing the ad were saying, "This isn't going to work." They wanted to do all these things that were embarrassing. They wanted to put in music, I said, "No." They wanted to put in waving flags, I said, "No." They wanted to put in car wrecks, "No." They wanted to have a car wreck flash on the screen, I said, "No." Because I have to try cases. I can't beat [name omitted, a prolific television advertiser based in Houston] and try cases. I can't have the car wrecks and the fist pumping and . . .

This lawyer also knew he would be risking his developing reputation as a plaintiffs' lawyer if his ad was seen as problematic by jurors or his peers.

It is not just younger lawyers who face the necessary evil. A midcareer lawyer in Austin said, "I don't like to advertise, but I've had to do television advertising from time to time." A Fort Worth lawyer was blunt in his statement, even though he recognized the potential downside: "I did it when I had to do it. . . . Ten years ago I had billboards. . . . I don't need to do it now, and if I needed to do it, I would." The potential downside comes when a juror asks whether a lawyer advertises. "They look at you with less suspicion when you tell them 'No, I don't advertise.'" A San Antonio lawyer who tries cases and who never had more than small, simple Yellow Pages ads in the past, said, "I don't like lawyer advertising. Okay? I just don't like it. I think that's something that hurts us." But at the time of the interview, he was contemplating embarking on his television advertising effort—buying into a plan with toll-free telephone numbers that prospective clients would call and have their cases initially screened by an employee of the plan, who would then direct the calls to lawyers in a sequence within a given zip code. For him, it was sheer necessity:

> I do it [plaintiffs' practice] because I like helping people. At one time, I thought that I would make good money at doing this. I made less money last year than I have made the five years preceding that. . . . Last year it went down significantly. I like practicing law; I like helping people, and at one time I thought you could make some money doing it. . . . But frankly, I question how much longer I can do it. Really, that is the reality of it.

He commented on the amount of advertising he sees "and lawyers getting cases that have no business getting that case because they don't know what to do with it. Because they advertise, they get the case." And of course, as a non-advertiser, he wasn't getting the cases. He said, "You have to start wondering, well, is it time to say I don't like it, but it's a necessary evil."

Image Advertising: Burnishing the Plaintiffs' Bar

We also found lawyers who took a longer-term view of necessity and a very different, but quite pragmatic, approach to advertising. For instance, a midcareer West Texas lawyer said, "We didn't want to advertise and don't like to advertise, but we do because other people are advertising and we want to get our name out there as well." His approach is more of a preemptive strategy than a reactive one. Whereas some lawyers may advertise even though they dislike the idea because they feel they have to because their business is already suffering, this lawyer wanted to advertise before his business was in trouble. It is a longer-term strategy related to his business *and* to the profession more generally. As he said, "We do a different type of advertising than most people probably do.... Ours is an image-type advertising." We found a number of lawyers doing roughly the same kind of public relations advertising. Like them, this lawyer is very much an insider with an excellent reputation.

In explaining his advertising strategy he said, "One of the ads that we run is if you were going to see a doctor ... you'd want to see a board-certified doctor, and all the lawyers in our law firm are board certified in personal injury trial law. That's basically it." It is a thirty-second television spot. Another one of his ads is an informational one about the jury system, and there is one "about trial lawyers—trial lawyers basically defend principles of who's right and personal injury and fairness." He readily admitted, "It's not a get-business type of deal." Its purpose is directed elsewhere. "We have gotten a lot of positive comments from people talking about our ads. They like our ads, and they say, you know, 'We like yours, and, boy, the other guy's ad, I can't stand it.'" Rather than get business in the short run, he said, "I think it's helped our public image a lot, which is what we wanted to do." Still, it may bring cases down the line. The advertising firm he used told him that "with this kind of campaign, you're not—the phone's not going to ring every time you run your ad. But over several years you'll generate this base of people that will, you know, that's how your business will come in. And that's pretty well proved to be true."

This approach not only helps his public image but also, he hopes, enhances the public image of plaintiffs' lawyers more generally. It presents the public with a positive image of a plaintiffs' lawyer as professional and serious, not simply looking for business. Another West Texas lawyer whose firm embarked on a similar advertising campaign said it was one that would stand in stark contrast to that of a typical television advertiser. He said,

It's gonna be something that when our children go to school, they're gonna be proud that they can see their dad on television doing that. They're—it's gonna be first class, it's gonna be tasteful, it's gonna be supportive of the legal system, or else we're not gonna do it.... And when we got the ads back and looked at 'em, we agreed these are—and each of us took 'em home to our respective spouses, said, "What do you think?" And they said, "These are fine, they don't bother us at all. These make us proud of what you do." And so that's how we advertise.

He added, "I live in a small town [a metropolitan area of just over 100,000] ... and I care more about being able to live in a small town." There is no reason to doubt this sentiment, but living in that small town also means trying cases before juries in the region.

Lawyers are advertising not just to get cases but to reinforce their reputation and counter both the effects of aggressive advertising for cases and the effects of the tort reform public relations campaigns. This takes the idea of tasteful advertising in a whole new direction. It is advertising—or public relations—in defense of the profession and professionalism, at least the plaintiffs' lawyers' version. Among these advertisers are some of the elite of the plaintiffs' bar. One of those lawyers said, "Unless those of us who have been in this practice a long time and did not advertise were willing just to abandon personal injury practice, we'd better figure out a way to advertise because there wasn't going to be any left.... It's all going to go away.... So we set out to try to figure out a way to do it in a tasteful ... to market in a tasteful way. And I think we have."

The campaign involved radio spots, and he admitted that the spots were not generating any business. But the spots were considered a success nonetheless. They were like infomercials in which the lawyer identifies himself and says he is going to answer a question that came into the firm recently, such as one dealing with the statute of limitations or one dealing with wrongful death cases. He said, "We're getting very positive comments from the bar and both sides of the bar and I think from citizens, although some don't like trial lawyers, and they don't like us to talk about anything that has to do with injury or death. But I think we're projecting a good positive image of trial lawyers in this community." This last idea is probably the most important—the positive image.

Necessity drives some lawyers to advertise, albeit reluctantly, because of the immediate need to get clients, but the community's normative values shape what they do and how they do it. Necessity drives other lawyers to advertise as a longer-term strategy in order to further and protect the community and its normative values. These lawyers hope to burnish the public perception of plaintiffs' lawyers with ads not immediately geared toward getting business but rather to serve some broader idea of public service—of course, as plaintiffs' lawyers see it. No one seems to object to advertising in the community's interest.

The Problem of Cost

The community's normative values have an important influence on the decisions lawyers make in meeting the challenge of getting a steady stream of clients, but they are not the only factor to be considered. There is also the very practical issue of cost. Advertising or other forms of client acquisition may bring in potential clients, but these techniques can be expensive. A lawyer must balance the cost of the advertising against its possible return. In our interviews, lawyers regularly raised the cost issue. As one lawyer said of his Yellow Pages ad, "We ran a full-page ad this year; cost us $3,000 a month to run that. We're making $2,000 a month off it, so we're running a $1,000 a month shortfall." Another said, "The Yellow Pages, of course, cost us a fortune. . . . It just makes me sick to write those checks. It's $20,000 to $25,000 we're spending on it." That expense is per month because this lawyer was advertising in five different telephone books in his metropolitan area, but he believes the ads bring in enough business—direct business from people who call based on the ads and indirect business from other people those clients may refer to this lawyer in the future—to justify the cost. Back covers of telephone books cost well over $100,000. Television advertising, of course, is the most expensive, with the most prolific advertisers spending well over $1 million a year just for the airtime in one of a number of markets in which they may advertise. More than anything, this may explain why so few lawyers use television advertising to any extent.[37]

Mass advertisers have additional costs, such as a marketing firm to oversee much of the advertising process. For instance, one television advertiser tried doing things on his own but quickly realized he could not. "So I got an expert. He tracks the trims. He's in Nashville. He gives me a sheet every month that tells me who's calling, what programs, where I get the calls. . . . [He does] it more scientifically as to what times to put advertising; what times not to put advertising; what times of the year are better than other times of the year; when can you get the best TV buys for the time." The marketing firm also works on the content of the ads and on targeting them toward a particular clientele or type of case.

For any lawyer who advertises to any degree, there are still more expenses —the costs of the personnel and infrastructure needed to handle the calls coming into the practice as a result of that advertising and screening those calls. A Dallas lawyer who advertises said,

37. Stephen Daniels & Joanne Martin, *It's Darwinism—Survival of the Fittest: How Markets and Reputations Shape the Ways in Which Plaintiffs' Lawyers Obtain Cases*, 21 L. & Pol'y 377, 388–390 (1999).

> Advertising is an expensive proposition. These guys that are running spots on TV, they are spending some big bucks. And when you spend that kind of money in the type of advertising, you gather up every kook in town; a lot of them with their shopping bags full of papers. A "shopping bag" case, as we refer to them. . . . How much are you going to have to pay someone to go through that shopping bag and determine that the statute ran ten years ago and they're still shopping it around?

One television advertiser averaged about 1,000 calls a month from his ads and was carrying $100,000 a month in overhead to process those calls.[38]

For many plaintiffs' lawyers, the costs involved are enough to deter them from advertising—or advertising to any great degree. Cost, together with the potential damage to one's reputation among other plaintiffs' lawyers and the response of jurors, provides a formidable barrier to advertising, especially on television. The fact that some lawyers still advertise to get clients and face the potential censure of their peers is an indication of just how precarious their situations may be.

CONCLUSION

In this chapter, we set out to do two things: first, explore how plaintiffs' lawyers get clients, and second, use that exploration as a window into professional identity. We found that plaintiffs' lawyers get most of their business from referrals and not from advertising or other controversial means. We also found that they have a distinct professional identity—a set of shared norms that help shape a community of practice and not just a practice area. These norms influence what many lawyers will do and show us that plaintiffs' lawyers cannot be understood simply as rational business actors. It is not clear that many rational business actors would enter this practice area or stay in it in a hostile tort reform environment. To the extent that these lawyers are not purely rational

---

38. When asked about the percentage of those calls that led to a signed agreement to handle the case, that lawyer said, "Probably, maybe 10 percent, 20 percent, something like that. It's pretty low." He added that 25 percent of those initially accepted would eventually be dropped upon further investigation or the lack of insurance for the defendant.

actors—in light of Professor Brickman's revealing assessment of tort reform's purposes—access is enhanced. Still, given the community's norms regarding client acquisition, access can also be dampened.

The community's approach to those norms, however, is decidedly pragmatic, and only a few lawyers will adhere strictly to them. Necessity tempers those norms because most plaintiffs' lawyers, like Otto Mullinax, want to make a good living as well as serve the professional goals that motivate them. If there is in fact a community of practice—a coherent plaintiffs' bar—and not just a practice area, the next question is what that community looks like. Chapter 5 answers this question and in doing so looks at some effects of tort reform on plaintiffs' lawyers.

5. "People Like Me Are Really the Majority of Plaintiffs' Lawyers"

Structure and Hierarchy in the Texas Plaintiffs' Bar

"People like me are really the majority of plaintiffs' lawyers. The Pat Maloneys, the Wendell Turleys, the Frank Bransons [well-known Texas plaintiffs' lawyers with high-end practices], those aren't the mainstay that represents the injured person. It's a guy like me. I've got one lawyer who works for me. I've got two secretaries." A San Antonio lawyer we interviewed in the late 1990s used these words in describing his practice and its place in the Texas plaintiffs' bar. There is a coherent plaintiffs' bar in Texas, and, as the lawyer's description reflects, it is one with an identifiable hierarchy.

It is a complex hierarchy, and there is much more to it than the ubiquitous (and at times outrageous) television advertisers like Brian Loncar of Dallas or Jim Adler of Houston.[1] There is more than the larger-than-life heavy hitters whose exploits in handling high-stakes and mass tort cases raise the ire of corporations, defense lawyers, and tort reformers—lawyers like the ones noted in the quotation or like John O'Quinn, Joe Jamail, John Eddie Williams, or Mark Lanier, who make headlines in the media—and especially the influential legal media like the *American Lawyer* or the *National Law Journal*. Such lawyers, along with the big advertisers, are the ones who attract, if not demand, our attention. It can be hard to ignore them, and it is easy to simply generalize from them in creating an image of the plaintiffs' bar.

Such an image, however, is far from accurate. If for no other reason than the specialization and market segmentation we find within the plaintiffs' bar's actual structure, some knowledge of these factors is needed to understand plaintiffs' lawyers' practices in the age of tort reform and what it means for their gatekeeping role and access (the best access tracks the plaintiffs' bar's

---

1. See Karen Olsson, *Jim Adler, Personal Injury Attorney*, Tex. Monthly, Aug. 2009, www.texasmonthly.com/story/jim-adler-personal-injury-lawyer, and Joanna Cattanach, *'Strong Arm' Flexing His Muscle Again: Rebounding from Collision, Injury Lawyer Loncar Is Back—and Out to Recover Claim*, Dallas Morning News, Nov. 29, 2008, www.wfaa.com/news/local/64539652.html.

market segmentation and structure). As the discussion of Texas tort reform in Chapter 2 showed, what happens to a practice may differ depending on its place in the hierarchy.

THE TEXAS PLAINTIFFS' BAR: SIZE AND STRUCTURE

The true size of the Texas plaintiffs' bar is hard to know with precision, in part because there is no simple definition of what a plaintiffs' lawyer is. Is it a lawyer who is certified in personal injury trial law by the Texas Board of Legal Specialization? If so, the plaintiffs' bar would be relatively small. In 2013, there were 1,678 lawyers certified in personal injury trial law.[2] However, even this number includes both plaintiffs' and defense lawyers.

Is it simply a lawyer who is a member of the Texas Trial Lawyers Association? TTLA would say this is not the case for no other reason than the lengthy list it maintains of lawyers who might be "prospects." This prospect list consists of lawyers who practice some amount of plaintiffs' law but who have never been members. These are the lawyers TTLA hopes to recruit. TTLA also keeps a list of former members.

Is it lawyers who do *any* amount of plaintiffs' work on a contingency fee basis? In a 2002 article, we roughly estimated that plaintiffs' lawyers made up no more than about 10 percent of the in-state members of the Texas bar, which would be about 6,200 lawyers.[3] Using that percentage and 2012 figures on the number of in-state members of the Texas State Bar, there would be no more than about 8,300 plaintiffs' lawyers, but again, this would be only a very rough estimate.[4]

Our interest is in lawyers for whom plaintiffs' work done on a contingency

2. Texas Board of Legal Specialization, *FAQ*, www.tbls.org/FAQs/FAQ.aspx?id=1#q-4general.

3. Stephen Daniels & Joanne Martin, *It Was the Best of Times, It Was the Worst of Times: The Precarious Nature of Plaintiffs' Practice in Texas*, 80 Tex. L. Rev. 1781, 1784 n. 12 (2002).

4. The Texas State Bar had 82,607 in-state members as of Dec. 31, 2012. *See State Bar of Texas Membership: Attorney Statistical Profile (2012–2013)*, State Bar of Texas Department of Research and Analysis, www.texasbar.com/AM/Template.cfm?Section=Demographic_and_Economic_Trends&Template=/CM/ContentDisplay.cfm&ContentID=23528.

fee basis accounts for a substantial part of their business. Among the lawyers we interviewed, none devoted less than 50 percent of their caseload to plaintiffs' work and some reported a concentration as high as 90 percent or more. As a threshold for our survey respondents, we required that they devote at least 25 percent of their practice time to contingency fee work. For the lawyers who responded to our surveys (pooling the responses from both surveys together, $n = 1,012$), the mean percentage of plaintiffs' work was 75 percent, and the median percentage was 90 percent. The lawyers in our surveys, therefore, are not simply those who occasionally do some plaintiffs' work. They are plaintiffs' specialists who devote most, if not all, of their practices to such work. The largest percentage (26 percent) reported doing plaintiffs' work exclusively, and another 25 percent reported that 90 to 99 percent of their practice was devoted to plaintiffs' work. Our letter writer from the Preface fits in here; he said that 99 percent of his work was plaintiffs' work. In short, it makes sense not only to talk of an identifiable Texas plaintiffs' bar, but to talk of one comprised of lawyers who have chosen to specialize in this particular area.

As the comments of the San Antonio lawyer that opened this chapter reflect, Texas plaintiffs' lawyers do not see themselves as fungible. There is a structure and a hierarchy within the plaintiffs' bar, and the best way in which to describe that structure is to categorize lawyers on the basis of the value of their average contingency fee case. Doing so will not capture everything that is important, such as a lawyer's reputation for professionalism and integrity, but it does seem to capture the most important indicator in the eyes of plaintiffs' lawyers of where someone is situated in the hierarchy. As one lawyer told us in explaining the referral process, "So what you'll have . . . is a handful of what everybody considers to be the 'heavy hitters.' The ones that for some reason always end up with big cases."

At the other end of the spectrum are the bread-and-butter lawyers, described by a Texas legal journalist as "the workaday PI [personal injury] lawyer—the lawyer whose bread is buttered by the run-of-the-mill car-wreck cases."[5] The San Antonio lawyer quoted earlier is a bread-and-butter lawyer, his typical case being what he called a "bread-and-butter automobile accident." In his words, "I guess the most typical case is your automobile accident case that will involve injury but not death, where the person probably was taken to the hospital in the EMS, probably didn't spend the night in the hospital but was

5. Joseph Calve, *Poured Out*, 18 Tex. Lawyer, Dec. 16,1996, at 1.

treated, examined, released, told to come back to their doctor—usual medical being all of $5,000" (about $7,600 in 2014 dollars). An Austin lawyer provided a similar picture: "The kinds of cases I have, the 'bread-and-butter,' so to speak, day-in, day-out cases are auto cases. They pay the bills."

For the lawyers who responded to our surveys, the average value of the typical case was $749,000 (in 2006 dollars).[6] However, few lawyers had a typical case value that high. The case value at the 75th percentile (meaning 75 percent of respondents had a case value below this figure) was $200,000, and the value at the 25th percentile (meaning 75 percent of respondents had a value higher than this amount) was $15,000. The median value (the 50th percentile, the value that splits the distribution in half) was $40,000 (about $47,000 in 2014 dollars). In short, most plaintiffs' lawyers' practices are not built on big, complex cases involving millions of dollars. They are built on more modest cases.[7]

We can use these figures on the distribution of case values to build a straightforward way of describing the structure of the plaintiffs' bar. The first group includes those with a typical case value of $14,999 or less—251 lawyers (the first quartile). The second group includes those with a typical case value between $15,000 and $40,000—258 lawyers (the next quartile). The third group includes those with typical case values between $40,001 and $200,000—243 lawyers (the third quartile). The final group includes those with typical case values over $200,000—258 lawyers (the fourth quartile). We label the lawyers with values below the median as "bread-and-butter" lawyers and divide them into two groups representing the first two quartiles—bread-and-butter 1 (BB1) and bread-and-butter 2 (BB2). The lawyers above the median we call "heavy hitters," and we divide them into two groups representing the third and fourth quartiles—heavy hitter 1 (HH1) and heavy hitter 2 (HH2).

A closely related aspect of a lawyer's place in the plaintiffs' bar structure is the geographic market in which he works.[8] The variation in the geographic

6. Unless otherwise stated, all dollars are in 2006 dollars, the year of our second survey. Our surveys asked lawyers for the value of their typical contingency fee case. The figure reported here is the average of the typical case values provided by respondents.

7. Because these case values deal only with plaintiffs' lawyers, our findings should not be taken as saying anything about the value of verdicts or settlements in Texas jurisdictions generally.

8. Texas plaintiffs' lawyers are overwhelmingly male—88 percent in our surveys—and to emphasize the gender imbalance, we will use the male pronoun.

scope of markets follows the size of the typical case. In the survey we asked lawyers to place their practices into one of three simple geographic markets: local, meaning most cases come from the county in which a lawyer's principal office is located or from adjacent counties; regional, meaning a substantial number of cases come from one or more Texas counties nonadjacent to the principal office site; and statewide/national, meaning a substantial number of cases come from all over Texas or from other states.

Table 5.1 shows the variations in geographic markets across the four groups of lawyers. As we go up the hierarchy, geographic markets become broader in scope, and the relationship between market and stratification group is a significant one.[9] Few lawyers in the lower two groups work statewide or beyond. Our San Antonio lawyer described his market as "fairly local—Bexar County" (the county in which San Antonio is located). Some lawyers are even more localized, concentrating on a particular neighborhood or ethnic community. Another San Antonio lawyer provides an example: "I think over time I've had a good many calls from people simply saying, 'I live in this area' or 'I pass your office,' etc. So I'm trying to build something more in terms of tapping the neighborhood." A Dallas lawyer, with a practice of more than twenty-five years in the same minority neighborhood, said when we interviewed him, "Most of my clients are minority. The reason that is so is because it has always been so. I represented Granddaddy. He sent his kids and his relatives and his friends, and I represented them. Now I'm working on the grandkids."

The heavy hitters are less likely to be so localized. Many HH1 lawyers, for instance, try to expand their markets by developing geographic niches. They target particular parts of the state either because they see a market opportunity or because they believe juries are more pro-plaintiff. For instance, a medical malpractice firm in Central Texas targeted East Texas and the Panhandle as market opportunities. One of the partners said, "We file a lot of suits and get a lot of cases from the Lubbock/Amarillo area [the Texas Panhandle] and from the Jasper/Lufkin area [East Texas] and we don't work too much down in South Texas. . . . Of course, Lubbock has got a big medical community up there and things happen. The East Texas area has terrible medical care period, so bad things happen there."

Another San Antonio lawyer talked about a regional practice that is based, in part, on places with friendlier juries. He described his geographic market as

9. Spearman's rho = .437, sig = .000.

TABLE 5.1. *Geographic Markets for Different Groups of Lawyers* (percent of lawyers in each market)

	BB1 (*n* = 251)	BB2 (*n* = 258)	HH1 (*n* = 243)	HH2 (*n* = 258)
Local	79	70	46	30
Regional	17	25	34	25
State/nation	4	5	21	45

Note: BB = "bread-and-butter"; HH = "heavy hitter."

"San Antonio and the counties within 50 or 100 miles, except we do a bunch of border work, which is Eagle Pass, Del Rio, and Laredo. Because there aren't very many lawyers there and those are very good counties for plaintiffs." Another San Antonio lawyer works in the same area for much the same reason: "It's still a decent place to try a case."

Lawyers handling larger, more complex cases may need an even broader geographic market in order to find enough of the cases in which they specialize. An HH2 lawyer located in San Antonio described his geographic market as "Well, it's Texas." At the extreme end of this spectrum, some of these lawyers have no real geographic boundaries to their market. Said one Austin lawyer about his caseload, "The pharmaceutical is national, and aviation is national." A lawyer specializing in serious injuries suffered by oil rig workers has cases from almost anywhere, even those involving injuries occurring in the North Sea. Still, as Table 5.1 shows, it is possible for a heavy hitter to have a more localized practice. A Dallas lawyer whose practice focused on medical malpractice cases said, "We only ever did Dallas and . . . there's enough in Dallas, you know."

THE TEXAS PLAINTIFFS' BAR: LAWYERS IN THE HIERARCHY

These examples all help to illustrate the differentiation and hierarchy in the Texas plaintiffs' bar. To flesh out the structure a bit more, we will describe some key practice characteristics of the lawyers in each of our four groups, relying upon Table 5.2, which presents data on those characteristics for each group. The data are organized to allow easy comparisons among the four groups.

TABLE 5.2. *Practice Characteristics and Place in the Hierarchy*

	BB1 (n = 251)	BB2 (n = 258)	HH1 (n = 243)	HH2 (n = 258)
Typical case value (2006$)	Median = $6.4K, Mean = $6.8K	Median = $23.4K, Mean = $24.2K	Median = $81.9K, Mean = $86.1K	Median = $585K, Mean = $2.8M
Solo (%)	56	47	33	19
2–5 lawyers in firm (%)	35	37	47	51
Plaintiffs' work (%)	Median = 80, Mean = 66	Median = 90, Mean = 72	Median = 95, Mean = 77	Median = 95, Mean = 84
Number of open cases	Median = 70, Mean = 126	Median = 43, Mean = 62	Median = 32, Mean = 64	Median = 17, Mean = 39
Number of calls/month	Median = 12, Mean = 30	Median = 10, Mean = 18	Median = 10, Mean = 20	Median = 10, Mean = 17
Calls signed to contract (%)	Median = 30, Mean = 34	Median = 20, Mean = 30	Median = 15, Mean = 25	Median = 10, Mean = 16
Certified Personal Injury Trial or Civil Trial (%)	24	39	33	37
Cases from (top two by %)	Clients: 34 Lawyers: 20 Advertising: 20	Clients: 33 Lawyers: 32	Lawyers: 42 Clients: 24	Lawyers: 56 Clients: 16
Using mail to other lawyers (%)	5	9	11	25
Caseload (top three by %)	Auto: 50 Criminal: 5 Commercial: 5 Commercial: 5 Domestic: 5	Auto: 44 Med mal: 8 Criminal: 5	Auto: 30 Med mal: 13 Products: 9	Med mal: 26 Products: 14 Auto: 14
Handling no auto cases (%)	13	9	18	47
Estimated income (2006$)	Median = $159K	Median = $159K	Median = $189K	Median = $265K

Note: BB = "bread-and-butter"; HH = "heavy hitter"; "Med mal" = Medical malpractice.

The BB1 Lawyer

This is the lawyer at the bottom of the plaintiffs' bar hierarchy, for whom the average value of contingency fee cases is quite modest (see Table 5.2). Among the four groups of lawyers, he is the most likely to be a solo practitioner and to work in a local geographic market (see Table 5.1).[10] While his practice is almost exclusively plaintiffs' work done on a contingency fee basis, it is less concentrated on this type of work than are the practices of lawyers in the other three groups.

As Table 5.2 shows, the BB1 lawyer has the highest volume of open cases, but again, these are cases of lower value. The BB1 lawyer handles simple, more mundane issues. Table 5.2 shows, for instance, that medical malpractice does not even make the list as one of the top three case types taken—on average, less than 5 percent of the BB1 lawyer's caseload. A number of these lawyers said they primarily handle "vanilla car wreck cases," meaning low-value cases without serious injury or death that will not often go to court. In fact, the typical BB1 lawyer's practice is built on auto accident cases. This is perhaps best illustrated by the fact that one-half of the BB1 lawyer's caseload is made up of such cases (Table 5.2, row labeled "Caseload"), more so than for the other three groups. As one such lawyer described his practice in the late 1990s, "We do anything from car wrecks to on-the-job injuries as long as it's not workers' compensation—we exclude that. . . . Probably on a percentage basis, 70 percent of my cases are car wreck. . . . It can be as small as $2,000." The nature of the BB1 lawyer's practice suggests that he primarily provides access to clients with particular needs. Other lawyers in the hierarchy may provide access for clients with different needs.

How choosy a lawyer is—the percentage of cases signed to a contract and the criteria used in making the decision—also has something important to tell

10. In 2000, 36 percent of Texas lawyers in private practice were solo practitioners. See State Bar of Texas Department of Research and Analysis, *Statistical Profile of the State Bar of Texas Membership* (2000–01) at 5, www.texasbar.com/AM/Template.cfm?Section=Archives&Template=/CM/ContentDisplay.cfm&ContentID=11533. The percentage was the same in 2005. *See* State Bar of Texas Department of Research and Analysis, *State Bar Members: Attorney Statistical Profile (2005–06)* at 2, www.texasbar.com/AM/Template.cfm?Section=Archives&Template=/CM/ContentDisplay.cfm&ContentID=11457.

us about access, and it is worth exploring. The BB1 lawyer does not get substantially more calls than lawyers in the other groups, however, he does sign a somewhat higher percentage of those calls to a contingency fee contract.[11] It is important to note, however, that the percentage is still rather low (about one-third). No plaintiffs' lawyer, regardless of place in the hierarchy, can take everything and maintain a profitable practice. So the BB1 lawyer, like lawyers elsewhere in the hierarchy, has to screen with care. The reason, one lawyer bluntly said, is simple: "We're getting increasingly selective. I front the costs and we lose, I eat the costs." Even high-volume, aggressive advertising lawyers are likely to turn away many potential clients. One explained that his firm tries "to screen them pretty good. With three investigators, we try to get out there, get the pictures, get witness statements. . . . The witness just says the light was green for the other guy . . . discover the [facts of the] case immediately. We usually tell [callers] within two to three weeks we'll tell them . . . after we've investigated it, whether it's a case or not. . . . Most of the time, unfortunately, they're not." In short, Kritzer would say, at least some amount of business rationality is always involved.

The screening process and specific factors involved vary considerably among lawyers—a BB1 lawyer handling auto accident cases will weigh a different set of specific factors than a HH2 lawyer specializing in medical malpractice cases. The basic idea, nonetheless, remains the same. As one lawyer said, "I try to evaluate. . . . I don't just look at the damages. I was taught a long time ago that in order to have a good personal injury case, you need three things: one, you need good liability; two, you need good damages; and three, you need a solid defendant [meaning solvent and/or insured]. It doesn't do any good to have two of three, so I try and evaluate all three of those factors in deciding whether or not to take the case."

We heard references to these basic factors over and over again in our interviews, although lawyers might differ on the balance between liability and damages. With BB1 lawyers, even in the late 1990s, there was a growing focus on damages—more precisely, on injuries—in the all-important bread-and-butter auto cases. The example typically given was a soft tissue injury case that

---

11. In his study of Wisconsin lawyers who handle contingency fee cases, Herbert Kritzer found that "lawyers reported accepting cases from a mean of 46% (median 45%) of the potential clients who contacted them." Herbert M. Kritzer, *Contingency Fee Lawyers as Gatekeepers in the Civil Justice System*, 81 Judicature 22, 24 (1997).

many were increasingly reluctant to take regardless of liability in light of the changes they were seeing in their working environment. The comments of one BB1 lawyer are illustrative.

> Low impact, soft tissue cases, we're very selective with because the insurance companies are not paying for those cases as well as juries are not giving money in those cases. . . . In today's climate, if someone goes in with that type of case, they're automatically cast out as a person that's only there for the money, regardless of the injury. . . . There's a very good chance that you're just not going to be able to achieve your full fee as per the contract.

The reference to "today's climate" and juries is a statement about the lawyer's view—shared by almost all his peers—regarding the success of the tort reform public relations campaigns in lobbying the jury pool. The BB1 lawyer, in general, appears to have been affected more by the tort reform public relations campaigns than by any specific piece of tort reform legislation.

Our San Antonio lawyer quoted at the chapter's opening would agree: "The fact of the matter is, I have to turn down all kinds of cases these days. I won't take them because I'll end up putting my money into them and not getting anything out of it." He contrasted this with the climate when he first started practicing plaintiffs' law. "Juries would award money for pain and suffering; they would award money for mental anguish. They wouldn't just open up their checking account. . . . [There's] never been . . . a situation where juries were just totally throwing money at you, but I feel that back then, they were more prone to give a decent verdict." All that, in his view, changed, "in large part . . . it's due to the propaganda that the insurance companies are putting out."

A major problem with the soft tissue cases is the issue of noneconomic damages—what people generically refer to as "pain and suffering." One lawyer became quite angry in talking about the issue:

> I mean, when I look at these jury verdict reports [pointing to the volumes of the local verdict reporter on his shelf] and see that a jury found the defendant was in a car wreck—100 percent negligent, the defendant ran a stop sign and hurt somebody. And they award $6,742 in property damages to the plaintiff and they award $1,192.50 in medical bills, zero pain and suffering, zero mental anguish, zero disability, zero physical impairment,

you know, whatever. I look at that like, good God, what have we come to? ... They didn't give a shit, you know. There are people on juries who say, "I couldn't award anything for pain and mental anguish." ... So, that's the biggest problem I see, it's just attitudes.

A struggling lawyer from Houston said the following about bread-and-butter cases and noneconomic damages: "It's going to be a full third of every jury that just quite frankly will tell you, 'I don't believe that pain and suffering exists, I don't believe it's anything that's payable, even if the law says it is.' ... These days after tort reform and everything that has happened to the state of mind of juries with reference to minor cases ... cases that used to be payable are no longer payable cases." Lawyers like these see a causal connection between the tort reform public relations campaigns and the changing landscape of jury verdicts.

They are not alone. A defense lawyer we interviewed told us jurors have heard about tort reform because there's been a lot of heavy advertising by business groups: "I mean advertising statewide. ... So they're aware of it, and of course part of that being aware of it is the 'insurance crisis.' ... Most of the people who are going to take the time and come down and serve on a jury are going to have insurance ... and they know they are paying. I think it affects them." He called the campaigns his "silent helper" and said, "[When I] was trying cases for the city ... they—jurors—are sitting there going, 'This is our tax money.' ... I never said that, but it's right there."

Similarly, a Dallas business principal interviewed as part of a 1998 Texas Department of Insurance study on the impact of tort reform commented, "Well, I think a big part of it is the education of jurors. ... I spoke about the movement—Citizens Against Lawsuit Abuse—I think that has ... my feeling, anyway, is that that has helped educate jurors to where they can associate big awards to the price of their car insurance."[12] A Lubbock judge/mediator also interviewed as part of that study said, "I don't think that you can say tort reform gets direct credit [for lower jury awards]. I think the propaganda asso-

---

12. Texas Department of Insurance, *Selected Quotations from Focus Group Sessions* (1998), at 55, quoted (with citation) in Stephen Daniels & Joanne Martin, *The Impact That It Has Had Is between People's Ears: Tort Reform, Mass Culture, and Plaintiffs' Lawyers*, 50 DePaul L. Rev. 453, 473, n. 79 (2000).

ciated with tort reform and the poisoning of the jury panels had an effect on bringing things down."[13]

A part of this concern over damages, soft tissue injuries, and juries is the client—even in a situation with good liability. A Houston attorney looks for "a client with no prior problems. . . . What they [jurors] don't want to see is Joe Blow who has a soft-tissue back injury but also had a soft-tissue back injury two years ago, and four years ago, and doesn't work and is unemployed, has three kids, and is on welfare. And those are a lot of the cases that get tried [and lost]. . . . You see it week after week in our Blue Sheets [the local verdict reporter]."

Noneconomic damages are one of the reformers' key targets, and they are of vital importance to the bread-and-butter lawyer. Such damages can make the difference between earning a profit on a given case or failing to realize any gain. Without some amount of noneconomic damages on low-value cases, the lawyer may not be able to recover enough to pay the client's bills, collect all or even most of the fee, and recoup his out-of-pocket expenses. The option of shortchanging the client by taking a fee from the award of economic damages intended to make the client whole is not something most lawyers want to do in what they see as a very competitive market for clients, a market in which the primary way of attracting business for a BB1 lawyer—as Table 5.2 shows—is through client referrals.[14] In fact, a number of lawyers indicated that they would, as one put it, "compromise your fee" in order to not shortchange the client.

The dangers inherent in shortchanging clients can be seen in the way a San Antonio solo practitioner described the importance of treating clients well and building a reputation for doing so. He said, "You represented somebody, did them a good job, and their brother or sister, friend at church has an accident, and they say, 'My lawyer did a good job, call him.'" The BB1 lawyer may even do things to cultivate that client base and stay in touch. One, for instance,

---

13. Texas Department of Insurance, *Selected Quotations from Focus Group Sessions* (1998), 29, quoted (with citation) in Daniels & Martin, *Id.* at n. 78.

14. For a comparative picture focusing on Wisconsin lawyers (finding that contingency fee lawyers get most of their business from referrals rather than from advertising), *see* Herbert M. Kritzer & Jayanth K. Krishnan, *Lawyers Seeking Clients, Clients Seeking Lawyers: Sources of Contingency Fee Cases and Their Implications for Case Handling*, 21 L. & Pol'y 347, 350–362 (1999).

sends "Christmas cards every year" to current and former clients. Another sends birthday cards as well as Christmas cards. During our interview in his office, he proudly pointed to a large cabinet where he kept updated information on his former clients and their families along with a supply of greeting cards for almost any occasion. Another San Antonio lawyer, whose practice concentrates on a working-class clientele, goes even further:

> We do a lot of pro bono work for our existing clients or our past clients. Let's say they have a little matter . . . a little fender bender with no injuries, and the other party won't talk to them. They'll come see us, we'll write letters here and there. We took a case to trial last year that was a matter of principle—people that only had property damage and we felt they were being very, very mistreated by the insurance company. We took it on knowing that it was going to be free and at a loss. But we were able to get them some money.

For him this is a matter of public service, but he also hopes those clients will refer more paying business to him.

Unlike the situation with the other three groups of lawyers, the second largest percentage of cases for this group comes from advertising (see Table 5.2, row labeled "Cases From"). However, for most BB1 lawyers, this strategy is not likely to involve intensive advertising using television. Only 14 percent of these lawyers reported using television advertising. On average, just 4 percent of the BB1 lawyer's business comes from television advertising. Only 10 percent reported getting more than 10 percent of their business in this way, but a handful of BB1 lawyers (6 of 251) reported getting half or more. One received all of his business from television advertising. The reason for the unimportance of television advertising is obvious: it's simply too expensive for most lawyers (as pointed out in the previous chapter).

Among all forms of advertising, the largest percentage of business comes from the Yellow Pages (18 percent of all cases), and these ads are not likely to be full-page or back-cover ads. Rather, the ads are likely to be small and discreet or even just a listing in the Yellow Pages under "Lawyers" set in boldface—like the lawyer noted in Chapter 3 whose listing was simply "Collins, John E." Heavy advertising and high volume go hand in hand—but the expenses of screening and handling a high volume of calls and cases must be taken into account in making the business model work. The high-volume, advertising lawyer quoted earlier regarding screening said his overhead (in the middle 1990s) was around $100,000 per month, and we will see later in the chapter that by the early 2000s, he was unable to make the business model work.

Surprisingly, though the use of lawyer websites is increasing, it does not appear that websites generate a lot of business for BB1 lawyers. In our 2006 survey, we asked specifically whether lawyers had a website, and just over one-half (51 percent) of BB1 lawyers answered affirmatively. We also asked what percentage of their caseload came from the website. The answer is very little— the average amount was a mere 3 percent, with only 10 percent of the BB1s saying that as much as 10 percent of their business came from the website. Over three-quarters (77 percent) reported getting no business from the website.[15]

Lawyer referrals, as Table 5.2 shows, were not as important as a source of business for BB1 lawyers compared to the other three groups. Still, such referrals are not unimportant, and they are tied with advertising for the second largest source of business. Some referrals come from lawyers whose practices focus on different types of cases, and some come from other plaintiffs' lawyers. Plaintiffs' lawyers higher in the structure may refer smaller cases down to BB1 lawyers—cases with good liability but with damages too low for the referring firm's needs (these referrals may be paid or unpaid). Other BB1 lawyers may refer even low-value cases that cannot be settled and need to go to trial. As our San Antonio lawyer put it, "There are some lawyers who just don't like to try cases, and they know that a case will need to be tried, and they'll refer it. It seems there's at least two different sets of folks. Well, I mean there are the settling lawyers and the trial lawyers." He's among the latter, and those among the former will refer cases to him.

Reflecting a more mundane practice, the BB1 lawyer is the least likely of the four to be certified as a specialist by the Texas Board of Legal Specialization. However, it is worth noting that even though the BB1 lawyer is the least likely to be board certified, he is far more likely to be certified than members of the

---

15. Most likely the frequency of website use has increased since the time of our surveys. Although we do not have figures specifically for BB1 lawyers, a 2012 update for all respondents to the 2006 survey showed advertising by firm website increased from 57 percent to 78 percent. *See* Stephen Daniels & Joanne Martin, "Plaintiffs' Lawyers and the Tension between Professional Norms and the Need to Generate Business," in *Lawyers in Practice: Ethical Decision-Making in Context,* eds. Leslie Levin & Lynn Mather (Chicago: The University of Chicago Press, 2012), 114.

Texas bar generally. As a point of reference, the State Bar's statistical profile reports that in 2000, only 9 percent of lawyers were certified in at least one area by the Texas Board of Legal Specialization, and by 2011 the percentage had not changed.[16]

In short, the BB1 lawyer is one with a local practice who handles relatively simple, more mundane cases. His net income from his legal practice was—on average—around an estimated $159,000 in 2006 dollars.

The BB2 Lawyer

Some differences begin to appear as we move up the hierarchy to the BB2 lawyer. Table 5.2 shows that he is less likely to be a solo practitioner than the BB1 lawyer but still more likely to be so than the lawyers in the two groups above him in the hierarchy. Like the BB1 lawyer's, his practice is almost exclusively plaintiffs' work done on a contingency fee basis, but more so; and while Table 5.1 shows that his geographic market is local, it is a bit less so than that of the BB1 lawyer. This lawyer has fewer open cases than the BB1 lawyer, meaning a smaller practice. Correspondingly, he receives somewhat fewer calls per month from potential contingency fee clients than the BB1 lawyer, and a smaller percentage of those calls result in a signed contingency fee contract. These differences, in part, reflect fewer really high-volume practices among BB2 lawyers. This is evidenced by the lower median for number of open cases in Table 5.2 and the lower figures for the 75th and 90th percentiles. For BB1s, the 75th percentile (meaning 75 percent of respondents reported a lower figure) is 160 cases and the 90th is 250 cases; for BB2s, the respective figures are 75 cases and 116 cases.

Like the BB1 lawyer, the largest percentage of the BB2 lawyer's cases come through referrals from former clients. Unlike the BB1 lawyer, however, the BB2 lawyer gets much more business from lawyer referrals. For one younger BB2 lawyer from Austin, this is a conscious strategy. He said, "My partner and I

---

16. For 2000, *see* State Bar of Texas Department of Research and Analysis, *Statistical Profile, supra* note 10; for 2011 (the most recent data available), *see* State Bar of Texas Membership: Attorney Statistical Profile (2011–12), 4, www.texasbar.com/AM/Template.cfm?Section=Archives&Template=/CM/ContentDisplay.cfm&ContentID=18559.

have established relationships with about eight or ten firms around town that regularly send us cases, and we have both made a bit of an effort to promote ourselves within the community and among lawyers." Consistent with this kind of strategy, the BB2 lawyer is a bit more likely to use mailings to other lawyers in the effort to attract referrals.

And like the BB1 lawyer, the largest percentage of the BB2 lawyer's caseload is made up of auto accident cases. The percentage, however, is not as large. The BB2 lawyer is a little more likely to try handling more complex matters— like medical malpractice—than is the BB1 lawyer. The BB2 lawyer is also more likely to be certified in either personal injury trial law or civil trial law. Regardless, the differences—mostly subtle—between BB1 lawyers and BB2 lawyers do not translate into a higher net income.

The HH1 Lawyer

The HH1 lawyer is different, in several key respects, from the BB lawyers. As Table 5.2 shows, his cases are worth much more. He is much less likely to be a solo practitioner and more likely to work in a small firm of two to five lawyers. While his practice is almost exclusively plaintiffs' work done on a contingency fee basis (a bit more so than the BBs), as Table 5.1 shows, he is much less likely to work primarily in a local geographic market than either type of BB lawyer and more likely to work in a statewide or broader market.

Perhaps reflecting the higher value of his cases, the HH1 lawyer's practice is modest in size in terms of the number of cases and the number of calls per month. While the largest percentage of this lawyer's caseload is made up of auto accident cases, it is at a rate much lower than that for the BB1 and BB2 lawyers. He handles fewer simple, mundane matters and more cases involving complex matters—like medical malpractice and products liability. Correspondingly, he is choosier in the percentage of cases signed to a contingency fee contract—the rate being lower than that of either type of BB lawyer.

As one might expect, the screening process is more intense as the potential damages and costs increase. The HH1 lawyer who does handle some more complex cases will invest more in screening those cases. One lawyer we interviewed, who handled some medical malpractice and some products liability cases that were not too large or too complex, described his approach to screening:

[For medical malpractice,] we have a nurse and several doctors that we have available to us on a contract basis. . . . They screen every case that comes to the office. Especially in the medical negligence cases, we go through two or three different screenings to make sure that they have the type of case that will be cost effective and in the end will yield a positive result. On the products cases, we have a better feel, but even there we've got to be very careful. We have to have a very serious injury for both cases, but for the products cases that's one of the very first requirements. For example, I don't take . . . let's say an aerosol can that is defective and explodes and blows away somebody's finger. That's not worth taking unless it's a little girl or small child. But if it's an adult, it's just not cost effective. . . . You have to realize that in today's climate, every case that you take, there's a 95 percent chance it will have to be tried to a jury. Our philosophy is we never take a case for settlement purposes because that's a good way to lose a lot of money, lose your time, and to have a very unhappy client at the end.

The screening process for lower-value cases is different but still concerned with identifying good cases in "today's climate."

No prospective client even comes to this lawyer's office unless the initial telephone screening done by a staff member shows potential for damages. That screening focuses on the level of injury as well as on the person involved. Because of the overhead this lawyer carries—four lawyers (including himself) and ten staff members—there must be some kind of substantial injury to justify accepting the case. This does not mean he simply turns away cases with less substantial injuries. Instead, he is likely to refer those cases to younger lawyers or lawyers lower in the hierarchy, like the BB2 lawyer quoted above who actively promotes his practice among other lawyers in the hope of receiving referrals. The HH1 lawyer just quoted said such lawyers "are willing to take those cases. Their overhead is not as high as mine, so they can cost-effectively handle those cases knowing the outcome will be lower because it costs less for them to put the cases together." As this reflects (and as the next chapter will show), the referral process works going down the hierarchy as well as up.

Although client referrals are important for the HH1 lawyer, in contrast to both BB1 and BB2 lawyers, the largest percentage of his cases comes from lawyer referrals. In fact, like the BB1 lawyer from San Antonio quoted earlier, some of these referrals may come from lawyers lower in the plaintiffs' bar hierarchy. For instance, one HH1 lawyer said,

> There are plaintiffs' lawyers that may not want to get into litigation. The gentleman who was just here talking to me is a friend from law school. He'll take a case until he has to file suit on it. Once he files suit, he sends it to us. A lot of lawyers are like that. They don't want that. They want to see if they can flip them with the insurance company and get them done. If it involves anything more, they will get rid of them. We have a ton of referring lawyers just like that.

Consistent with a greater reliance on lawyer referrals, the HH1 lawyer is more likely to use mailings to other lawyers as a marketing tool and less likely to rely on advertising as a source of business.

Interestingly, the HH1 lawyer is slightly less likely than the BB2 lawyer, but more likely than the BB1 lawyer or lawyers generally, to be board certified. Overall, the differences between the HH1 lawyer and the BB1 and BB2 lawyers do translate into a noticeably higher income.

The HH2 Lawyer

The HH2 lawyer is very different from BB lawyers, and in some respects he is also different from the HH1 lawyer. He is highly unlikely to be a solo practitioner. Rather, he is likely to work in a small firm of two to five lawyers—and maybe even a larger firm. His practice is almost exclusively plaintiffs' work done on a contingency fee basis, and he is the least likely to work primarily in a local geographic market and the most likely to work in a statewide or national market. One of these heavy hitters described his practice as "pretty well statewide. . . . In a two-week period, I tried three cases. I tried a legal malpractice case for the plaintiff . . . in Dallas; I tried a personal injury case in Amarillo involving two pickups that came together on a country road; and I tried an intentional infliction of mental distress case in Austin. . . . All these were big cases." For some HH2 lawyers, their practice can be national. Said another, "In the last year, I've tried three cases in Philadelphia, Pennsylvania, and then I've tried two here in Beaumont, Texas, and one in Jackson, Tennessee, so you know, kind of all around the place." At the extreme, a lawyer may have offices in multiple states.

The HH2 lawyer's caseload is quite modest in size in terms of the number of cases and calls per month, with the exception of those handling mass torts. Most HH2 lawyers (78 percent) reported no involvement with mass torts. A small number (18 HH2 lawyers), however, reported a substantial involvement with mass torts. Eighteen lawyers reported that one-half or more of their business involved mass torts, and these lawyers have caseloads much higher than the norm for HH2 lawyers. Table 5.2 shows that the average number of cases for HH2 lawyers is 39, but for those eighteen lawyers, the average caseload is 132.

Whether it is mass torts or something else, the HH2 lawyer is a high-end, complex case specialist. Cases that are important for lawyers in the lower tiers of the hierarchy make up only a small proportion of this lawyer's business. Unlike the caseloads of lawyers in the other three groups, the largest percentage of this lawyer's caseload is not made up of auto accident cases. In fact, as Table 5.2 shows, almost one-half of HH2 lawyers handle no auto cases. The largest percentage of his caseload is made up of medical malpractice cases, followed by products liability and auto cases (only 14 percent of caseload on average). For all HH2 lawyers, mass torts make up, on average, 8 percent of caseload. The average value of his contingency fee cases is far larger than the values for the other groups, reflecting the greater complexity of the cases.

Consistent with the focus on complex, high-end cases, the HH2 is the choosiest in signing calls to a contingency fee contract. He must be because the value of his typical contingency fee case is far larger than the values for the other groups, reflecting the greater complexity of the cases. He is also likely to have a much higher overhead because of the needs of a practice that must screen and handle complex cases very carefully (business rationality is especially important for him). For example, the HH1 lawyer mentioned earlier said he has medical professionals available on a contract basis to screen medical malpractice cases. HH2 lawyers may internalize this need by having one or more nurses on staff or even nurse-lawyers or physician-lawyers as employees of the firm. For instance, one HH2 lawyer said, "I have two nurses that work here full-time, and every case that comes in the office, every call that comes in, is run by one of the nurses to see if it is a case that would even get someone's attention and . . . then if it does that, we will get the medical records."

Another HH2 lawyer, a medical malpractice specialist, has a quite extensive screening process. It is worth quoting his description at length:

We have nine lawyers now that do almost nothing but medical malpractice. Two of our lawyers are doctor-lawyers; one is a nurse-lawyer; we have three nurse-paralegals. Anytime anybody makes a call . . . they're going to talk to a nurse-paralegal; they're not going to talk to a lawyer. The nurse-paralegal gets that call and screens that call. A large number of those calls, the nurse-paralegal tells them over the phone that what they're describing is not medical malpractice. They may be mad at their doctor, you know, because they looked at them the wrong way or pinched them the wrong way. Or a frequent thing is that somebody went in for back surgery and they are not any better after the back surgery. Those things are not medical malpractice. So those are screened out over the phone. If the nurse-paralegal thinks that the case sounds like it may potentially have merit, then she will either on her own or after consulting with one of the doctor-lawyers get a medical authorization from the potential client and get the medical records to review.

We don't take a contract first and then obtain the records and review them. We don't want to take a contract and give a client the sense of hope unless we know what the case is about, we've analyzed it, believe it will be a successful case. So the medical records are obtained, and then the normal process is that those records are going to be reviewed by one of the nurse-paralegals and by one of the MD-JDs, and then either the records themselves or those initial reviews are going to be reviewed by the senior MD-JD and it's going to be reviewed by me. And then we meet once a month, what we call our nonlitigation meeting; in any given month we're going to have seventy or eighty cases under consideration for the ones we're going to take. We talk about all of them. There has to be an agreement from the medical side and from my side, the legal side of it, that we're going to pursue that case—that not only is the medicine favorable in terms of we believe that there has been a medical screw-up but that we can find an expert that will say that, or we've already found an expert that will say that. At that point, we will have done research through Medline and the medical journals and the medical texts, and we will have medical literature that says what was wrong.

And then I look at it from a damages standpoint, a venue standpoint, and an economic standpoint. Only if we agree on all of that, and basically . . . everybody in the room reaches agreement, do we then decide we're going to then get the client in and sign the client up.

With such an investment in firm infrastructure, it is easy to see why this lawyer has a minimum of $1 million in potential damages as a threshold for cases he will take. The successful cases have to help pay for this overhead.

Consistent with the focus on complex, high-end cases, most of the HH2 lawyer's cases come through referrals from other lawyers (as Chapter 6 will show, such referrals are especially important for access by getting cases to the lawyers best able to handle them). For instance, one Houston medical malpractice specialist said, "Probably 90 percent of our cases are from other lawyers." The lawyer quoted earlier about his three trials in two weeks said, "Over 75 percent of my practice was and is referrals from other lawyers." The lawyer who said he had three trials in Philadelphia handles products liability cases (mostly pharmaceutical), and he gets the "vast majority of my docket through referrals from other attorneys who are familiar with the firm and my reputation . . . primarily just from advertising lawyers that are primarily case brokers." He explained, "You know how it works. They go out and they buy a lot of ad time and say that they, you know, handle certain kinds of cases, and then when they get them, they end up referring them to somebody who really handles those types of cases." For this lawyer, even his referral network extends beyond the state. "Most of 'em are in Texas. I do have some from out of state that I've formed relationships with in the past on mass torts."

A lawyer so reliant on lawyer referrals may invest heavily in cultivating lawyer referrals and in marketing himself and his firm. One Dallas lawyer sent a brochure to every lawyer in private practice in Texas seeking referrals of medical malpractice cases. A Houston lawyer, more modestly, sent his brochure just to lawyers practicing in San Antonio and in areas farther south in Texas. Another was more systematic in his marketing.

Last year . . . we spent about $80,000 on programs that were designed to touch our former clients—our referring lawyers—and make sure that we were, you know, they were sure that we wanted their business. . . .
If my referring lawyers go away, I'm in trouble. . . . I'll always have to be thinking about new referring lawyers. . . . That's why we're spending a lot

of time, energy, and money on them. . . . We have this year a new business development program in which each lawyer sat down with . . . our consultant and said, 'Okay, where am I most likely to be able to improve my business sources?' . . . We've been working to tailor a new business development program around each lawyer [in the firm] and then a couple of programs around the partners, like we're going to do a little golf tournament with some of the tried-and-true referring lawyers. We're mentioning them in our newsletter. . . . They really get stroked for sending us business.

Consistent with this, as Table 5.2 shows, the HH2 lawyer is by far the most likely to use mailings to other lawyers as a way of generating business. As we might expect, referrals from former clients are much less important for the HH2 lawyer. Advertising is even less important, producing an average of only 9 percent of cases (as Table 5.2 shows, the figure for BB1 lawyers is 20 percent). He is the most likely among the four groups of lawyers to use the Internet for marketing purposes, which is consistent with a greater reliance on lawyer referrals for business. In answer to the question in our 2006 survey about a firm website, two-thirds (67 percent) said they had one, but firm websites do not generate much business. On average for the HH2 lawyers in the 2006 survey, websites accounted for only 4 percent of business.

The HH2 lawyer is slightly more likely than the HH1 lawyer to be board certified but slightly less likely than the BB2 lawyer. Still, like the lawyers in the other three tiers of the hierarchy, he is far more likely to be certified than lawyers generally. Finally, the differences between the HH2 lawyer and those in the other three groups translate into a substantially higher income.

As we move up the hierarchy within the plaintiffs' bar, we find important differences in lawyers' practices. Practices in the higher tiers are very different from those in the lower tiers. How a lawyer gets his business changes, moving from word-of-mouth client referrals to lawyer referrals and the use of marketing rather than advertising. Those in the lower tiers work mostly in a consumer market in which the person bringing the case to the lawyer is the injured party. Those in the higher tiers work mostly in a referral or a lawyer's market in which the person bringing the case to the lawyer is another lawyer. As we go from a consumer's market to a referral—or lawyer's—market the geographic scope of a lawyer's practice broadens. The nature of business also changes, away from the simple, more mundane and low-value cases to the more complex and higher-value cases and away from the mainstay of auto cases to those involving more complex issues like medical malpractice, products liability, and commercial matters. As we move up the hierarchy, the lawyer receives fewer calls from potential clients on a monthly basis and signs fewer of those to a contingency fee contract. The lawyer becomes choosier about the cases he will take.

What ties the different segments of the plaintiffs' bar together is a professional identity that does not vary across the hierarchy and the referral process that moves cases among lawyers both up and down the hierarchy. The next chapter investigates the referral process, but before that—following up the observation in Chapter 2 that the impact of tort reform may vary based on where lawyers are in the hierarchy—the remainder of this chapter explores changes that may have occurred in lawyers' practices during the time of our research and what it might mean for access. It does so by looking at the practices of BB1 lawyers as compared to HH2 lawyers.

CHANGING PRACTICES: BB1 AND HH2 LAWYERS

Aggregate Patterns

We would expect lawyers to alter their practices if, in their judgment, the key factors affecting the market in which they work are changing. More simply, if they perceive changes that provide more opportunities for financial success, we might expect an expanding market. On the other hand, if they see the changes as negative in character, meaning an environment with fewer opportunities for financial success, we might expect a contracting market. Needless to say, Texas plaintiffs' lawyers see their working environment as increasingly negative because of legislative actions, the rightward shift of the Texas Supreme Court, and the reformers' public relations programs. Given the differences between BB1 lawyers and HH2 lawyers, comparing them offers an interesting way of exploring changes in practices while keeping in mind the idea that the plaintiffs' bar is not a monolithic or uniform entity and that changes in practices can have important consequences for access. We can do this by focusing on the questions asked in both of our surveys, many of which appeared in Table 5.2:

- questions that speak to the basic nature of their practice: percentage of caseload made up by contingency fee cases and percentage of caseload

made up by different kinds of cases; solo status; certification; and market; and
- questions that speak generally to how well their practices are doing: the value of their typical contingency fee case (and, concomitantly, their stratification group); their income; the number of cases; the number of calls received per month; the percentage of calls signed to a contract; and the sources of their cases.

Perhaps the most basic and important indicator of change is the percentage of caseload made up of plaintiffs' work. Did that percentage change in the aggregate for either BB1 or HH2 lawyers? For BB1 lawyers, the answer was yes. There was a significant, although not large, decrease in the percent of caseload made up of plaintiffs' work—from 70 percent on average in 2000 to 61 percent on average in 2006.[17] The percentage of BB1 lawyers reporting that they did 100 percent plaintiffs' work also declined from 22 percent to 17 percent. The main component of BB1 lawyers' business remained auto accident cases—staying at one-half of caseload on average. No other type of case made up more than 8 percent on average in 2000 or 2006. It is important to remember that even though the percentages of caseload made up by auto and other cases (the basic mix of business) did not change, the overall percentage of caseload made up by plaintiffs' work did change.

We saw earlier that BB1 lawyers said they were becoming increasingly leery of soft tissue cases. The reason they gave was their sense of a changing climate because of the tort reform public relations campaigns. In each of our surveys, we asked lawyers about this. More precisely, we used the same question to ask lawyers whether they would take a low-value auto accident case that involved only soft tissue injuries and minimal property damage. Importantly, the question was designed to largely take liability out of the equation. It stated that the case was one in which liability appeared to run to another party who was adequately insured. In the 2000 survey, a point in time at which lawyers were already saying they were becoming reluctant to take such cases, two-thirds of the BB1 respondents said they would take the case. In the 2006 survey, the percentage dropped to 50 percent.[18]

17. The difference is statistically significant (T-Test) at >.05.
18. The difference is statistically significant (Fisher's exact) at >.05.

The value of the typical case for the BB1 lawyer declined from an average of $7,642 to $5,758 between 2000 and 2006, and so did the lawyer's income—from a median of $142,000 in 2000 to $120,000 (in 2006 dollars).[19] The BB1 lawyer's caseload shrank from an average of 141 cases in 2000 to 108 in 2006, although the difference is not significant (still, in combination with the change in the percentage of caseload made up by plaintiffs' work, this suggests a diminution of access). Even though caseload shrank, it was not because the BB1 lawyer was receiving fewer calls from prospective plaintiffs. The BB1 lawyer's sources did not dry up. Referrals from clients remained the most important source of business, but the percentage of business from this source declined (from 36 percent to 25 percent).[20] The percentage of business from lawyer referrals and from advertising was virtually unchanged. There was a significant increase in the number of calls per month (from twenty-two to forty on average).[21] The BB1 lawyer, however, became choosier in terms of how many of those calls would be signed to a contingency fee contract (from 38 percent to 29 percent).[22]

Although the BB1 lawyer's market broadened a little, it still remained overwhelmingly local. The BB1 lawyer also remained predominantly a solo practitioner, with a slight—but not significant—increase from 55 percent of BB1s to 58 percent. There was a slight—but again not significant—decrease of BB1s working in firms of two to five lawyers, from 35 percent to 29 percent. The BB1 lawyer in 2006 was a bit more likely to be board certified in either personal injury trial law or civil trial law (27 percent) compared to the number from 2000 (23 percent). In short, the BB1 lawyer's existence became a bit more precarious and less remunerative.

For HH2 lawyers at the other end of the spectrum, the situation is quite different. For HH2 lawyers, there was actually a slight (but significant) increase in the percentage of caseload made up by plaintiffs' work—from 82 percent to 87 percent.[23] The percentage of HH2 lawyers reporting that they did 100 percent plaintiffs' work also increased, from 38 percent to 46 percent. The main com-

19. The difference in case value is significant (T-test) at >.05 and median income at >.05.
20. The difference is statistically significant (T-test) at >.05.
21. The difference is statistically significant (T-test) at >.05.
22. The difference is statistically significant (T-test) at >.05.
23. The difference is statistically significant (T-test) at >.05.

ponents of the HH2 lawyer's caseload remained medical malpractice, products liability, and auto accident cases. Auto accident cases, of course, made up a far smaller proportion of the HH2 lawyer's caseload than the BB1 lawyer's. For HH2, it was 15 percent in 2000 and 13 percent in 2006, and for BB1 it was 51 percent in 2000 and 50 percent in 2006.

The value of an HH2 lawyer's typical case declined (significantly) from an average of $4.5 million to $764,000,[24] but his income rose from a median of $284,000 in 2000 to $371,000 in 2006. The decline in case value was the result of fewer very high case values in 2006, when the highest typical case value reported by a respondent was $5 million. In 2000, 10 percent of the case values were higher than this, with the highest 5 percent exceeding $35 million (four of the six lawyers reporting case values in excess of $35 million in 2000 were commercial litigation specialists). There was no change in the number of calls, but these lawyers became choosier, signing a smaller percentage of calls to a contract in 2006 than in 2000 (20 percent to 12 percent).[25] Referrals from lawyers remained the main source of business (55 percent and 56 percent), and a noticeable minority continued to use direct mail to other lawyers (25 percent and 25 percent).

The HH2 lawyer's decidedly nonlocal market became even more so, with over one-half (53 percent) reporting their market as statewide and beyond compared to 39 percent in 2000.[26] Although the HH2 lawyer was slightly more likely to be a solo practitioner in 2006 (22 percent) than in 2000 (16 percent), he was far less likely to be so than was the BB1 lawyer. Just over one-half of HH2 lawyers at both points in time worked in firms of two to five lawyers (51 percent and 53 percent). Finally, like the BB1 lawyer, the HH2 lawyer was more likely to be board certified in 2006 (40 percent) than in 2000 (34 percent), and the HH2 was more likely to be certified than the BB1 lawyer at either point in time. Interestingly, this change in certification suggests that although lawyers in each group may be choosier in the cases and clients they take, the quality of the representation may have increased for the clients they do take.

24. The difference is statistically significant (T-test) at >.05.
25. The difference is statistically significant (T-test) at >.05.
26. The change in market is statistically significant—chi square = 5.279, $2df$ >.05.

Individual Changes

We do see shifts between each survey in the aggregate, but we do not see much in the way of fundamental change at this level. Nor should we expect to see such change; the plaintiffs' bar is too deeply institutionalized to simply disappear or change dramatically in a short amount of time. Still, even shifts can have important consequences, and so we need to ask what might be happening within that aggregate picture. Are individual lawyers' practices changing? If so, are they changing in ways that resemble the BB1 lawyer—or are they more like the HH2 lawyer? And what might those changes mean in terms of access? We cannot make inferences about individual lawyers and their practices from the aggregate picture, and the more pertinent question is about change in individual practices. Unfortunately, we know little about changes in the plaintiffs' bar as a whole and virtually nothing about changes in the practices of individual plaintiffs' lawyers, but we can at least shed some light on this issue.

Whatever the aggregate picture, the changes for a given lawyer could be quite significant. For instance, one lawyer we interviewed twice (the aggressive advertiser quoted earlier about screening cases) saw his high-volume, lower-case value practice—built on a sophisticated, television advertising plan— collapse by the early 2000s. We interviewed him first in the middle 1990s, and when we interviewed him the second time, almost ten years later, he was working as a solo practitioner with a low volume of cases: "Well, I used to have more of a volume practice." He had 20 employees and between 400 and 500 cases when we first interviewed him. Most of those cases, of course, settled and provided the month-to-month cash flow to cover his overhead and support the few more serious cases he handled that were more likely to go to trial (this lawyer was double certified in personal injury trial law and in civil trial law).

At the second interview he told us, "Now, I trimmed down. . . . I have a secretary. . . . I have maybe 30 cases instead of 400 to 500. . . . They're, you know, car wreck cases. I do primarily car wrecks, premises liability—slip and falls." He went on to say, "I don't advertise anymore. . . . The cases come from, just from other people I've handled in the past [clients]. And then from other lawyers—I get referred cases." Even though he could retire, he hasn't. "Some of my friends are retiring, and they go, 'You know, why are you still doing this?' and I said, ''Cause I wanna do it.' I mean, these people need me you know, and I want you to know I wanna help 'em, and I have a way." He said, "A lotta this tort reform has me fired up."

His high-volume practice collapsed because he could no longer generate the needed cash flow by settling cases at a favorable level. "You always looked at how many cases you were taking in; you looked at how many cases you were settling; you looked at how much money was in the bank. You had all these checks that you could look at and see how you were doing. And, you know, as long as you were taking cases in, then the money in the bank generally stayed pretty good." What made his settlement strategy work was the possibility of a third party suit alleging bad faith by defendant's insurance company, which would entice the insurance company to accept a settlement within or at the policy limit rather than risk a jury verdict in excess of the policy limit. When the insurance company did not settle and the defendant lost at trial for an amount exceeding the policy limits, this lawyer would then go to the defendant and have the defendant sign over the right to sue the insurer for bad faith for not accepting the settlement offer. Again, this lawyer is an experienced litigator double certified in personal injury trial law and civil trial law.

"The thing that I think really changed my practice was a case down here called *Maryland Casualty v. Head*, where the Texas Supreme Court eliminated third-party bad faith."[27] This, he said, began to change insurance companies' approach to settlements. With the possibility of the third-party bad faith suit eliminated, insurance companies became increasingly more likely to offer only lowball settlements and go to trial. This meant smaller checks and less money in the bank each month. Eventually this meant the inability to meet the overhead of a high-volume practice ($100,000 a month): "You know, it just kept snowballing."

Another lawyer we interviewed closed his downtown Dallas practice that focused on medical malpractice after the 2003 reforms passed by the state legislature were enacted. He had five lawyers and over twenty staff members in a practice that would have fifteen medical malpractice cases a year and five to six nursing home cases. His monthly overhead was over $60,000. "I had a half a floor in a downtown building, just all kinds of crap." The firm also had over 100 auto accident cases at the time, and these covered the overhead and provided cash flow: "We tried to keep enough car wrecks to make that . . . to cover the nut." This kind of business model is an old one. In the years before workers' compensation disappeared in the early 1990s, a number of firms would have

27. 938 S.W.2d 627 (Tex. 1997).

a relatively high volume of workers' compensation cases for cash flow and the financial resources to handle higher-value cases. These firms would use the compensation cases to identify third party cases that would come up in a work injury situation. Needless to say, this version of the model broke down with the end of workers' compensation as a profitable area.

By 2004, this lawyer's version of this business model was no longer working. The medical malpractice cases became too expensive and risky with the changing rules—especially the damage cap—and the juries grew increasingly hostile. The lawyer's income, after expenses and overhead, dropped all the way to $11,000. "So at that point I decided that it was just clearly not worth it," he told us. "If you're looking for known-about changes in the practices of individual plaintiffs' lawyers who went broke as a result of the reforms. I sort of ... I didn't go broke, but ... we started again here in a sublet [actually an office sharing arrangement costing $1,700 a month] with me and two of my best paralegals [and half-time bookkeeper], and we're not doing any more medical malpractice ... no nursing home cases."

The results of our two surveys provide a way to at least explore patterns in individual lawyers' practices more broadly at two points in time. Even though the samples for the two surveys were drawn from independent lists, 424 lawyers appeared in both samples, and 163 responded to both surveys. These "repeaters" are not a representative sample of all Texas plaintiffs' lawyers, but comparing their responses to common questions in the two surveys still provides a unique opportunity to carry out this exploration. This allows us to say, for example, that the proportion of caseload composed of contingency fee cases decreased or increased for *x* percentage of repeaters rather than simply saying the proportion changed in the aggregate for all lawyers. This involves taking that proportion for each individual lawyer in the 2000 survey and subtracting it from the proportion for that lawyer in the 2006 survey—a positive number means an increase and a negative number a decrease. We can then look at what percentage of all repeaters had an increase and what percentage a decrease (and where appropriate the mean and median amount of change).

As with the aggregate comparison above, we will focus on BB1 lawyers and HH2 lawyers. We will see identifiable shifts of some lawyers doing better and some worse and of some being choosier in the cases they take and some less so; but in general, the trend leans toward lawyers doing worse and being choosier, with a substantial minority not following the trend.

We can start by looking briefly at Table 5.3 and all 163 repeaters on some key

TABLE 5.3. *Nature of Change for Selected Practice-Related Characteristics: 163 Survey Repeaters* (percent of respondents with increase, decrease, or no change)

	Increase	No Change	Decrease
Total caseload	29	1	70
Typical case value	36	0	64
Income	39	6	58
Number of calls per month	35	10	55
Calls signed (%)	37	11	52
Caseload medical malpractice (%)	18	34	47
Caseload plaintiffs' (%)	27	27	46
Caseload auto (%)	42	15	43

practice-related characteristics to provide a general context. Table 5.3 shows the percentage of repeaters who for each characteristic experienced an increase, a decrease, or no change. The general trend suggested by Table 5.3 leans toward a worsening situation (the table is organized with the largest decrease at the top and the smallest at the bottom). By far, most repeaters have smaller caseloads in 2006, with less than one-third having larger caseloads. Just over one-half had fewer calls coming to them, and almost one-half saw the percentage of their caseload comprised of plaintiffs' work decrease (only 27 percent saw an increase). Just over one-half of the repeaters signed fewer calls to a contract for their plaintiffs' work. Almost two-thirds saw the value of their typical case value decline, and over one-half saw their income decline. Though not documented in Table 5.3, most repeaters stayed in the same geographic market (54 percent), and equal percentages (23 percent) saw their market either broaden or narrow.

Table 5.3 also shows the change in percentage of caseload comprised of medical malpractice cases. Only a small percentage of the repeaters experienced an increase, with the largest percentage experiencing a decrease. Because many lawyers never handled medical malpractice cases, more telling is what happened with the 104 repeaters who reported handling any amount of medical malpractice in the 2000 survey. Eighty-four percent reported a decline in the proportion of their caseload made up by medical malpractice in the 2006 survey. Of the fifty-nine lawyers reporting no medical malpractice in the 2000 survey, only thirteen reported they were handling at least some medical malpractice in the 2006 survey—with the highest proportion of caseload being 20 percent and the remainder 11 percent or less. The story for auto accident

TABLE 5.4. *Nature of Change for Selected Practice-Related Characteristics: 40 BB1 Survey Repeaters* (% of respondents with increase, decrease, or no change)

	Increase	No Change	Decrease
Total caseload	33	0	67
Typical case value	62	0	38
Income	40	2	58
Number of calls per month	27	8	65
Calls signed (%)	49	8	43
Caseload medical malpractice (%)	22	43	35
Caseload plaintiffs' (%)	23	24	53
Caseload auto (%)	22	22	56

cases—the mainstay for bread-and-butter lawyers—is less clear, with almost equal percentages of repeaters with either a higher percentage or a lower one.

Of the repeaters who were BB1 lawyers in 2000 (there were 40), over one-half (58 percent) remained so in 2006. Most (72 percent) stayed in the same geographic market, and in 2006, most of the 2000 BB1 lawyers (73 percent) worked in a local market. As Table 5.4 shows, two-thirds of the BB1 repeaters saw the size of their caseload decrease, and just over one-half reported doing less plaintiffs' work in 2006 than in 2000. Twenty-three percent reported doing more, with the rest reporting the same percentage. Unlike the pattern for all repeaters, well over one-half saw the value of their typical case increase. Nonetheless, most still handled modest cases in 2006 (mean value, $46,600; median value, $10,000), and over one-half saw their income decrease.

Fifty-six percent of the BB1 repeaters decreased the proportion of their caseload made up by auto accident cases (56 percent), with equal percentages having a larger proportion or the same proportion (22 percent each). Still, auto accident cases remained the mainstay for the 2000 BB1 repeaters (on average, 50 percent of caseload in 2006). Fifty-five percent reported doing at least some medical malpractice in the 2000 survey (on average, 7 percent of caseload), but almost two-thirds of these lawyers reported doing less in 2006 (on average, 4 percent of caseload). One-half of those reporting at least some medical malpractice in 2000 reported doing none in the 2006 survey. Finally, unlike the general pattern for all repeaters, just under one-half of 2000 BB1 repeaters (49 percent) increased the proportion of calls signed to a contract (43 percent decreased the proportion).

TABLE 5.5. *Nature of Change for Selected Practice-Related Characteristics: 41 HH2 Survey Repeaters* (% of respondents with increase, decrease, or no change)

	Increase	No Change	Decrease
Total caseload	38	3	59
Typical case value	8	0	92
Income	39	3	58
Number of calls per month	27	3	65
Calls signed (%)	38	16	59
Caseload medical malpractice (%)	10	39	51
Caseload plaintiffs' (%)	25	28	47
Caseload auto (%)	44	36	20

Of the repeaters who were HH2 lawyers in 2000 (there were forty-one), just under one-half (49 percent) remained so. Just over one-quarter (27 percent)—like the example of the former medical malpractice specialist—experienced drastic change in their practices and dropped all the way down to the BB level. As Table 5.5 shows, over one-half of the HH2 repeaters saw the size of their caseload decrease, compared with two-thirds of the BB1 repeaters (Tables 5.4 and 5.5 list practice-related characteristics in the same order as Table 5.3). As was the case for the BB1 repeaters, the largest percentage of HH2 repeaters reported a smaller proportion of their caseload made up by plaintiffs' work in the 2006 survey (although at a somewhat lower figure than for the BB1 repeaters). Almost all of the HH2 repeaters saw the value of their typical case decrease, an amount greater than that for all repeaters and quite different from what we saw above for BB1 repeaters. Nonetheless, most still handled higher-end cases in 2006 (mean value, $448,000; median value, $150,000). For those who dropped to a group lower in the hierarchy, however, the typical case value was substantially lower—dropping to the BB level means a typical case value under $38,000 (the lowest case value for an HH1 lawyer). Most (59 percent) stayed in the same geographic market, but almost one-third (31 percent) narrowed their market. In 2006, 41 percent worked in statewide or broader markets, and 39 percent worked in a local market.

Unlike the BB1 repeaters and all repeaters, the largest percentage of HH2 repeaters increased the proportion of their caseload made up of auto accident cases—again, one can look to the earlier example of the former medical malpractice specialist. For those HH2 repeaters who reported handling medical malpractice cases in the 2000 survey, most (72 percent) reported handling none on the 2006 survey (and only two of those handling medical malpractice in the earlier survey reported doing more in the later survey). Nonetheless, higher-value, complex cases remained the mainstay for the 2000 HH2 repeaters, with auto accident cases making up only 20 percent of caseload on average in 2006 for these lawyers (of course, it is possible that the auto cases taken were higher-value cases). Finally, unlike the 2000 BB1 repeaters and like the general pattern for all repeaters, just under one-half of the 2000 HH2 repeaters decreased the proportion of calls signed to a contract.

The trends we have seen can have consequences in terms of access and how wide the doors of the courthouse will be open. To return to the blunt statement from one Texas plaintiffs' lawyer we quoted in Chapter 1, "Unless there's a way to make money practicing law, rights don't make any difference." Some lawyers like the two discussed at the beginning of this section, have experienced dramatic changes in their practices. At the extreme, like the lawyer whose situation opened the Preface, a few are even leaving the practice of law. More generally, though the specifics may vary by where lawyers are in the hierarchy, we see that individual repeaters have smaller caseloads, with plaintiffs' work making up a smaller percentage of that caseload. As we noted above, there are identifiable shifts of some lawyers doing better and some worse. Some are being choosier in the cases they take and some less so. Nonetheless, in general the trend leans toward doing worse and being choosier, with a substantial minority not following the trend. The trends we have seen can have consequences in terms of access and the plaintiffs' lawyers' gatekeeping role.

CONCLUSION

As the comments of the San Antonio lawyer that opened this chapter reflect, the Texas plaintiffs' bar is not some monochromatic entity. It is one with an identifiable, complex hierarchy that includes the small, modest, and localized practices, like the lawyer whose practice was built on auto accident cases and client referrals. It is one with practices that narrowly specialize in a particular kind of high-value, complex case, like medical malpractice, in a market that is statewide or broader—even international—built more on lawyer referrals. Different kinds of lawyers provide access for different clients with different issues.

Cutting across the structure we have outlined is specialization. It is not just that lawyers choose to specialize in plaintiffs' work; many specialize further in the kinds of cases they build their practices around. We have seen BB1 lawyers building their practices around auto accident cases and HH2 lawyers building theirs around medical malpractice cases. Such specialization runs counter to the idea of plaintiffs' lawyers as business actors building their practices around a diversified portfolio of cases. Plaintiffs' lawyers have chosen, for better or worse, to deal with cost and risk by specializing.

In this regard, they are part of a well-documented, more general trend toward increasing specialization in the legal profession. A 1964 American Bar Foundation report, for example, said, "In the mid–twentieth century circumstances favoring specialization became even more favorable. Many lawyers narrowed their practices to particular fields of law (such as corporation law, patent law or tax law) and some limited themselves in regard to the 'side' of the cases they handled. In the personal injury field, certain lawyers became known as 'plaintiff's lawyers' and others as 'defendant's lawyers.'"[28] This is reflected and institutionalized in Texas, as we noted earlier, with the Texas Board of Legal Specialization, which was established in 1974. It certifies lawyers in twenty-one different areas; a total of 7,237 lawyers were certified in 2013. This represents approximately 9 percent of Texas lawyers, whereas 34 percent of the respondents to our surveys were board certified at the time of the survey in either personal injury trial law or civil trial law or both. Table 5.2 shows that even the BB1 lawyer is far more likely to be board certified than are lawyers generally.

We can also look at specialization in a more practical and detailed way by looking at what plaintiffs' lawyers do, remembering that they shape their practices around the kinds of cases they seek and actually handle. To explore the extent of specialization within the plaintiffs' arena, we looked at how lawyers' caseloads were distributed across twenty different practice areas.[29] A lawyer who had 50 percent or more of his caseload in an area was considered a specialist in that area. Using this approach, two-thirds of the respondents to our surveys (66 percent) reported having 50 percent or more of their caseload

28. Glenn Greenwood & Robert Frederickson, *Specialization in the Medical and Legal Professions* (Chicago: Callaghan & Co. 1964), 51.

29. Each of our surveys asked respondents to indicate the distribution of their caseload across the same list of substantive areas.

in one area. Only four areas had 5 percent or more of the respondents. Auto accident cases, reflecting their place at the heart of the plaintiffs' bar, represented the most important area of specialization—36 percent of respondents reported having 50 percent or more of their caseload in this area at the time of the survey. Nine percent of respondents specialized in medical malpractice; 6 percent specialized in commercial cases (handled on a contingency fee basis); and 5 percent specialized in products liability.[30]

As we might expect, specialization does track the hierarchy. For instance, 54 percent of BB1 lawyers were auto accident specialists. Four percent specialized in commercial cases, 3 percent in criminal cases, and 3 percent in domestic cases. At the other end of the spectrum, only 12 percent of HH2 lawyers specialized in auto accident cases (high-value ones). Twenty-four percent specialized in medical malpractice cases, 12 percent specialized in commercial cases, and 11 percent specialized in products liability cases.

For specialization to be a successful strategy—especially for those specializing in complex, high-end cases like medical malpractice—there must be a way for the cases to get to the specialist. It is unlikely that the typical client—a one-shot client who is not a sophisticated consumer of legal services—will know who the specialists are. This is the information problem that specialists must solve if they are to have an ongoing supply of business. There needs to be a way of matching opportunities to talent and enhancing access for clients. In his classic 1974 article on repeat players and the reasons why the "haves" come out ahead, Marc Galanter was not optimistic about the development of specialization on the plaintiffs' side. In addressing the possibility of specialization on the plaintiffs' side, Galanter asked, "Might we not expect the existence of specialization to offset RP [repeat player] advantages by providing OS [one-shotters] with a specialist who in pursuit of his own career goals would be interested in outcomes that would be advantageous to a whole class of OSs? Does the specialist become the functional equivalent of an RP?"[31] Galanter's answer to his own question was no. Most importantly, because of the low state of informa-

---

30. The patterns in the 2006 survey were not significantly different from those in the 2000 survey, although there was a bit more specialization in the 2006 survey. Sixty-three percent of the 2000 respondents had 50 percent or more of their caseload in one area, and 69 percent of the 2006 respondents did (with the same four areas predominating).

31. Marc Galanter, *Why the "Haves" Come Out Ahead: Speculation on the Limits of Legal Change*, 9 L. & Soc'y Rev. 95, 115 (1974).

tion among "one-shotters" (injured people), would-be specialists would have problems mobilizing a clientele. There is simply no reason, Galanter asserted, for one-shotters to know who the real specialists are.[32]

Regardless of what may have been the situation when Galanter wrote forty years ago, there clearly are lawyers who specialize as plaintiffs' lawyers, and there are even some who specialize further in a particular type of case. Referrals among lawyers are a key mechanism for dealing with the information problem. As Table 5.2 shows, lawyer referrals are an important source of business for plaintiffs' lawyers, and as we go up the hierarchy, such referrals become more important. Specialization and referrals go hand in hand, and as we noted earlier in this chapter, referrals are a factor (along with professional identity) in tying together the different segments of the plaintiffs' bar. Specialization and referrals are also important for enhancing access—getting cases to the lawyers best able to handle them. Referrals and specialization are the focus of the next chapter.

32. *Id.* at 116–117.

6. "If My Referring Lawyers Go Away, I'm in Trouble"

Reputation, Specialization, and the Referral of Cases

The statement in this chapter's title comes from an interview with a well-established and successful lawyer whose practice is built on high-end, complex cases that may come from anywhere in Texas—he is a heavy hitter. We quoted him in the last chapter in the discussion of HH2 lawyers (the top of the plaintiffs' bar hierarchy) and how they get business: "Last year . . . we spent about $80,000 on programs that were designed to touch our former clients—our referring lawyers—and make sure that we were, you know, they were sure that we wanted their business. . . . If my referring lawyers go away, I'm in trouble." As that discussion pointed out, he is not alone among high-end plaintiffs' lawyers in relying heavily on lawyer referrals as a source of business.

It is not, however, just the high-end lawyers who rely on such referrals. Lawyer referrals, as Table 5.2 showed, are important for lawyers at all levels of the plaintiffs' bar hierarchy. Even the San Antonio lawyer whose statement about his much lower place in the hierarchy opened Chapter 5 noted, "There are some lawyers who just don't like to try cases, and they know that a case will need to be tried, and they'll refer it. . . . Well, I mean there are the settling lawyers and the trial lawyers." He is among the latter, but in a complex referral system that moves cases up *and* down the hierarchy, he may also get a referral of a lower-value case from that heavy hitter. The referral system, especially paid referrals, and a widely shared professional identity help tie together the different segments of the Texas plaintiffs' bar. It is a system that generally works to the benefit of clients by moving cases to the lawyers best able to handle them—thereby enhancing access.

This system supports the specialization undergirding the hierarchy within the plaintiffs' bar, and the key to the system's working is reputation—a reputation for being successful. Cases are referred to specialists because of their reputation among other lawyers. Certain lawyers are recognized as having the expertise and resources to successfully handle particular kinds of cases that most lawyers believe they themselves cannot handle as well or at all. As Lynn

Mather and her collaborators found in their study of divorce lawyers, "Reputation within the legal community matters enormously."[1]

Most obviously, one thinks of the lawyers who handle complex, high-end cases beyond the means and expertise of many others. As one younger bread-and-butter lawyer put it, "Of course, there's the handful of heavy hitter guys, that, you know . . . live on the referrals—like your Frank Bransons and Wendell Turleys, those type of guys. Where the smaller fish will get a case that's over their head and kick it to those guys. There's a few of those guys, and they don't really have significant advertising to speak of. It's more their reputation." But there are also the lawyers at the other end of the hierarchy, like that San Antonio lawyer, who have built a reputation for successfully handling certain kinds of lower-value cases.

Sara Parikh's research on referrals within the plaintiffs' bar in Chicago reinforces the importance of specialization and referrals in understanding the Texas plaintiffs' bar.[2] Drawing on social network theory, which emphasizes the relational nature of social structure, Parikh observes that there is in Chicago—as there is in Texas—a clearly identifiable hierarchy that structures the plaintiffs' bar. As one ascends the hierarchy, the value of cases handled increases and it becomes more likely that a lawyer will specialize in a complex arena like medical malpractice. Referrals, which can go up or down the hierarchy, are the glue that helps hold this structure together. In her words:

Personal injury lawyers also refer cases to other personal injury attorneys in recognition of the existing stratification in the personal injury bar. Attorneys practicing in the low-end sector often secure smaller cases from high-end attorneys who do not handle smaller cases. . . . Likewise, attorneys practicing in the high-end sector often secure larger, more complex cases from low-end attorneys who do not feel comfortable, or do not have the resources to handle larger cases. This happens most often with medical malpractice and product liability disputes because of

1. Lynn Mather, Craig McEwen & Richard Maiman, *Divorce Lawyers at Work: Varieties of Professionalism in Practice* (New York: Oxford University Press, 2001), 127.

2. Sara Parikh, *How the Spider Catches the Fly: Referral Networks in the Plaintiff's Personal Injury Bar*, 51 N.Y.L. Sch. L. Rev. 244 (2006–2007).

the complexity of the cases, the financial expenditures, and the level of expertise required.[3]

In her view, the referral system plays the important role of reinforcing and reproducing the stratification within the plaintiffs' bar and the kind of specialization upon which it is built.

The importance of the referral system in understanding the plaintiffs' bar and its gatekeeping function is reason enough to explore it in some detail, but the Texas Supreme Court's efforts to fundamentally change the rules governing paid referrals in Texas (outlined in the context of tort reform in Chapter 2) provide an additional reason. Those efforts were aimed primarily at ending Texas's long history of explicitly allowing pure forwarding fees, a practice at odds with the American Bar Association's equally long history in its model ethics standards of prohibiting such fees. The Court was concerned that Texas remained an outlier in the treatment of referral fees and the issues underlying their prohibition: client consent, receiving a fee for nothing other than the referral, additional cost to the client, and the unprofessional nature of such fees. The Court was also concerned with the brokering of cases to the highest bidder by those whose practices involved little more than aggressively advertising for cases to refer. Interestingly, commentators have long pointed out that practicing lawyers have not universally condemned referral fees and that the practice of paying referral fees has persisted regardless of the formal prohibitions in many states.[4]

To recap the story told in Chapter 2, the Texas Supreme Court's Proposed Rule 8a for the Texas Rules of Civil Procedure dealt with paid referrals. It would have, most importantly, capped fees for paid referrals at $50,000 or 15 percent of the successful attorney's fee, whichever is less, with one exception. Rule 8a would also have imposed reporting requirements in which any paid referral arrangement or fee paid was to be filed with the court handling the case, and it allowed the court to conduct evidentiary hearings on the matters covered, including the amount of the referral fee. Even a fee under the cap

---

3. *Id.* at 260–261.

4. *See* Texas Supreme Court, *Proposed Rule 8a of the Texas Rules of Civil Procedure,* 67 Tex. B. J. 116 (2004).

could then be lowered even further if the court found it unconscionable given the circumstances of that case.[5]

Because of its treatment of referral fees, the proposed rule had the potential of seriously affecting the referral system, and because of what it would mean for the movement of cases among lawyers, it would affect access as well. Whether intended or not, plaintiffs' lawyers would have been hit the hardest by the changes, as would the clients in the kinds of cases most likely to be involved in the referral system, such as medical malpractice and products liability. The proposal's hard cap was an approach to fees fundamentally different from the traditional working practice in Texas. The long-standing practice has been that the fee to the referring lawyer would generally be one-third of the referred-to lawyer's fee if he or she were successful. While the actual fee could vary, this is exactly what our 2006 plaintiffs' lawyer survey (hereafter the 2006 survey) shows. For the survey's respondents, the typical referral fee paid is 32 percent to 33 percent of the successful lawyer's fee, as was the typical referral fee received.[6]

As Chapter 2 explained, Proposed Rule 8a never went into effect. In the face of staunch opposition from the Texas Bar, the Supreme Court agreed to the creation of a special task force to hold hearings, study referral fees, and make recommendations about changes. The recommendations of that task force were the ones that went into effect in 2005, and the resultant rule was different from Proposed Rule 8a. Rather than being a part of the Texas Rules of Civil Procedure, as Rule 8a would have been, the new rule was made a part of the Texas Disciplinary Rules of Professional Conduct (additions to the former can be made by the Court alone, whereas additions to the latter are made after a vote of the membership of the State Bar of Texas).[7] It requires full disclosure to the client of all lawyers involved and the fees, as well as consent by the client to those arrangements. The rule also states that a fee may be shared in two situations: (1) in proportion to the work of each lawyer or (2) if all lawyers involved

5. Amendments to the Texas Rules of Civil Procedure, Texas Supreme Court, Misc. Docket No. 03-9207 (2003).

6. Specifically, the results were: referral fee paid, mean = 32 percent, median = 33 percent; referral fee received, mean = 32 percent, median = 33 percent.

7. Since Texas is a mandatory bar state, this means a vote of all attorneys licensed in the state.

assume joint responsibility for the services provided.[8] There were also changes in the rules governing lawyer advertising to deal with the issue of brokering— lawyers advertising heavily for cases they would not themselves handle but would simply refer to other lawyers for a fee.[9]

The 2005 changes put the Texas rules much more in line with the American Bar Association's Model Rules of Professional Conduct, especially by adopting standards for shared work or joint responsibility that mirror the ABA's standards. As a result, it might be assumed that the occurrence of pure forwarding fees would diminish, if not disappear altogether. The idea is that being jointly and severally responsible for any liability arising out of the handling of the case would be a disincentive for pure forwarding fees. The referring lawyer would not want to exchange the possibility of a fee for the potential of full financial responsibility for liability arising out of the handling of the case by the lawyer to whom it was referred. Better to be involved with a fee based on the actual services rendered or to not refer the case at all with the expectation of a fee.

It seems, however, that the Texas rule may not work this way. Because of previous changes in Texas dealing with joint and several liability (changes made as part of tort reform legislation in 1995 and 2003), a commentary that appeared shortly after the new rules took effect noted that a "referring lawyer would now be jointly and severally liable in only two circumstances: (1) if the percentage of responsibility attributed to the referring lawyer is greater than fifty percent; or (2) if the referring lawyer, with specific intent to do harm to others, acted in concert with another person and committed violations of certain provisions of the Texas Penal Code."[10] So long as the required consent from the client is obtained, the referring lawyer may, in practice, face no

8. Texas Disciplinary Rule of Professional Conduct Rule 1.04(f); *Approval of Referendum on Proposed Changes in the Texas Disciplinary Rules of Professional Conduct,* 67 Tex. B. J. 838 (2004). *See also* Richard Pena, *The New Referral Fee Landscape in Texas, State Bar of Texas,* 3rd Annual Advanced Workers' Compensation Course, Aug. 24–25, 2006, Austin, TX. Pena was a member of the State Bar of Texas Referral Fee Task Force.

9. Supreme Court of Texas, Order Promulgating Amendments to Part VII of the Texas Disciplinary Rules of Professional Conduct. Misc. Docket No. 05-9013-A (2005). *Also see Approval of Referendum, id.*

10. *See* Rachel Bosworth, *Is the Model Rule Outdated? Texas Carries Referral Fee Responsibility into the Limited Liability Era,* 84 Tex. L. Rev. 509, 537 (2005).

real threat of joint responsibility, and pure forwarding fees will survive unless additional changes are made.[11] It is also worth mentioning again that commentators have long pointed out that, whatever the rules governing referral fees, most lawyers do not disapprove of them, and those rules may simply be ignored in many instances.[12]

As we will see, there is—and has been—a robust referral system in Texas, and it involves more than just plaintiffs' lawyers, although they clearly dominate. According to the 2004 Texas Survey of Referral Practices done for the State Bar's Referral Fee Task Force (hereafter Texas Referral Survey), tort cases are by far the largest category of cases referred for a fee by *all* lawyers in private practice in Texas.[13] More specifically, medical malpractice cases are the most referred across the board—and not just the most referred kind of personal injury case. Automobile accident cases are next, followed by products liability cases. In addition, plaintiffs' lawyers are by far the most likely to refer a case for a fee (with medical malpractice being the case they would most likely refer, followed by products liability). Indeed, with one exception, plaintiffs' lawyers account for the largest percentage of referrals for all types of cases, including family cases and real estate cases. The exception is criminal defense matters, with criminal defense lawyers accounting for the largest percentage of criminal case referrals. We will examine the survey's findings in more detail shortly.

Our surveys of Texas plaintiffs' lawyers show that lawyer referrals are the most important source of business for the respondents overall. On average, for the lawyers responding to our surveys, 38 percent of their business comes from

11. In this regard, Bosworth noted, "Eleven states do not require that fees be divided based on services performed or joint responsibility, but each provides guidelines for fee amounts or client notification. Texas was previously among the latter group but is now in its own category—it requires joint responsibility but redefines it so as not to include vicarious liability." *Id.* at 520.

12. *See* Texas Supreme Court, *supra* note 5; F. B. MacKinnon, *Contingent Fees for Legal Services: A Study of Professional Economics and Responsibilities* (Chicago: Aldine, 1964), at 181, 203; Thomas Hall & Joel Levy, *Intra-Attorney Fee Sharing Arrangements*, 11 Valparaiso U. L. Rev. 1 (1976); Stephen Spurr, *Referral Practices among Lawyers: A Theoretical and Empirical Analysis*, 13 L. & Soc. Inquiry 87 (1988).

13. All findings in this paragraph come from the 2004 Texas State Bar Referral Practices Survey, *see* https://www.texasbar.com/AM/Template.cfm?Section=Archives&Template=/CM/ContentDisplay.cfm&ContentID=11493.

lawyer referrals, followed by client referrals at 27 percent of their business. For higher-end plaintiffs' lawyers, lawyer referrals are even more important. For the HH2 lawyers we described in Chapter 5, lawyer referrals account for over one-half of their business on average (56 percent), with one-third responding that 75 percent or more of their business comes from that source. For those who specialize in medical malpractice (meaning 50 percent or more of their caseload is medical malpractice), the percentage of business generated by lawyer referrals is equally high (on average, 58 percent of business), with one-third of malpractice specialists getting 80 percent or more of their business from lawyer referrals. After our examination of the Texas Referral Survey, we will turn to a detailed examination of the results of our 2006 survey, which included a special section on the referral system.

This chapter is not about rehashing the long-standing arguments for and against paid referrals. Rather, it looks at reputation, specialization, and the referral system as key parts of plaintiffs' practice in the context of tort reform. The remainder of the chapter has two main sections. Each will address five basic questions about paid referrals: what gets referred, who refers, who gets the referrals, why cases are referred, and how the target lawyer for the referral is chosen. The answers will give us the basic contours of the system and what drives it. With regard to access, the consequences of eliminating the system or fundamentally changing the rules governing it will become obvious as those contours become clear—access will be seriously comprised. The first section will draw from the 2004 Texas Referral Survey and the second section will draw from our 2006 survey. Throughout, the term *formal referrals* will appear, meaning paid referrals. This is the term many lawyers use, and it was used in the Texas Referral Survey and our 2006 survey, each of which defined it as meaning paid referrals.

THE GENERAL PICTURE: THE TEXAS REFERRAL SURVEY

What Kinds of Cases Are Referred?

The Texas Referral Survey is unique in seeking general information on referrals, and it involves a sample of all licensed Texas lawyers, not just plaintiffs' lawyers. Relevant for our purposes are the responses of the 861 lawyers in pri-

TABLE 6.1. *Referrals by Case Type: Texas Referral Survey, 2004* (% of 3,874 reported referrals)

Probate	2
Real estate	3
Consumer	3
Other	4
Commercial	5
Workers' compensation	5
Family	7
Employment	7
Criminal	9
Personal injury other	11
Products liability	12
Auto accidents	14
Medical malpractice	17

vate practice within the state. The survey asked lawyers to report the number of cases referred with the expectation of a fee in the twelve months prior to the survey for a wide variety of case types. Table 6.1 presents information on those case types for which there were twenty or more referrals reported being made with expectation of a fee during this period. Specifically, it shows the percentage of all reported referrals made with expectation of a fee ($n = 3,874$) for each of those case types. Two important things are evident in Table 6.1. First, it shows that the market for paid referrals in Texas is dominated by cases in the personal services sector. Second, within this sector, personal injury cases are the most frequently referred cases. Over one-half (54 percent) of all referrals reported in the survey are personal injury cases, with medical malpractice cases being the most-referred type of case.

To place the role of personal injury cases in the referral market in a context that emphasizes their importance in that market, we can compare the relative magnitude of referrals to the relative magnitude of cases filed in the Texas District Courts—the trial courts of jurisdiction. As noted, all personal injury cases make up 54 percent of the referrals in the survey. The Texas Office of Court Administration collects annual filing figures for two categories of cases that cover this ground: injury or damage involving a motor vehicle and injury or damage other than motor vehicle. Together these two categories of cases made up just 7 percent of civil filings and 5 percent of all filings in 2004 (civil and criminal). These percentages clearly show the disproportionate role of these cases in the referral market. In contrast, family cases made up 7 percent of the referrals in Table 6.1, 53 percent of civil cases filed, and 37 percent of all cases filed. Criminal cases made up 9 percent of referrals and 32 percent of all cases filed.[14]

Who Refers Cases?

One key finding of the Texas Referral Survey is that not all lawyers in private practice participate in the referral market—defined as referring one or more cases with the expectation of a fee in the twelve months prior to the survey. Just over one-half of the 861 private practice respondents to the Texas Referral Survey did not—58 percent reported making no referrals with the expectation of a fee. The mean number of referrals for the 366 respondents making at least one referral is eleven referrals and the median number was four. Only a handful of lawyers regularly made a large number of referrals per year. For those making at least one referral per year, the 75th percentile is eight referrals and the 90th percentile is twenty-four. Sixteen lawyers referred 50 or more cases (4 percent of those participating in the market). Only four respondents reported making 100 or more.[15]

Participation in the referral market varies by practice area, with plaintiffs' lawyers being the predominant players.[16] Table 6.2 shows that 80 percent of the plaintiffs' lawyers in the survey made at least one referral of some kind with the expectation of a fee. They account for 40 percent of all referrals, with a mean of twenty referrals and a median of seven referrals while being only 21 percent of the 366 lawyers in the survey making at least one referral. The

14. For 2004, the year of the Texas Referral Survey, 14,678 auto accident cases were filed in the Texas District Courts, and 14,837 non-auto tort cases were filed, for a total of 29,515 tort cases. A total of 225,462 divorce and other family matters were filed. Overall, 421,699 civil cases were filed along with 195,969 criminal cases for a grand total of 617,668 cases filed.

15. Ten of these heavy players are plaintiffs' lawyers.

16. The differences among lawyers in different practice areas for their participation in the referral market are statistically significant. Using one-way ANOVA, the differences among practice areas for whether lawyers will make at least one referral are significant at .01 ($F = 10.541$, $df = 14$) as are the differences in the number of referrals made by those who refer at least one case ($F = 2.795$, $df = 7$).

TABLE 6.2. *Participation in Referral Market by Referring at Least One Case: For Lawyers in Referral Survey Percent in Primary Practice Areas**

Real estate	24
Probate	30
General litigation	33
Personal injury defense	37
Family	45
Criminal	58
General practice	60
Personal injury plaintiff	80

*Practice areas with 5% or more of respondents to the Texas Referral Survey.

next highest levels of participation are among criminal lawyers (60 percent participating) and general practitioners (58 percent participating).[17] However, these two groups account for much smaller percentages of all referrals, 14 percent and 12 percent, respectively (no other group accounted for as much as 10 percent of referrals). The mean and median numbers of referrals are also lower than those for plaintiffs' lawyers—criminal lawyers had a mean of sixteen referrals and a median of five, and general practitioners had a mean of six referrals and a median of three. At the other extreme are probate lawyers (30 percent participation and 2 percent of all referrals) and real estate lawyers (24 percent participation and 3 percent of all referrals). The nature of their practices is such that individuals do not bring them the kinds of cases most often referred for a fee—personal injury cases.

The high level of participation in the referral market by plaintiffs' lawyers cuts across case types. With the exception of criminal cases, personal injury plaintiff lawyers referred the largest proportion of every kind of case listed in Table 6.1. They referred over 40 percent of medical malpractice cases, over 40 percent of family cases, and over 80 percent of products liability cases. General practice lawyers account for 20 percent of the medical malpractice referrals, meaning that these lawyers and plaintiffs' lawyers together referred over 60 percent of the medical malpractice cases. With the exception of criminal cases, plaintiffs' lawyers referred at least twice as much of every case as the next highest percentage.

17. Criminal lawyers were the only group other than plaintiffs' lawyers that accounted for a percentage of referrals higher than their percentage of all respondents (12 percent of referrals and 6 percent of respondents).

Who Gets Referrals?

The relationship between the referral system and specialization becomes evident when we look at where referrals go. As was the case with making referrals, plaintiffs' lawyers are *the* key players with regard to accepting referrals for which a fee is expected in return.[18] Over three-quarters of plaintiffs' lawyers reported accepting at least one such referral, with a mean of twenty-five acceptances and a median of five (the highest for each). For no other practice area did more than 39 percent of the respondents report accepting at least one case on referral for a fee. In addition, plaintiffs' lawyers accepted almost 60 percent of the 3,264 accepted referrals reported in the Texas Referral Survey. No other practice area accounts for more than 10 percent of acceptances. Four practice areas are noteworthy for the small percentage of referred cases accepted by lawyers in these practice areas. Family lawyers, probate lawyers, real estate lawyers, and personal injury defense lawyers together account for only 8 percent of all acceptances. Individually, none of these practice areas account for as much as 3 percent of acceptances.

The link between referrals and specialization is especially clear in light of the percentage of acceptances taken by plaintiffs' lawyers for the three specific personal injury case types—medical malpractice, auto accident, and products liability. Plaintiffs' lawyers stand out. They accepted nearly three-quarters of medical malpractice cases and over 80 percent each of auto accident cases and products liability cases. They also accepted 91 percent of referred workers' compensation cases. In contrast, plaintiffs' lawyers account for a relatively low percentage of acceptances for non–personal injury cases. The highest percentage is 17 percent for referrals of commercial cases. Plaintiffs' lawyers accepted no referrals for criminal, real estate, or probate cases.

Why Refer a Case?

A possible and obvious answer to the question of why a case is referred is the one that animates much of the criticism of paid referrals and the effort to cur-

---

18. The Texas Referral Survey asked only about referrals accepted and did not distinguish between referrals accepted by a lawyer and referrals made to the lawyer but not ultimately accepted. The 2006 survey asked about both.

tail or eliminate them—greed. The idea is that the prospect of a fee for little or no work beyond the referral of the case is the driving force, and that lawyers will just refer the case to the highest bidder with little or no concern for the client's best interest. This answer is too simple since it presumes nothing else is involved. The empirical literature, scant though it is, provides an alternative to this crude, yet plausible, idea—and it deals with reputation. Herbert Kritzer emphasizes the importance of reputation for lawyers working on a contingency fee basis—it is the key to getting business on a regular basis. Those lawyers need to have satisfied clients, he says, and "more important, the lawyers want the clients to *stay* satisfied. A lawyer who settles cases too cheaply will have trouble maintaining the reputation necessary to create the flow of potential clients that is in the lawyer's long-term interests."[19] The logic easily applies to lawyers who rely on referrals from other lawyers. Reputation is important for all lawyers. It is also good for the client.

Referring a case that is too complex, too expensive, or out of a lawyer's realm of expertise allows a lawyer to significantly reduce risk and cost while offering the potential for a meaningful return. That return is twofold: a fee for the referring lawyer and a satisfactory outcome for the client. Even if a lawyer's sense of professional identity does not include concern for the client's best interest, practical considerations do. A happy client benefits the referring lawyer's reputation, and a happy referring lawyer benefits the referred-to lawyer's reputation. If a lawyer shortchanges or provides suboptimal service to his or her referring lawyers, those referring lawyers will take their business elsewhere and suggest that others do the same. This is why the heavy hitter at the chapter's opening is so concerned with how his referring lawyers—his clients, as he calls them—are treated. Whether it is a situation involving a contingency fee or any other fee situation, a lawyer with a reputation for poor service and suboptimal results will find it difficult to keep getting business.

Table 6.3 presents the responses to the Texas Referral Survey regarding a list of different reasons for referring a case (the next section deals with the money issue and how the lawyer to receive the referral is chosen). Respondents were asked to check all the reasons that applied, so the percentages will not add up to 100 percent. Three-quarters of the respondents listed "out of practice area" as a reason and this motivation overshadows all of the others. The possibility

---

19. Herbert Kritzer, *Risks, Reputations, and Rewards: Contingency Fee Legal Practice in the United States* (Stanford, CA: Stanford University Press, 2004), 67.

TABLE 6.3. *Reasons for Referring Cases: Lawyers in Referral Survey Making at Least One Formal Referral* (% of 366 respondents choosing each)

Conflict of interest	1
Refers most cases	1
Case value too high	11
Caseload too high	16
Case value too low	18
Location of case	32
Case too complex	36
Case out of practice area	75

of a fee provides a financial incentive to move the case to a lawyer better able to serve the client. "Out of practice area" is also the primary reason for referrals from each of the practice areas listed in the earlier tables. With one exception, personal injury defense lawyers (68 percent), over 70 percent of the respondents in each practice area cited it as a reason for referring cases.

This response further underscores the connection between specialization and referrals, as does the second most popular reason. Just over one-third of the respondents said that they referred cases that were too complex or technical. To be more precise, the wording in the survey is "case was in my practice area but was too complex/technical." This points to the existence of varying degrees of specialization within a practice area and to the idea that some lawyers may be "super-specialists"—focusing on very particular kinds of cases within a practice area.

Referrals, then, move within practice areas, as Parikh's work shows, as well as between them. Most plaintiffs' lawyers, for instance, can handle a straightforward auto accident case, but the same is not true for cases like medical malpractice that are highly complex and very expensive to prepare. Even most plaintiffs' lawyers are likely to refer such a case to a plaintiffs' lawyer who specializes in medical malpractice. Some of these super-specialists may handle little other than medical malpractice (or whatever their special focus is). The possibility of a fee provides a financial incentive to move the case to a lawyer better able to serve the client (as well as the referring lawyer).

Just under one-third of the respondents said that they referred cases because the cases are in another geographic area, and smaller percentages reported their caseload or a conflict of interest as the reason for referring. Eighteen percent said they referred cases because the dollar value of the case was too low.

This means that the referring lawyer normally does not handle certain cases because their value is too low and so refers them to another lawyer who does handle lower-value matters. Nonetheless, the referring lawyer still expects a fee. Plaintiffs' lawyers and general litigation lawyers have the highest percentage of respondents citing this reason—30 percent for each.

Another 11 percent of the 366 respondents who made at least one referral said they will refer a case if the dollar value is higher than the lawyer normally handles. In these situations, the referring lawyer may not have the resources, especially the financial resources, to handle a higher-value case. For instance, one Houston lawyer we interviewed said, "We don't take any medical malpractice cases. We refer them. . . . They are way too technical for our expertise. . . . They are also very, very expensive to handle. Easily you can spend $100,000 without blinking on those kinds of cases, and typically we don't have that kind of cash lying around." In these situations, referring lawyers are looking for target lawyers with the needed resources. Once more, the possibility of a referral fee provides a financial incentive to move the case to a lawyer better able to serve the client.

How Is a Target Lawyer Chosen?

More is involved in understanding why cases are referred than simply the referring lawyer's financial interest, but the referring lawyer's financial interest is still there. If we return to the view of the traditional critics of paid referrals, the answer to the question of how the target lawyer is chosen is the highest bidder—the lawyer offering the highest referral fee. But again, the literature suggests an alternative way of understanding how a target lawyer is chosen, and it points once more to reputation—here the reputations of potential target lawyers. If, as Kritzer, Mather et al., and others argue, it is important for a lawyer to build and maintain a reputation in order to keep business coming in, then that argument presumes, of course, that reputation does in fact attract business. This does not mean a reputation for simply offering the highest referral fees.

In fact, a referring lawyer may not want to go to the highest bidder. Instead, he may go to the lawyer providing the best chance of succeeding and hence of paying the referral fee. What makes a lawyer an attractive referral partner is that lawyer's reputation for success and for having the resources and expertise

TABLE 6.4. *Criteria for Choosing a Target Lawyer: Lawyers in Referral Survey Making at Least One Formal Referral* (% of 366 respondents choosing each)

	Important	Neutral	Not Important
Lawyer's reputation	97	3	1
Compatibility with client	56	26	18
Reciprocity between lawyers	19	19	63
Size of fee offered	14	23	63

needed to be successful. This maximizes the referring lawyer's chance for a fee, but it also benefits the client. In addition, there are other possible reasons for choosing a target lawyer not involving the highest fee offered. For instance, the lawyers involved may have a reciprocal relationship—each handles different cases and each refers cases to the other.

Table 6.4 presents data on the relative importance of different criteria used for selecting a target lawyer. For lawyers in the Texas Referral Survey who made at least one referral, Table 6.4 clearly shows that the most important reason for choosing a target lawyer is the target lawyer's reputation in his or her practice area, followed by compatibility between the client and the target lawyer. In contrast, the two criteria most immediately tied to the referring lawyer's self-interest—the size of the expected fee and reciprocity (the expectation of future referrals from the target lawyer)—are relatively unimportant.

Reputation is also the most important criterion for the lawyers referring medical malpractice cases, auto accident cases, and products liability cases. The same is true for those referring completely different kinds of cases, like family and real estate cases. For the lawyers referring each of those types of cases, reputation was identified as an important criterion by at least 94 percent for each case type. In contrast, no more than 18 percent of the referring lawyers listed size of the fee as an important factor for any of the case types (the highest percentage was 18 percent of the lawyers referring auto cases). No lawyer referring real estate cases listed the size of the fee offered as an important factor in choosing a target lawyer.

The importance of reputation should not be surprising given that many lawyers, including plaintiffs' lawyers, refer cases because those cases are out of their practice area—or, if they are in the lawyers' practice area, they are too complex to handle. Sending the case to a lawyer seen as capable of being successful serves the referring lawyer's interest because it maximizes his or her chance of receiving a fee with little or no risk or cost. This also, obviously, serves the client's interest by getting the case to a lawyer best able to handle the case. And, importantly, there is typically no additional cost to the client in terms of lawyers' fees. When asked in the Texas Referral Survey whether those respondents accepting paid referrals increase the fee charged to the client to cover all or some of the referral fee, only 3 of the 241 lawyers (1.2 percent) accepting paid referrals responded yes and another 15 (6.2 percent) said it depends.[20]

In Texas there is a robust market for referrals that allows lawyers to specialize by providing a system that helps them get business even though most consumers will not know who the specialists are. The system works to move cases from lawyers less able to handle them to lawyers better able to do so. The referral fee provides the incentive to move cases, but it is lawyers' reputations—not the size of the fee—that really makes the system work. Using our 2006 survey data, the next section looks more deeply into how this system works within the plaintiffs' bar. In a number of instances, our 2006 survey used the same question wording as in the Texas Referral Survey to allow for comparisons.

PLAINTIFFS' LAWYERS AND REFERRALS: THE 2006 SURVEY

What Kinds of Cases Are Referred?

The Texas Referral Survey shows plaintiffs' lawyers referring personal injury cases more than other types of cases. Our 2006 survey paints a similar picture. Table 6.5 shows that the respondents, for the most part, referred personal injury cases, with over two-thirds of the referrals (69 percent, not counting workers' compensation cases, which accounted for an additional 13 percent of referrals) being some kind of personal injury. Less than one-fifth of the referrals (18 percent) did not involve some kind of personal injury or workers' compensation.

20. The three lawyers responding "yes" were one plaintiffs' lawyer, one general practice lawyer, and one commercial lawyer. The fifteen lawyers responding "depends" were four general practice lawyers, two plaintiffs' lawyers, one family lawyer, two criminal lawyers, three general litigation lawyers, one probate lawyer, one intellectual property lawyer, and one lawyer unknown.

TABLE 6.5. *Referrals by Case Type: Plaintiffs' Lawyer Survey, 2006* (% of 3,034 reported referrals)

Commercial	1
Consumer	3
Employment	6
Other non–personal injury	8
Products liability	10
Workers' compensation	13
Other personal injury	16
Medical malpractice	21
Auto accident	22

More specifically, the largest percentage of referrals involves auto accident cases, which is not surprising because they are the most frequently occurring type of injury case. Table 6.5 shows that just over one-fifth of the cases referred by respondents to the 2006 survey are auto accident cases (22 percent), but it also shows that almost as large a percent of the referred cases are medical malpractice cases (21 percent), which occur far less frequently than auto cases. Together, auto and medical malpractice cases account for 43 percent of the referrals. If we add referrals of products liability cases, the three together account for over one-half of all referrals. Auto and medical malpractice cases also account for the largest number of referrals in the Texas Referral Survey, although medical malpractice was higher. Nonetheless, far more of the lawyers responding to the 2006 survey referred at least one medical malpractice case than referred an auto case or any other type of case. This is similar to what we see in the Texas Referral Survey.

Who Refers?

Forty-four percent of respondents to the 2006 survey referred at least one case with the expectation of a fee, with a mean of fifteen referrals and a median of five for these lawyers. As noted above, while auto cases make up the largest proportion of all cases referred, more lawyers referred at least one medical malpractice case than one auto case—26 percent of all respondents referred at least one malpractice case for a fee compared to 16 percent referring at least one auto case. Thirteen percent referred at least one products liability case.

If we look at the four stratification groups in the Texas plaintiffs' bar hierarchy outlined in Chapter 5, we find no significant difference among them in terms of whether they referred at least one case with the expectation of a fee. It is enough to say at this point that plaintiffs' lawyers across the board refer cases. As we will soon see, however, the important differences and patterns are in who refers what and in who receives what referrals. This is where specialization, and the importance of referrals for specialization, will be clearly evident.

Who Gets Referrals?

The findings from the Texas Referral Survey show how, in the broadest sense, the referral system is tied to specialization. Although the symmetry is not perfect, more often than not, particular types of cases move from lawyers who do not regularly handle those cases to lawyers who do regularly handle them—to the clients' benefit. The 2006 survey allows us to look at the tie between referrals and specialization in more detail by looking at lawyers who specialize not simply in personal injury cases but in certain types of cases, especially the most complex, expensive, and risky cases like medical malpractice and products liability.

This is where the importance of reputation is most evident. Cases are referred to specialists because of their reputation among other lawyers. Certain lawyers are recognized as having the expertise and resources to successfully handle particular kinds of cases that most lawyers believe they themselves cannot handle as well or at all. It is worth repeating the remarks of a bread-and-butter lawyer we quoted near the chapter's beginning: "Of course, there's the handful of heavy hitter guys, that, you know . . . live on the referrals—like your Frank Bransons and Wendell Turleys. Those types of guys, where the smaller fish will get a case that's over their head and kick it to those guys. There's a few of those guys, and they don't really have significant advertising to speak of. It's more their reputation." Those reputations are often tied to some kind of specialization.

A useful way of exploring the connection between receiving referrals on one hand and having a reputation as a specialist on the other is to ask where referrals go (the next section will look at why cases are referred). More specifically, are referrals *received* (regardless of ultimately being accepted or not) distributed in a roughly equal fashion across the plaintiffs' bar? The most obvious way to answer this question is to see if the receipt of referrals varies by whether a receiving lawyer is certified by the Texas Board of Specialization in either personal injury trial law or civil trial law (the two most relevant certifications in Texas). Certification is important because in Texas it signals a well-understood level of expertise and experience in a particular area of practice, and gaining certification does much to enhance a lawyer's reputation. In addition, at the time of our research the rules governing advertising mandated that in any advertisement, a lawyer had to specifically note whether or not he was board certified. In other words, the noncertified lawyer, if he advertised, had to state unequivocally that he was *not* board certified. The board certified lawyer could unequivocally state that he was certified by the Texas Board of Legal Specialization in a particular practice area. To provide an illustration, we asked one midcareer lawyer if he was receiving referrals from other lawyers. He replied, "I'm starting to, and the reason is . . . I just achieved board certification." He is certified in personal injury trial law.

Respondents to the 2006 survey reported receiving a total of 11,346 referrals. Almost all of these cases are personal injury cases: 10,413, or 92 percent. In itself, this tells us something obvious but important—these lawyers are not attracting a broad array of referrals. They are receiving personal injury referrals, and these personal injury referrals do not appear to be evenly distributed among all respondents. The 172 respondents in the 2006 survey who were board certified in either personal injury trial law or civil trial law (37 percent of all respondents) received a disproportionate share of these referrals. These lawyers received 49 percent of the personal injury referrals, and they are somewhat more likely to receive such referrals than their noncertified peers.[21]

There is, however, much more to the story because specialization can go deeper than certification in personal injury trial law or civil trial law. One of the first lawyers we interviewed in the mid-1990s told us, "I used to feel like I could handle. . . . I thought PI [personal injury] was narrow enough. . . . It's just . . . it's hard enough to keep up your own little narrow field much less all of PI." He went on, "There's a lot more specialization," and added, "I did a good

---

21. There is a significant, though not strong, relationship between being certified in either of these areas and receiving at least one referral of a personal injury case: Cramer's $V = .118$, sig = .013. There is also a significant, but not strong, relationship between certification and the number of personal injury referrals received: Pearson's $r = .082$, sig = .042.

bit of medical malpractice, but I'm much more comfortable just referring it out now. . . . That is getting to be so much of a specialty that it pretty much has to go to people who do nothing but that." He said he referred any medical malpractice cases to a well-known specialist in his city. He said of the plaintiffs' lawyers in his city, "We recognize each other's specialty. Like nursing home cases, X [another well-known lawyer] is sort of developing a nursing home specialty. And I'm not saying I wouldn't take a nursing home case, but I might as well just refer it over to him. I get a third, and he'll do a good job." Another plaintiffs' lawyer in the same city had a similar view. "Once in a while, if it's something—an insurance bad faith case—I will refer to lawyers who are doing a bunch of those cases because I have done some, but I really don't want to re-create the wheel all the time."

We can look at this in more detail by examining where referrals for specific kinds of cases go. For instance, do lawyers who handle more medical malpractice cases receive more medical malpractice referrals? The answer is yes, and the relationship is a significant one.[22] In contrast, there is no relationship between handling more auto accident cases and receiving more medical malpractice referrals, but there is the expected relationship between the number of auto accident cases handled and receiving more auto accident referrals.[23]

More important are the forty-three respondents to the 2006 survey whom we labeled as medical malpractice specialists because they reported that medical malpractice cases made up 50 percent or more of their business at the time of the survey. They represent 9 percent of all respondents, yet they got 47 percent (1,721 of 3,654) of all medical malpractice referrals received in the survey.[24] If we look at the issue in terms of the book of referrals received by these forty-three specialists, we find that almost all of the referrals they received are medical malpractice cases (91 percent of a total of 1,881).

Auto accident specialists received another one-third of the medical malpractice referrals (1,196). However, a single auto accident specialist received just over one-half of these referrals. He was a medical malpractice specialist

22. Pearson's $r = .272$, sig $= .000$.
23. Pearson's $r = .191$, sig $= .000$.
24. There is a significant relationship between being a 2006 medical malpractice specialist and receiving at least one medical malpractice referral: Cramer's $V = .264$, sig $= .000$. There is also a significant relationship between being a specialist and the number of such referrals received: Pearson's $r = .227$, sig $= .000$.

before the 2003 medical malpractice reforms were enacted (before 2003, all of his business was medical malpractice). Although he completely changed his practice, he continued to receive medical malpractice referrals, but the change in his practice was so dramatic that he actually accepted only two of those referrals. If we remove the referrals he received from the total for auto accident specialists, then the remaining auto accident specialists received just 16 percent of the medical malpractice referrals. And if we add that lawyer's referrals to the total for medical malpractice specialists—effectively counting him as a medical malpractice specialist for the moment—then these specialists received 64 percent of medical malpractice referrals. In contrast, the thirty-two lawyers who reported that commercial cases handled on a contingency fee basis made up 50 percent or more of their business received less than 1 percent of medical malpractice referrals.

There are 173 auto accident specialists in our 2006 survey respondent pool (37 percent of respondents). They received 61 percent of the 3,371 auto accident referrals in the survey.[25] If we look at the book of referrals received by the 173 auto accident specialists, we find that one-half are auto accident cases. But if we remove from the total for all auto accident specialist referrals the medical malpractice referrals of the lawyer noted above (again, counting him as a medical malpractice specialist for the moment), auto accident referrals increase to 59 percent of all referrals received by these lawyers. Commercial specialists received less than 1 percent of the auto accident referrals.

There are twenty-nine products liability specialists in the respondent pool (6 percent of respondents). They received 69 percent (1,448 of 2,096) of the products liability referrals in the survey.[26] In terms of their book of all referrals, 82 percent are products liability cases. The commercial specialists received less than 1 percent of the products liability referrals.

The symmetry may not be perfect, but there are identifiable patterns showing that the receipt of referrals is not distributed in a roughly equal fashion

25. There is a significant relationship between being an auto specialist and receiving at least one auto accident referral: Cramer's $V = .329$, sig $= .000$. There is also a significant relationship between being an auto specialist and the number of auto accident referrals received: Pearson's $r = .156$, sig $= .001$.

26. There is a significant relationship between being a products liability specialist and receiving at least one products liability referral: Cramer's $V = .295$, sig $= .000$. There is also a significant relationship between being a products liability specialist and the number of products liability referrals received: Pearson's $r = .359$, sig $= .000$.

across the plaintiffs' bar. There are clear and significant patterns showing that referrals do flow toward substantive specialization. Reputation and specialization may draw referrals, but we would not expect specialists to actually take everything that comes to them—and this is the case. For all respondents, there were 11,346 referrals received but only 4,401 accepted, for a rate of 39 percent. The acceptance rates for specific kinds of cases can be lower—reflecting the complexity and costs involved—for example, 10 percent for medical malpractice and 31 percent for products liability. The acceptance rates for some also can be higher—56 percent for the less complex, less costly auto accident cases.

Why Are Cases Referred?

In the 2006 survey, we presented the respondents with the same list of reasons for referring a case that was used in the Texas Referral Survey, with the exception of conflict of interest. Table 6.6 shows the results of that inquiry, and again, since respondents were asked to check all reasons that applied, the percentages do not add up to 100 percent. Like lawyers in the broader survey, just over three-quarters of the respondents identified "out of practice area" as a reason for referring a case. Across the board, lawyers will refer cases because the case is outside their practice area—for those making at least one referral, there is no significant relationship between stratification group and giving this as a reason.

The connection between specialization within the plaintiffs' bar and referrals is reinforced by those respondents who listed "case was in my practice area but was too complex/technical" as a reason for referring. As one goes up the hierarchy, it is *less* likely that this reason will be given. For those making at least one referral, there is a significant relationship between the group a lawyer is in and listing "too complex/technical" as a reason for referring a case.[27] This should not be surprising because those specializing in the most complex areas like medical malpractice and products liability are likely to be found in the hierarchy's upper echelons.[28] These are the lawyers who handle the more

27. Cramer's V = .308, sig = .000.

28. The correlation between group and being either a medical malpractice or products liability specialist is positive: Spearman's rho = .359, sig = .000—meaning these specialists are more likely to be in the hierarchy's higher echelons. The correlation

TABLE 6.6. *Reasons for Referring Cases: Lawyers in Plaintiffs' Survey Making at Least One Formal Referral* (% of 202 respondents choosing each)

Refers most cases	1
Case value too high	10
Caseload too high	14
Case too complex	32
Case value too low	45
Location of case	57
Case out of practice area	78

complex and demanding cases; these are the lawyers to whom lawyers in the lower echelons are likely to refer such cases.

One noticeable difference between the respondents to the 2006 survey and those in the Texas Referral Survey is found in the percentage listing geographic location as a reason for referring a case. While approximately one-third of the Texas Referral Survey respondents listed location as a reason for referring a case, over one-half of the 2006 survey respondents did so. Unfamiliarity with local juries and the tightening of the rules for venue may encourage some plaintiffs' lawyers to refer a case rather than handling it in an unfamiliar jurisdiction, or the referral may simply be a result of the cost of handling a case at a distance in a state in which distances can be great.[29]

Like the respondents to the Texas Referral Survey, few of those responding to the 2006 survey reported that the size of their caseload was a reason for referring or that most of the cases they took were referred. Still, it is important to remember that heavy advertising and referring most cases—brokering cases—remains a business model for a small number of plaintiffs' lawyers, and as the discussion of norms and professional identity in Chapter 4 showed, it is a business model that is controversial within the plaintiffs' bar.

Unlike respondents to the broader survey, a higher percentage of the 2006 survey respondents (45 percent versus 18 percent) reported that "case dollar value was less than I usually handle" as a reason for referring a matter. As

---

between being an auto accident specialist and group is negative: Spearman's rho = −.411, sig = .000—meaning these specialists are more likely to be in the lower echelons.

29. There is no significant relationship between listing this reason and a respondent's group, type of specialization, or geographic scope of practice.

might be expected, there is a significant relationship between a respondent's place in the hierarchy and giving this reason—the higher one goes up the hierarchy, the more likely this reason will be given.[30] A heavy hitter we quoted in Chapter 5 about his screening process for the occasional medical malpractice or products liability cases he takes provides the simple reason: he refers lower-value cases back down the hierarchy to younger lawyers just starting out. He said, "They are willing to take those cases. Their overhead is not as high as mine, so they can cost-effectively handle those cases, knowing the outcome will be lower because it costs less for them to put the cases together." Correspondingly, a younger lawyer told us, "Because my partner and I are on the younger end of the career ladder, older lawyers with much higher thresholds for the cases they take send us smaller damages cases."

The patterns for specialists are consistent with this idea. There is a significant relationship between being a medical malpractice specialist or a products liability specialist and being more likely to list "case dollar value was less than I usually handle" as a reason for referring a matter.[31] As we might expect, the same is not true for the auto accident specialist, whose cases generally tend to be of lower value than those handled by the medical malpractice and products liability specialists. He is unlikely to list "case dollar value was less than I usually handle" as a reason for referring a matter and for the relationship.

Although only 10 percent of respondents who referred at least one case gave as a reason that the "case dollar value was more than I usually handle," the expected relationship is there—the higher one goes in the hierarchy, the less likely this reason will be given for referring a case.[32] Virtually no medical malpractice or products liability specialist listed this as a reason for referring a case—just one each. Thirteen percent of auto accident specialists who referred at least one case gave this as a reason.

In summary, the reasons given for referring a case are consistent with a hierarchical plaintiffs' bar that includes some members who clearly specialize in certain kinds of complex cases. Those lower in the hierarchy are more likely to refer certain matters up, and those higher in the hierarchy are more likely to refer certain matters down. Most importantly for clients and for access, re-

---

30. Cramer's V = .381, sig = .000.

31. Medical malpractice specialist, Cramer's V = .155, sig = .028; products liability specialist, Cramer's V = .198, sig = .005.

32. Cramer's V = .289, sig = .000.

ferrals are made because the referring lawyer is seeking someone better able to handle the case. The next section on the importance of certain factors in deciding on the attorney to whom to refer the case will provide further evidence for the idea of seeking someone better able to handle the case.

How Is a Target Lawyer Chosen?

In the earlier discussion of the Texas Referral Survey and how a target lawyer is chosen, we emphasized the importance of reputation—and not simply a reputation for offering the highest referral fees. If a lawyer is motivated to refer a case because doing so offers a good way of balancing cost and risk against potential gain, then the more attractive referral partner is the lawyer with a reputation for success and for having the resources needed to be successful. This maximizes the referring lawyer's chance for a fee, but it also benefits the client. The findings from the Texas Referral Survey were quite consistent with the idea that reputation was overwhelmingly the most important factor in deciding the lawyer to whom a case would be referred, and the findings from our 2006 survey bolster this idea.

The 2006 survey asked the same questions used in the Texas Referral Survey concerning the criteria used for choosing the target lawyer. Table 6.7 shows the results of this inquiry. Like the results for the Texas Referral Survey shown in Table 6.4, it shows that reputation is by far the most important reason for choosing a target lawyer, followed by compatibility between the client and the target lawyer. As in Table 6.4, the two criteria most immediately tied to the referring lawyer's self-interest—the size of the expected fee and reciprocity (the expectation of future referrals from the target lawyer)—are less important in comparison.

These two criteria, however, are more important for the plaintiffs' lawyers responding to the 2006 survey than for the broader array of respondents to the Texas Referral Survey. In the broader survey, 14 percent of respondents said that the size of the fee offered is important, while 25 percent of the respondents to the 2006 survey answered affirmatively to the same question (63 percent in the broader survey said the fee was not important, as compared with 49 percent in response to the 2006 survey). Reciprocity is important for 19 percent of the respondents in the broader survey, whereas it is important for 34 percent of those responding to the 2006 survey.

TABLE 6.7. *Criteria for Choosing a Target Lawyer: Lawyers in Plaintiffs' Survey Making at Least One Formal Referral* (% of 202 respondents choosing each)

	Important	Neutral	Not Important
Lawyer's reputation	97	3	0
Compatibility with client	53	32	16
Reciprocity between lawyers	34	26	40
Size of fee offered	25	27	49

Needless to say, with the overwhelming majority of respondents saying that a lawyer's reputation in a particular practice area is important as a criterion for choosing a target lawyer, there is no significant relationship between position in the plaintiffs' bar hierarchy and citing reputation as a criterion. Nor is there a significant relationship between position in the hierarchy and identification of any of the three other criteria as a reason for targeting a lawyer. The results are the same in terms of lawyers who are medical malpractice, products liability, or auto accident specialists—there were no significant relationships, with one exception, a very weak negative relationship between being an auto accident specialist and rating reputation as an important criterion.[33] For non-specialists (meaning that no single type of case accounted for 50 percent or more of their caseload), there is also one significant relationship: a very weak negative relationship between being a non-specialist and rating reputation as an important criterion.[34]

In general, the picture for plaintiffs' lawyers is similar to the one we saw earlier in the Texas Referral Survey for all lawyers in private practice. The differences, to the extent they exist, are a matter of degree. The same two criteria are the most important in each survey—reputation (97 percent important in each) and compatibility between client and the target lawyer (56 percent in the Texas Referral Survey and 53 percent in our 2006 survey). The two criteria that go directly to the referring lawyer's self-interest—reciprocity and especially the size of the referral fee offered —are less important. It is worth noting, again, that each of these two criteria are seen as more important in the plaintiffs' lawyers survey than in the more general survey.

Still, there is the question about referrals going to the lawyers offering the

33. Spearman's rho = −089, sig = 047.
34. Spearman's rho = −088, sig = 050.

highest referral fees without regard to specialization or substantive reputation. Table 6.7 suggests that the fee paid is not entirely unimportant. More precisely, given the fears of the critics of paid referrals, can we reject the hypothesis that the number of referrals received increases as the size of the fee increases? The relationship between the size of the typical referral fee offered and the number of referrals received is relatively clear and shows that we can do so. Except for auto accident referrals in some situations, a higher fee does not translate to a higher number of referrals.

If we look at the 318 respondents who provided a figure for the typical referral fee they offer, we find that all received at least one referral of some kind. For them, there is no relationship between size of fee and the number of personal injury referrals received. Nor is there a relationship between size of fee offered and the number of medical malpractice referrals received for those who received at least one such referral. The same is true for the number of products liability referrals received. There is, however, a significant—but not strong—relationship for auto accident referrals: the higher the fee, the more referrals received.[35]

If we limit the analysis to just those respondents who provided their typical referral fee and who received at least one relevant referral, then we can look at the importance of the fee paid by the lawyers active in a given practice area. For example, for those receiving at least one medical malpractice referral, did more such referrals flow to the higher fee paid? For those lawyers providing the size of their fee and receiving at least one personal injury referral, the number of referrals does not go up as their fee rises. For those lawyers receiving at least one medical malpractice referral, there is a significant relationship between the size of the fee offered and the number of medical malpractice referrals received. The relationship, however, is a negative one, meaning that those receiving more such referrals offer lower fees.[36] There is no significant relationship between higher fees and more referrals for those receiving at least one products liability referral or for those who received at least one auto accident referral.

If we limit things even further to just the specialists in the three areas, there are no significant relationships. The one other situation in which there is a significant relationship between higher fees and more referrals received is for

35. Pearson's $r = .115$, sig = .024.
36. Pearson's $r = -.182$, sig = .023.

those lawyers who were non-specialists and auto accident referrals.[37] In short, with the minimal exceptions noted, we can reject the hypothesis that the number of referrals received increases as the size of the fee increases.

CONCLUSION

The referral of cases among lawyers is an important source of business for many lawyers, and there is a robust referral system in Texas. Lawyers across different practice areas participate in this system by either referring cases or accepting referrals. Plaintiffs' lawyers, however, are clearly the key players, and personal injury cases—especially medical malpractice and auto accident cases—dominate the system. Referrals are tied closely to specialization in the legal profession: specialization could not exist without referrals, and the fee provides a useful incentive for referring cases. As the plaintiffs' lawyer quoted in the chapter's title said, "If my referring lawyers go away, I'm in trouble." This is why he and others like him invest in building and maintaining a reputation and in making their interest in receiving referrals known. Even bread-and-butter lawyers will invest in developing their reputations and marketing themselves in order to attract referrals.

Lawyers refer cases primarily because those cases are out of their own practice area or are too complex for the lawyer to handle even if within their practice area. In other words, cases tend to move from lawyers unable or unwilling to handle cases to those with a reputation for successfully handling those cases—the specialists. The possibility of the fee provides the incentive to do so. While the fee may serve the referring lawyer's interest, it also serves the client's interest. Referrals do not generally go to the lawyer offering the highest fee but to the lawyer with the stronger reputation—one who tends to be a specialist.

In short, the referral system in Texas operates in ways that enhance access, and fundamentally changing that system would diminish access. Since plaintiffs' lawyers are the primary players in the referral system, any substantial changes in the rules governing the system—especially with regard to fees—would fall hardest on those potential clients needing the services of a plaintiffs' lawyer. These potential clients, then, would be the real victims—some might

---

37. Pearson's $r = .116$, sig $= .05$.

say the "hidden victims"—of reform because it will be their cases not getting to the lawyers best able to handle them.[38] At the extreme, in some situations, the hidden victims may not be able to find any lawyer to take their case. In Chapter 7 we explore this possibility in more detail in an examination of lawyers' responses to the 2003 legislation in Texas that capped noneconomic damages in medical malpractice cases.

38. On the idea of "hidden victims," *see* Lucinda M. Finley, *The Hidden Victims of Tort Reform: Women, Children, and the Elderly,* 53 Emory L.J. 1263, 1313 (2004).

7. "The Juice Simply Isn't Worth the Squeeze in Those Cases Anymore"

Damage Caps, "Hidden Victims," and the Declining Interest in Medical Malpractice Cases*

The simple statement in this chapter's title is taken from a 2006 interview with a medical malpractice lawyer in East Texas. He was referring to medical malpractice cases involving children, the elderly, and women who work in the home and why he was no longer handling such cases—clients who are the so-called "hidden victims" of tort reform.[1] He also said he was handling fewer medical malpractice cases of any kind and attributed that change in his practice to the 2003 cap on noneconomic damages in health care cases discussed in Chapter 2 (a piece of legislation commonly known as House Bill 4, or simply HB4).[2] A 2009 journalistic examination of the factors driving current health care costs that focused on McAllen, Texas, raised the number of medical malpractice suits as a possible consideration. Reflective of the change in our informant's practice, one of the physicians interviewed for the article dismissed this idea and characterized the number of such suits being filed after the 2003 cap as going "practically to zero."[3]

Malpractice cases have not dropped "practically to zero," but the available empirical evidence does strongly suggest a marked decline in Texas in medical malpractice insurance claims and a corresponding decline in the number of medical malpractice lawsuits. Although annual data on the number of medical malpractice filings for the entire State of Texas are unavailable prior to

---

*An earlier and somewhat different version of this chapter appeared in Stephen Daniels & Joanne Martin, *It Is No Longer Viable from a Practical and Business Standpoint: Damage Caps, "Hidden Victims," and the Declining Interest in Medical Malpractice Cases*, 16 Int'l J. Legal Prof. 187 (2010).

1. *See* Lucinda M. Finley, *The Hidden Victims of Tort Reform: Women, Children, and the Elderly*, 53 Emory L.J. 1263, 1313 (2004).

2. Tex. Civ. Prac. & Rem. Code Ann. § 74.301(a)–(c), Vernon 1986 & Supp. 2003. As shorthand, we will use the term "medical malpractice" as including both medical malpractice and nursing home cases.

3. Atul Gawande, *The Cost Conundrum: What a Texas Town Can Teach Us about Health Care*, The New Yorker, June 1, 2009 at 38.

2011, they are available from a number of sources for Harris County, which includes Houston, the most populous county in Texas as well as the third-most-populous county in the United States.[4] The numbers from these sources indicate that filings for medical malpractice lawsuits clearly and substantially declined in Harris County after the implementation of the 2003 cap. For the first five years after the cap was put into place—2004 to 2008—the average annual number of medical malpractice filings was 233, representing a 46 percent drop compared with the 1997 to 2002 annual average of 435. Similarly, a decline in filings was reported in Cook County, Illinois (Chicago), after Illinois enacted a cap on noneconomic damages in 2005.[5]

A 2012 article by a team that has done extensive research on closed malpractice claims in Texas, and which we highlighted in Chapter 1 as a target of Governor Rick Perry's ire, reports that closed medical malpractice claims and payouts per claim for Texas declined after the 2003 cap went into effect. The declines affected medical malpractice claims generally but are especially acute for the elderly.[6] The authors note:

> The 2003 tort reforms had a dramatic impact on claim rates and payouts per claim. We expected the impact to be larger for elderly plaintiffs, because a higher proportion of their damages are non-economic. We find evidence consistent with that expectation. There is evidence of a steeper drop in claim rates for the elderly, especially the very elderly. We also find

4. The Texas Office of Court Administration collects annual data on court filings. It breaks tort cases down into only two categories: auto cases and non-auto cases. However, data are available for Harris County's trial courts of general jurisdiction from the Harris County District Clerk; the Harris County Justice Information Management System; *see also* Terry Carter, *Tort Reform Texas Style: New Laws and Med-Mal Damage Caps Devastate Plaintiff and Defense Firms Alike*, A.B.A. J. (2006), http://www.abajournal.com/magazine/article/new_laws_and_med_mal_damage_caps_devastate_plaintiff_and_defense_firms_alike.

5. *Crain's Chicago Business* (a business weekly) reported in 2006 that "medical malpractice lawsuits in Cook County dropped 25 percent—to their lowest level in at least a decade—in the year following the passage of a new state law that limits how much juries can award plaintiffs for pain and suffering." *Cook Co. Med Mal Suits down 25 Percent*, Sept. 18, 2006; www.chicagobusiness.com/cgi-bin/news.pl?id=22109.

6. Myungho Paik et al., *How Do the Elderly Fare in Medical Malpractice Litigation, before and after Tort Reform? Evidence from Texas*, 14 Am. L. & Econ. Rev. 561, 580 (2012).

a larger drop in per claim payouts for the elderly, and in total payouts to the elderly as a group.[7]

Consistent with our East Texas informant's comment about the juice not being worth the squeeze, they speculate that, in part, "the falloff in claims reflects judgments by Texas plaintiffs' lawyers (presumably as smart, motivated, and good looking as lawyers elsewhere) that many cases are no longer worth bringing."[8]

Our focus in Chapter 7 is on investigating the proposition that caps on noneconomic damages will lead plaintiffs' lawyers to stop handling medical malpractice cases, especially those involving certain kinds of clients. Such caps dramatically alter the incentive structure for plaintiffs' lawyers, and this is the key to understanding the consequences—and perhaps the purposes—of limitations on damages. Chief among those consequences is the closing of the courthouse doors if lawyers are discouraged from handling these cases. As we have emphasized throughout this book, these lawyers hold an important key to access and function as the civil justice system's gatekeepers, and the doorway will widen or narrow depending on the profitability of plaintiffs' lawyers' practices. Damage caps directly affect profitability and can create a situation in which business necessity trumps some of the key values underlying professional identity that we saw in Chapter 4.

Finally, in terms of consequences, there are the normative concerns raised by some critics of litigation-limiting reforms like caps on damages. Taking a very different stance than Professor Brickman, these critics point to the plight of hidden victims and to issues of fairness, equality, responsibility, and justice in the civil justice system. They provide an important additional reason for examining the effect of caps on plaintiffs' lawyers.[9]

This chapter is divided into five substantive sections, and at its core are the responses to questions included in our 2006 survey based on a set of hypothetical situations that probe lawyers' decisions to take certain kinds of cases—especially those involving hidden victims. As a context for those questions, the first section briefly discusses the logic of damage caps—their stated and

7. *Id.* at 595.
8. *Id.* at 596.
9. *See* Finley, *supra* note 1, at 1313; Tom Baker, *The Medical Malpractice Myth* (Chicago: University of Chicago Press, 2005), 117.

other purposes along with the problems caps pose for plaintiffs' lawyers. The second section explores that context further by outlining a series of questions about the effects of caps and whether those effects will result in diminished access to the rights and remedies the law provides—in other words, closing of the courthouse doors. The third section presents the hypothetical situations at the chapter's core. The fourth section analyzes lawyers' responses to the hypothetical situations, and the fifth section presents additional evidence from our surveys to bolster that analysis.

THE LOGIC(S) OF DAMAGE CAPS

The Stated Claims for Caps

Reformers claim that noneconomic damages (commonly referred to as "pain and suffering") have risen dramatically, causing medical malpractice insurance premiums to rise accordingly. In turn, these higher premiums threaten access to affordable health care—and in some situations access to health care itself. Caps are needed, they say, to counteract these severely negative consequences of increasing damage awards. The reformers' logic says such caps will result in greater access to medical malpractice insurance and lower insurance premiums for physicians because the caps will limit the amount of money insurance companies will need to pay out to those injured by medical negligence. This, in turn, will result in substantial benefits to people generally and not just to physicians and insurance companies. More readily available and affordable insurance will prevent physicians from abandoning the practice of medicine, relocating from one state to another, changing medical specialties, or leaving already underserved places like rural areas.

The purported benefits of the caps for Texas are clearly seen in Governor Rick Perry's statement made as he signed HB4 into law in 2003:

> This lawsuit reform measure is good for patients, consumers, doctors and job creators. . . . Because of the medical malpractice reforms of House Bill 4, our hospitals and clinics will remain open to the patients who need them. Pregnant women will not have to worry about finding an obstetrician to help them deliver their newborn children. And Texans who suffer a trauma can know that when their life is on the line, the

specialist they need will be on call.... By capping non-economic damages and providing greater protections for many of our hospitals that provide charity care, we are taking strong actions to lower malpractice insurance rates and keep doctors, nurses and hospitals doing what they do best: providing health care to Texans in need.[10]

HB4 imposed a "hard cap" of $250,000 per incident on noneconomic damages (up to $750,000 if there are multiple defendants). A "hard cap" means an unchanging one—not pegged to inflation or the cost of living.

According to supporters of caps, the threat to accessible and affordable health care comes not simply from exorbitant noneconomic damage awards but from greedy plaintiffs' lawyers filing frivolous lawsuits and, in Perry's words, "playing the lawsuit lottery with Texans' access to health care."[11] In his view, "the only folks hurt in the pocketbook by this lawsuit reform measure are the plaintiff trial lawyers who have profited from frivolous lawsuits and by gaming of the legal system." As we noted in Chapter 1, Governor Perry and reform proponents have declared the cap an unqualified success. In an early 2013 op-ed piece titled "Tort Reform Sparked 'Texas Miracle'" in the *Austin American-Statesman*, the president of the Texas Public Policy Foundation touted highly the claimed results of HB4 for health care and for the Texas economy (the "miracle").[12] Speaking before a physicians' political action committee in July of 2012, Perry said,

In 2003, Texas was facing a real crisis, one that we met with a specific solution.... The crisis involved a dramatic drop in the number of doctors practicing medicine in our state.... Even more concerning, the greatest loss occurred among doctors practicing in high-risk specialties. Patients in dire need were discovering the only local doctors who could help them had either left the state or ceased treating their types of ailments.... The crisis' prime culprit was skyrocketing malpractice insurance rates that

10. *Gov Perry Speaks at Med Mal Bill Signing*, July 11, 2003, http://governor .state.tx.us/news/speech/10637/.

11. *Id.*

12. Brooke L. Rollins, *Rollins: Tort Reform Sparked the "Texas Miracle,"* Austin American-Statesman, Mar. 24, 2012, www.statesman.com/news/news/opinion/rollins-tort-reform-sparked-texas-miracle/nWzRP/.

reflected Texas' status at the time as a lawsuit haven. To remedy this, we took the bold step of instituting tort reforms to limit lawsuit abuse and bring malpractice insurance rates down to a manageable level. And it was an overwhelming success. . . . The reform wasn't good news for trial lawyers.[13]

Chapter 1 noted the critical examinations of the claims about the reform's success that raise serious doubts as to their veracity. Key among those critical examinations is a study by Paik and his colleagues (again, the researchers attacked by Governor Perry). Using closed malpractice insurance claim data compiled by the Texas Department of Insurance in conjunction with Medicare data on cost, they examined the impact of the 2003 Texas malpractice reforms on cost to see if in fact costs declined after 2003. In their words, "no matter how we slice the data, we find no evidence that the Texas 2003 tort reforms 'bent the cost curve' downward."[14] Placing their findings in the context of other studies beyond Texas, they conclude that the "accumulation of recent evidence finding zero or small effects suggests that it is time for policymakers to abandon the hope that tort reform can be a major element in health-care cost control."[15] In a separate piece, this research team reports that the noneconomic damages had not increased in the years prior to 2003, as reformers claimed.[16] In a third piece, the team could find no connection between tort reform in Texas and physician supply—even for neurosurgeons, orthopedic surgeons, obstetrician/gynecologists, primary care physicians, and rural physicians.[17]

13. Rick Perry, *Tort Reform Has Had Just the Impact We Desired,* Austin American-Statesman, July 16, 2012, www.statesman.com/news/news/opinion/tort-reform-has-had-just-the-impact-we-desired/nRqBq.

14. Myungho Paik, Bernard S. Black, David A. Hyman & Charles Silver, *Will Tort Reform Bend the Cost Curve? Evidence from Texas,* 9 J. Empirical Legal Stud. 173, 175 (2012).

15. *Id.* at 175–176.

16. Bernard S. Black, David A. Hyman, Charles Silver & William M. Sage, *Stability, Not Crisis: Medical Malpractice Claim Outcomes in Texas, 1988–2002,* 2 J. Empirical Legal Stud. 207 (2005).

17. David A. Hyman, Charles Silver, Bernard Black & Myungho Paik, *Does Tort Reform Affect Physician Supply? Evidence from Texas,* Northwestern University Law School Law and Economics Research Paper No. 12-11, Feb. 2014, at 3, http://ssrn.com/abstract=2047433.

Caps and the Problem for Plaintiffs' Lawyers

Regardless of the veracity of the reformers' political claims, caps may still achieve their most immediate goal (reform opponents would argue the only real goal): fewer medical malpractice lawsuits. The reason for this, in the words of David Hyman and Charles Silver, is simple and blunt: "It's the incentives, stupid."[18] As Governor Perry said with regard to HB4, "We are now removing the incentive that personal injury trial lawyers have to file frivolous lawsuits and run health care providers out of business."[19] Caps are clearly about changing the incentive structure for lawyers handling medical malpractice cases on a contingency fee basis to such a degree that lawyers will handle fewer, if any, medical malpractice cases.

At first glance, a cap of $250,000, like the one in Texas, may not seem very low or at all problematic, but it can be problematic in medical malpractice and similar high-stakes areas. As Herbert Kritzer characterizes it, a contingency fee based practice is a constant balancing of cost, risk, and potential return.[20] For a practice based around medical malpractice cases, it is more like a high-wire act with no safety net. If a lawyer cannot strike and maintain the right balance across these factors, the fall can be fatal to a practice. Although the return on investment can be substantial in these cases, they are also especially risky and costly. As one plaintiffs' lawyer told us, "We all know that the hardest case to win is a med mal case at a trial because the juries just don't want to believe that doctors can make mistakes." Plaintiffs are likely to lose medical malpractice cases that go to trial, generally losing two-thirds of the time and in Texas losing an even larger proportion of the time.[21]

---

18. David Hyman & Charles Silver, *Medical Malpractice Litigation and Tort Reform: It's the Incentives, Stupid*, 59 Vanderbilt L. Rev. 1085, 1085 (2006).

19. *Gov Perry Speaks, supra* note 10.

20. Herbert Kritzer, *Risks, Reputations, and Rewards: Contingency Fee Legal Practice in the United States* (Stanford, CA: Stanford University Press, 2004), 1–8.

21. Even in the years before Texas enacted major medical malpractice reforms, plaintiff win rates in medical malpractice cases tried to a jury were very low. For instance, for the years 1988 to 1990, the plaintiff win rate (defined as winning at least $1) was 25 percent or lower in Texas's three largest jurisdictions: Harris County (Houston), Dallas County, and Bexar County (San Antonio). In comparison, the win rates for auto accident cases during the same time period were no lower than 48 percent. *See* Stephen Daniels & Joanne Martin, *Civil Juries and the Politics of Reform* (Evanston, IL: Northwestern University Press, 1995), 83.

Lawyers can deal with this risk and the substantial requirements for bringing a medical malpractice suit only by carefully and thoroughly screening and preparing their cases. As a result, their costs of doing business are high compared to those for lawyers handling other types of cases, such as automobile accident cases. As a Houston medical malpractice specialist said, "There's no other case in the system as expensive as malpractice." It starts with the cost of screening cases. The lawyer must choose cases that offer a realistic potential for success at an amount that will compensate the client for his or her losses as well as providing the lawyer's fee and covering the disbursements required to prepare and try the case. The successful cases must also cover the costs of the cases the lawyer screens and then chooses *not* to take.

Because of the costs and risks involved, as the example of the HH2 lawyer in Chapter 5 showed, lawyers screen medical malpractice cases quite stringently. Our 2006 survey shows that lawyers regularly handling medical malpractice cases (those for whom these cases make up at least 50 percent of their business) take on average fewer than 10 percent of the cases that come to them, and some take as few as 1 or 2 percent. An initial outlay of $10,000 or more is typical just for the initial expert reviews, and this figure does not include the time spent by anyone in the lawyer's firm. This means that a lawyer may spend thousands of dollars in deciding *not* to take a case—money the lawyer will not get back. One specialist reported, "Last year we spent in excess of $100,000 in cases that we didn't take."[22]

Because of the many requirements for bringing a medical malpractice case in Texas, the disbursements required to appropriately prepare such a case can easily approach $100,000 or more if the case is especially complex. For instance, one lawyer who specializes in brain injury cases said, "We always escrow $300,000 for each case." Another specialist provides an idea of how high the costs can get when you actually go to trial: "I've tried . . . I think the most I've had was around $600,000 or $700,000. We prevailed on that one, thank goodness." More typical is the lawyer who said, "You're talking about $100,000 that you're gonna spend on technical expertise to write reports, to give depositions, you know, to explain the standard of care and how it's been breached.

22. In addition, some lawyers—like the one in Chapter 5—who regularly handle high-value personal injury cases internalize a part of the cost of screening by having nurses, nurse-lawyers, or even a physician-lawyer on staff. This, of course, increases the overhead they have to cover every month.

You're talking about a lot of money, and—in other words—it makes the juice not worth the squeeze."

In addition to these costs, there is also the likely expense of a fee to be paid to another lawyer who referred the case (typically around one-third of the successful lawyer's fee if there is a settlement or an award). As noted in Chapter 6, medical malpractice cases are the most referred tort cases in which a fee is involved, and medical malpractice specialists rely heavily on referrals as a source of business. If the cap is set low for cases that are very costly to pursue (such as a $250,000 cap on noneconomic damages in malpractice cases), the plaintiffs' lawyer may face a serious dilemma. The choice is to maximize his own profit by shortchanging the client or a lawyer expecting a referral fee, or to make the client whole and pay the referring lawyer while shortchanging himself.

The latter result undermines a lawyer's ability to remain profitable and stay in business because in a capped environment there isn't enough money to go around. The former undermines the lawyer's ability to keep the steady stream of clients and referrals needed to stay in business.[23] Shortchanging has negative consequences because of the importance of referrals in maintaining a steady stream of clients, and the key to referrals of any kind is reputation. Shortchanging in this manner to enhance a lawyer's own gain seriously harms a lawyer's reputation as someone who treats clients and referring lawyers fairly. The importance of reputation, as Chapter 6 showed, cannot be underestimated. Lawyers who build their practices on complex matters like medical malpractice must rely heavily on lawyer referrals because consumers are unlikely to know who the specialists are, but other lawyers will. To reiterate two facts noted in previous chapters: on average more than half of cases for medical malpractice specialists come from lawyer referrals, and the most important factor in choosing a lawyer to whom to refer a malpractice case is that lawyer's reputation.

If indeed it is about the incentives for plaintiffs' lawyers, then pushing for the implementation of a low, hard cap like the one in Texas suggests that the reformers work on the assumption plaintiffs' lawyers are rational actors who

---

23. To deal with this problem, perhaps lawyers could cut costs, raise prices (the amount of the contingency fee), or a combination of both. However, most plaintiffs' practices are small, lean operations, making substantial savings from significant cost-cutting unlikely. The highly competitive nature of the plaintiffs' lawyers' market makes raising the fee charged to the client problematic.

need to make a profit. Caps are intended to alter the balancing of cost, risk, and potential return and thereby make the targeted cases economically unattractive—so much so that plaintiffs' lawyers will abandon them in favor of more profitable cases. The lower the cap in the face of the costs and risks involved, the more effective a cap will be. The reason is simple. Damage caps are, in practical effect, a limitation on the contingency fee that is at the heart of the plaintiffs' lawyers' business model. And that limitation can be severe enough to override the normative values at the heart of the plaintiffs' lawyers' professional identity.

For most lawyers, the only way to escape the dilemma created by damage caps and the inability to successfully balance cost, risk, and potential return may come from making changes in their practices by not taking the types of cases posing that dilemma. This can mean avoiding medical malpractice cases altogether—precisely the response hoped for by the reformers. For critics of caps like Professor Lucinda Finley, the concern is that the burden of this dilemma will fall disproportionately on certain types of people—she calls them the hidden victims of tort reform. Finley, like the reformers, sees plaintiffs' lawyers as rational actors focused on their own bottom line, and she is worried about the impact of caps on injured people for whom noneconomic damages make up the bulk of the potential damages. Such victims of medical negligence reflect the effects of the dilemma in their starkest form. Even if some lawyers continue to handle medical malpractice cases, those lawyers may decide to avoid these potential clients. In Finley's words, this will leave the avoided clients "shut off from seeking redress and recognition through the tort system." Again, for her, this is perhaps the most profound consequence of caps because it undermines "fairness and equality of our civil justice system."[24] In short, there are important normative issues at stake when talking about access.

HAVE THE COURTHOUSE DOORS CLOSED?
QUESTIONS ABOUT THE EFFECTS OF DAMAGE CAPS

The discussion so far suggests that if "it's the incentives, stupid," then Finley's fears and the reformers' hopes are plausible. To pursue this plausibility further,

24. Finley, *supra* note 1, at 1313.

it is useful to think of Finley's fears and the reformers' hopes in terms of four basic questions that probe more deeply into the handling of medical malpractice cases generally by plaintiffs' lawyers as well as the attractiveness of certain kinds of clients specifically.

Two of the four questions provide a needed context for both Finley's concerns and the reformers' interest in the potential effects of reform. Concerns about hidden victims in medical malpractice matters presume that such clients were attractive in the past and have become less so in the face of a cap on noneconomic damages. It also presumes a robust interest on the part of plaintiffs' lawyers in malpractice cases generally. It is possible, however, that such clients have always been considered less than ideal by plaintiffs' lawyers regardless of the kind of case, and that malpractice cases—because of their complexity, risk, and cost—have always been of limited interest to most members of the plaintiffs' bar. The other two questions ask more specifically about the attractiveness of hidden victims in medical malpractice cases—presuming, of course, that such clients and cases were ever attractive.

First and perhaps most importantly, we need to know if Texas plaintiffs' lawyers handle medical malpractice cases generally, and not just those involving certain kinds of clients. As we have noted, such cases are expensive and risky, and one can see the possibility that many plaintiffs' lawyers may avoid them. Given our interests, there are two parts to the question: (1) whether medical malpractice cases were generally unattractive before the implementation of the cap in 2003 and (2) whether they were generally unattractive after the cap. If plaintiffs' lawyers were reluctant to take these cases both before and after the cap, then the recently enacted caps on noneconomic damages in medical malpractice cases are not likely to make much difference in terms of access to the justice system for individuals injured through medical negligence. If medical malpractice cases generally became less attractive after the caps were enacted, then the caps may well be an important factor. This is the effect the reformers hope for. The impact of this shift in the behavior of plaintiffs' lawyers would be felt by all kinds of clients and not just those who resemble hidden victims, even though the hidden victims may be hit harder.

Second, perhaps it is not the type of case that is unattractive but rather the type of client. We need to know whether Texas plaintiffs' lawyers always turned away certain client types because of profitability issues—those like Finley's hidden victims without the potential for substantial economic damages— regardless of the type of case. In the context of a practice built on the contingency fee, one can see this possibility regardless of the presence of a damage cap. In the context of our interests, this question also has two parts (1) whether such clients were generally considered unattractive in Texas before the 2003 cap and (2) whether they were generally deemed unattractive afterward. If plaintiffs' lawyers identified these client types as generally undesirable both before and after 2003, then the recently enacted caps on noneconomic damages in medical malpractice cases are not likely to make much difference in terms of access to justice concerns for these individuals. If anything, the enactment of the cap would simply aggravate an existing problem tied to profitability and the incentive structure within which plaintiffs' lawyers work.

Obviously, our inquiry could end at this point depending on the answers to the first two questions. Presuming that hidden victims have not been generally considered undesirable clients and that medical malpractice cases have not been avoided by most plaintiffs' lawyers, there is a third, more specific, question: whether certain types of clients were unattractive specifically in medical malpractice cases before the 2003 cap. If not generally considered unattractive clients, perhaps Finley's hidden victims have always, nonetheless, been unattractive clients in medical malpractice cases regardless of any cap. Her concern with the consequences of caps for the hidden victims of tort reform presumes that noneconomic damage caps affect the viability of cases involving these specific types of clients. It could be that their unattractiveness after the cap is just more of the same—a deeper problem that may be aggravated by caps but ultimately not caused by them.

Finally, if certain client types were not always pushed out of the civil justice system as generally undesirable, if medical malpractice cases were not seen as generally unattractive, and if clients with cases presenting little potential for economic damages were not totally unattractive in medical malpractice cases before the cap—did they become undesirable after the cap? This is Finley's ultimate concern.

"HIDDEN VICTIMS" HYPOTHETICALS

With these matters in mind, we used a "difference in differences" strategy and included in our 2006 survey a series of very specific questions asking respondents to indicate whether they would take cases with certain kinds of clients five years prior to the survey and whether they would take them at the time of the survey (Time 1 and Time 2). Rather than simply ask the survey respondents generally about clients and cases, greater analytic purchase was gained by presenting them with a series of questions based on hypothetical situations that would allow for controlled comparisons involving different combinations of cases and clients.

To construct the hypotheticals in a way that would resonate with plaintiffs' lawyers receiving the survey, we sought the assistance of ten Texas plaintiffs' lawyers practicing in different parts of the state (selected because of their reputations as successful and experienced litigators).[25] The hypotheticals were designed around variations in client and case type, holding severity of injury and liability constant. The hypotheticals went through a number of iterations based on discussions with and pretesting by these consultants. When finalized, the hypotheticals permitted comparisons involving three different kinds of clients (two resembling Finley's hidden victims and one not) and two different kinds of cases.[26]

With medical malpractice as one of the cases, the other had to be a specific type of personal injury case that remained untouched by the cap on noneconomic damages in health care cases and could function as a control. Otherwise, there wouldn't be a needed clear and unambiguous comparison. After discussions with the consultants, the comparison chosen was an auto accident case involving a collision between an automobile and an eighteen-wheel tractor-trailer truck (what in Texas is called an "18-wheeler case") resulting in severe injuries to the driver of the automobile. All of the consultants agreed that this is, and has been, a very attractive type of personal injury case—one

25. Because of promises of complete confidentiality, which were required for human subjects purposes, detailed information about the ten consultants cannot be provided.

26. It was not possible to randomize the hypotheticals in the survey or the order of questions for each hypothetical as a way to avoid biasing responses (or priming the respondents). To deal with this issue we placed the scenarios in the section of our 2006 survey entitled "Case Acquisition," which included a long series of questions focusing primarily on referrals (the material in Chapter 6 from our 2006 survey on referrals came from this section). The respondents would have to respond to thirteen detailed questions (most with multiple subquestions) before getting to the two scenarios— each of which included the option of referring the case in the scenario. The questions following the scenarios asked about completely different topics related to case acquisition.

that juries continued to respond to favorably in an environment otherwise perceived to be anti-plaintiff. This perception is consistent with what we learned from our lawyer interviews. An accident case of this type, although resulting in severe physical harm, is a less complex case carrying much less risk and requiring far less in the way of case preparation expenses than a medical malpractice case.

The comments of a Texas plaintiffs' lawyer interviewed in 2006 are illustrative of the general view held across the plaintiffs' bar with regard to 18-wheeler cases:

> Let me tell you. The one area that is still, has a lot of meat on the bones, is representing folks in accidents with trucking companies. Texas is a terrible place to drive down a freeway. It's just a terrible place. The egregious nature of the number of miles these guys drive, the lack of following the rules, the lying on the logs, driving eighty miles an hour in a construction zone just lead to horrendous accidents and, unfortunately, business for me.

Such cases have the potential for substantial settlements and awards, and more importantly they appear to be unaffected by the tort reform rhetoric and public relations campaigns seen in Texas since at least the mid-1980s. "Everybody seems to be able to connect with an 18-wheeler that's out of control. You know, we hit one for $20 million that we got paid on, and you know, even Republicans were voting for us on that one," said a Houston lawyer.

As for the client types to be used in the hypotheticals, there had to be variation in the potential for *economic* damages to allow for the comparisons necessary to address the questions we wanted to investigate. The key to Finley's argument is the idea that certain kinds of clients will become highly unattractive in the wake of a cap on noneconomic damages because their cases do not offer much potential for economic damages. This meant that the hypotheticals needed to incorporate not only client types that might become unattractive after the cap but, as a point of comparison, a client type likely to remain attractive even after the cap. This client, unlike the hidden victims, would still offer the potential for economic damages.

We worked with the consultants to choose three different client types for the hypotheticals. One is a client who would generally be considered financially attractive—almost the ideal client—a forty-five-year-old married male, fully employed, with dependents. This client should be attractive in both the 18-wheeler case and the medical malpractice case. Even with a cap on noneconomic damages, this client type might remain attractive because of the potential for economic damages and can be used to represent the bottom-line attractiveness of medical malpractice itself—he would become unattractive only if medical malpractice cases generally became unattractive.

One straightforward counterpoint for the employed, married male with dependents that changes the potential for economic damages is a forty-five-year-old female with dependents who is not employed outside the home—a stay-at-home mom. This is the second client type. Given the existence of dependents, there may be some additional potential for economic damages but certainly not as great as that for an individual who is employed. The final comparison client type is more extreme: a seventy-year-old male who is retired and without dependents. Beyond basic medical bills related to an injury, the potential for economic damages with this client type is minimal.[27]

The two overarching hypotheticals hold constant the type of harm suffered by the potential plaintiff—serious injuries requiring six months of rehabilitation and ultimately resulting in obvious permanent facial disfigurement. The idea was to create a situation in which noneconomic damages—here for permanent facial disfigurement—would be a prominent factor for all three plaintiffs. Facial disfigurement is recognized in Texas as a type of noneconomic damage covered by the 2003 cap involving health care cases.[28] What would clearly differ in the hypotheticals is the potential for economic damages. Finally, the questions in the survey were arranged so that the lawyers were asked about each type of client in each type of case at the time of the survey

27. These three potential clients are not literally the client types Finley discusses in talking about "hidden victims." She has a special interest in gender issues and emphasizes situations in which such issues arise in the absence of substantial economic damages. Our concern is with the underlying logic of case and client selection and how lawyers make choices based on an assessment of profitability. We are not suggesting the absence of gender disparities. Rather, we want to explore more fully the underlying economic reasons that may explain their existence. Where the data allow, we will address variations that may speak to gender.

28. Said a medical malpractice specialist interviewed in 2005: the cap "includes physical disfigurement, physical impairment, loss of consortium, conscious pain and suffering, mental anguish—every single kind of thing for which you cannot put an exact dollar figure on is now capped at $250,000, total, combined."

and five years earlier (before and after the enactment of the 2003 cap on non-economic damages without specifically mentioning the cap).

In summary, the hypothetical situations posed in the survey involved the following:

1. Three kinds of potential plaintiffs—a seventy-year-old retired male for whom economic damages would be minimal; a forty-five-year-old employed, married male, for whom there could be significant economic damages; and a forty-five-year-old married stay-at-home mom for whom economic damages would be present but low.
2. The same injury (as outlined above) unquestionably caused in one of two ways—by a physician in a medical malpractice case or by an 18-wheeler in a car wreck case; and
3. Two time periods—Time 1 being five years prior to the 2006 survey and before the implementation of caps in 2003 and Time 2 being the time of the survey.

For each situation at each point in time, respondents were asked whether they would take the case, take it but refer it to another lawyer, or not take it at all. The possibility of referring the case was included in order to present the respondents with a realistic set of choices.

RESPONSES TO THE HYPOTHETICALS

Figure 7.1 presents the responses to the two hypotheticals for all respondents. Those responses will help us answer our four basic questions: the general attractiveness of medical malpractice cases, the general attractiveness of hidden victims, the attractiveness of hidden victims in medical malpractice cases before the cap, and the attractiveness of hidden victims in medical malpractice cases after the cap. It shows the aggregate patterns in the attractiveness of each type of client in each type of case at the time of the survey and five years earlier (before and after the cap—Time 1 and Time 2). The "attractiveness" measure includes the percentage of responding lawyers who would have taken or referred each client in each of the case types at Time 1 and Time 2. We combined the two possibilities because we knew there is a substantial and brisk market for referring medical malpractice cases. Reading from the left to right, the re-

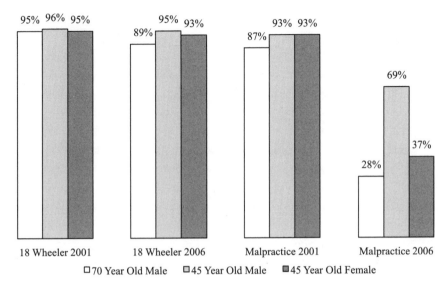

95% 96% 95%   95% 93%   93% 93%
        89%   87%

                                        69%

                                                37%
                            28%

18 Wheeler 2001   18 Wheeler 2006   Malpractice 2001   Malpractice 2006

□ 70 Year Old Male   ▢ 45 Year Old Male   ▪ 45 Year Old Female

FIGURE 7.1. *Attractiveness of Clients by Case Type in Light of Damage Caps*

sults are arranged by client type and case with a bar for each point in time that allows for easy comparison of the acceptability of that client type at Time 1 and Time 2.[29]

Comparing the two sides of Figure 7.1, one immediately notices the lack of any real change in the 18-wheeler case with regard to all of the client types between Time 1 and Time 2. Such a case was *very* attractive for both time periods regardless of the type of client. This is consistent with what we heard in our interviews with Texas plaintiffs' lawyers and what our consultants said in suggesting such a case as a comparison for medical malpractice. While the 18-wheeler case shows the lack of significant change between the two time periods, Figure 7.1 presents a very different picture for the medical malpractice case, in which there appears to be substantial change between Time 1 and Time 2. The analyses needed to answer our four questions will help us understand those changes.

29. The more detailed analysis of the results and the statistical analyses can be found in Stephen Daniels & Joanne Martin, *It Is No Longer Viable from a Practical and Business Standpoint: Damage Caps, 'Hidden Victims,' and the Declining Interest in Medical Malpractice Cases*, 16 Int'l J. Legal Prof. 187 (2010).

Question 1: The General Attractiveness of Medical Malpractice Cases

The first question marks a threshold that asks about the general attractiveness of medical malpractice cases and whether lawyers would turn away these cases in the absence of a cap regardless of the client's economic damage potential. The response to this question is best captured in the medical malpractice cluster for Time 1 in Figure 7.1—before the enactment of the damage cap—with the middle bar for the forty-five-year-old male. As we noted earlier, this client can be used as a rough indicator of the attractiveness of medical malpractice cases generally, the idea being that if a lawyer would not take a client with the potential for substantial economic damages, he is unlikely to take any medical malpractice cases. Over 90 percent of all the respondents found this client attractive (64 percent would take the client and 29 percent would refer the client). This suggests that at Time 1 medical malpractice cases were generally attractive and few would have completely turned away the medical malpractice case with the "best" client, at least at Time 1. The 18-wheeler cluster in Figure 7.1 also shows substantial attractiveness for this client type.[30]

At Time 2 (after the implementation of the cap), however, there was change in the attractiveness for the "best" client in the medical malpractice case (the relevant bars for the forty-five-year-old male on the medical malpractice side of Figure 7.1). Far fewer of the respondents (69 percent) found this "best" client attractive, compared to 93 percent at Time 1. This indicates that while the "best" client did not become completely unattractive, he did become less attractive after the implementation of caps.[31] For the same client in the

---

30. One way to test for any fundamental difference between the attractiveness of medical malpractice cases as compared with 18-wheeler cases is to look for a statistically significant association between take/refer the "best" client at Time 1 for each type of case. If there is a meaningful difference in attractiveness, we would *not* expect a statistically significant association between the choice to take/refer this client in one type of case compared with the other. Again, to simplify matters for the purpose of looking at differences in attractiveness, we have combined "take client" with "take and refer client"—meaning the two alternatives are to take or refer the client on one hand or to turn the client away on the other. We found the relevant statistically significant relationship. *Id.*

31. To test for a fundamental change in attractiveness in Time 2 compared to Time 1, we looked for a statistically significant relationship between the two times. If there were a fundamental change, we would *not* expect to find a statistically significant rela-

18-wheeler case, there was virtually no change between the two time periods. It appears safe to say that even though medical malpractice cases did not become completely unattractive, they became less attractive after the implementation of damage caps.

The attractiveness of the other two client types in medical malpractice cases will be addressed directly in the discussion of Question 3. Before that, however, we need to address the prior question of whether the forty-five-year-old female and the seventy-year-old male were attractive as clients as a general proposition.

Question 2: The General Attractiveness of "Hidden Victims"

The second question is also a threshold question and asks whether Texas plaintiffs' lawyers turn away certain client types generally—those without substantial economic damages—because of profitability issues regardless of case type. A simple way to address this question is to see whether lawyers found such clients attractive in the 18-wheeler case—a less complex, less risky, and less costly case in which most lawyers would generally be interested. If lawyers would not take these clients in this type of case, then it is unlikely that they would take them in any less attractive type of case, such as medical malpractice, that is more complex, more risky, and more costly.

Focusing on the 18-wheeler side of Figure 7.1, we see that the vast majority of respondents reported that they would have taken any of the three clients in an 18-wheeler case at either point in time. In addition, there is no fundamental change in attractiveness from one time period to the other.[32] We can therefore reject the assertion that plaintiffs' lawyers would turn away clients with lim-

---

tionship between the attractiveness of the "best" client in the medical malpractice case at Time 1 and at Time 2. In other words, attractiveness at Time 1 would not predict attractiveness at Time 2. We did find the relevant statistically significant relationship. *Id.*

32. There was only a very slight decline in the attractiveness of the two "hidden victim" clients. If there was a fundamental change in attractiveness for any client, we would *not* expect there to be a statistically significant association between the choice to take that client at Time 1 and the choice to take the client at Time 2—attractiveness at Time 1 would not predict attractiveness at Time 2. We did find the relevant statistically significant relationship for each type of client. The statistical relationship is strongest for the forty-five-year-old male, reflecting his status as the "best" client. *Id.*

ited economic damage potential (like the two in the hypothetical) as a general proposition.

One of Finley's special concerns with regard to hidden victims is gender disparity. Figure 7.1 provides at least a limited look at the general possibility of gender disparity in terms of lawyers' choices about clients in an appealing type of case. It allows us to compare the forty-five-year-old male (the "best" client) with the forty-five-year-old female in the 18-wheeler case. For the earlier time period, the percentage finding either client attractive is virtually identical (96 percent and 95 percent), and the same is true for the later period (95 percent and 93 percent).[33] With regard to the seventy-year-old male, the percentage of respondents finding this client attractive is at least 89 percent at both points in time.[34] We will look at gender and age disparities in medical malpractice cases as we address Questions 3 and 4.

Question 3: "Hidden Victims" in Medical Malpractice Cases at Time 1

Seeing that medical malpractice cases in general were not unattractive at Time 1, our third question asks whether clients with limited economic damage potential were nonetheless unattractive in medical malpractice cases at Time 1. To answer this question, we again look to the Time 1 cluster for the medical malpractice side of Figure 7.1. It shows that the vast majority of lawyers found both the seventy-year-old male and the forty-five-year-old female to be attractive clients before the cap, even though they had limited economic damage potential. In addition, we see no apparent gender disparity in lawyers' client choices in the medical malpractice situation before the cap. Identical percentages of respondents would take or refer the forty-five-year-old male or the forty-five-year-old female.

Question 4: "Hidden Victims" in Medical Malpractice Cases at Time 2

The fourth question asks whether the clients with limited economic damage potential became unattractive in medical malpractice cases after the cap. The

---

33. Again, we found the relevant statistically significant relationships between client types indicating no difference in attractiveness. *See* Daniels & Martin, *supra* note 29.

34. Again, we found the relevant statistically significant relationships between client types indicating no difference in attractiveness. *Id.*

medical malpractice cluster for Time 2 in Figure 7.1 indicates that the answer is a clear yes. Whereas most of the respondents found the seventy-year-old male and the forty-five-year-old female attractive at the earlier time, over a majority would simply turn either client away at the later time (over 70 percent for the seventy-year-old male).

These are fundamental changes in attractiveness of medical malpractice matters involving certain types of clients,[35] especially with regard to the seventy-year-old male. Fewer than 10 percent of the respondents reported that they would take such a client, and fewer than 20 percent would even refer this client. The forty-five-year-old female fared little better than the seventy-year-old male. Like the elderly client, the nonworking forty-five-year-old female does not present the likelihood of substantial economic damages (such as lost wages) that would make the case financially attractive to lawyers after the 2003 cap. As we have seen, there are no similar changes with regard to these client types shown in Figure 7.1 for the 18-wheeler case.

These dramatic changes in the attractiveness of the two types of clients give credence to the comments of one plaintiffs' lawyer interviewed in 2006: "They essentially closed the courthouse door to the negligence that would kill a child, a housewife, or an elderly person." The reason: "There are no medical expenses, no loss of earning capacity, and unless it's drop dead negligence that you can prosecute with one or two experts, that's just not a case that I think in Texas right now is a viable case." Every lawyer interviewed in 2005 to 2006 agreed with this assessment. These changes with regard to medical malpractice matters suggest exactly the effect of a damage cap that bothers opponents like Finley—the rights of identifiable groups of people are being diminished because of the change in the incentive structure for plaintiffs' lawyers and the concomitant change in their practices. The changes are also consistent with the findings of the previously mentioned research using closed medical malpractice claims for Texas.

If we turn to the possibility of gender disparity, the picture is more nuanced. While the forty-five-year-old male, the "best" client among the three,

---

35. Here we found no statistical relationship for the association between attractiveness at Time 1 and attractiveness at Time 2 for the seventy-year-old male or for the forty-five-year-old female. In other words, these two clients became so unattractive as to be almost toxic. This was not the case for the forty-five-year-old male, but as we saw earlier, he did become less attractive. *Id.*

became less attractive after the cap, he did not become unattractive. There was a fundamental change in the attractiveness of the forty-five-year-old female, suggesting gender disparity, and the change was even greater for the seventy-year-old male, suggesting age disparity as well.[36] The suggestion, however, is that all three became less attractive. The reluctance to take these clients—even the best one—indicates the possibility—as the reformers hoped—that medical malpractice cases more generally were becoming less attractive to plaintiffs' lawyers after implementation of the cap.

Individual Respondent Changes Regarding Acceptance of Clients

There remains the question of how individual respondents may have changed their minds regarding each type of client in a medical malpractice case after the cap. Figure 7.2 provides the data to answer this question,[37] and unlike Figure 7.1, it is organized to show the percentage of lawyers who did *not* change their minds regarding the attractiveness of (i.e., whether they would take or refer) each of the three clients after the cap (Time 2) as compared to before the cap (Time 1). More specifically, for each of the cases it shows the percentage that found each client type attractive at both points in time. For instance, 98 percent of the lawyers found the forty-five-year-old male attractive at both points in time in the 18-wheeler case, and 73 percent found this same client attractive at both points in time in the medical malpractice case.

Comparing the bars in Figure 7.2 for the 18-wheeler case with those for the medical malpractice case shows the dramatic shifts after the implementation of the cap for medical malpractice cases. There was very limited change in the attractiveness of any of the clients in the 18-wheeler case. In contrast, the bars

36. We did find a statistically significant association between the attractiveness of the forty-five-year-old female and the attractiveness of the forty-five-year-old male at Time 1 and at Time 2, but the strength of the relationship at Time 2 is weaker. This suggests the possibility—but only the possibility—of gender disparity. A similar set of analyses for the forty-five-year-old male and the seventy-year-old male also suggest the possibility of age disparity. *See* Daniels and Martin, *supra* note 29.

37. All of the crosstabs for the tables underlying Figure 7.2 are significant at .000 (chi square). *Id.*

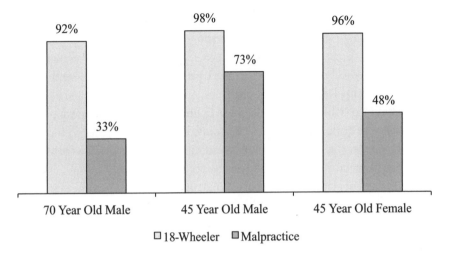

FIGURE 7.2. *Percent of Individual Lawyers Still Finding Different Clients Attractive in Light of Damage Caps*

for medical malpractice show that far fewer lawyers found either the seventy-year-old male or the forty-five-year-old female clients attractive in 2006—especially the elderly client. More specifically, in looking inside the data underlying Figure 7.2, three-quarters of those who would have taken (and not simply referred) the seventy-year-old male at Time 1 and over one-half of those who would have taken the forty-five-year-old female at Time 1 said that they would simply turn the clients away at Time 2 (and not even refer them). To further indicate the unattractiveness of these two client types at Time 2, that inside look reveals that very, very few lawyers responded that they would switch from referring or not taking the client before the cap to taking the client after the cap.

The forty-five-year-old male—the "best" client—fared somewhat better than the other two client types in the medical malpractice context, but still became less attractive. Looking again at the data underlying Figure 7.2, just a bare majority (53 percent) of the lawyers who would have actually taken (and not referred) the forty-five-year-old male before the cap would still take this client after the cap. A little less than 30 percent of those who would have taken this more desirable client before the cap would simply turn the client away (not take or even refer) after the cap. This highlights the idea that—as the reformers would hope—malpractice cases generally have become less attractive. In contrast, almost all (98 percent) of those who found the forty-five-year-old male attractive in the 18-wheeler case still did so at Time 2.

In summary, in terms of the questions at the heart of our discussion, we found the following with regard to all respondents:

1. That medical malpractice cases were generally attractive before the cap but became less so after the cap;
2. That in 18-wheeler cases, clients with limited economic damage potential were quite attractive at both points in time;
3. That even clients with limited economic damage potential were attractive in medical malpractice cases before the cap; and
4. That clients with limited economic damage potential became significantly less attractive in medical malpractice cases after the cap, whereas there was no comparable change for these clients in the 18-wheeler case, and that even the "best" client became less attractive in medical malpractice cases, but not to the same degree as the other client types.

OTHER EVIDENCE OF CHANGE

It is possible to read the results from the survey's hypotheticals with a skeptical eye and assume that plaintiffs' lawyers' responses were guided more by their political opposition to caps than by actual changes in their approach to certain kinds of clients and to medical malpractice cases. However, responses to other questions from the 2006 survey were unlikely to be guided by political views, and they reinforce the findings drawn from the hypotheticals. The survey asked lawyers to indicate the distribution of their caseload by percent across twenty substantive areas relevant to plaintiffs' practice. When asked about their caseload mix in the 2006 survey, just over one-half of the 460 respondents (250, or 54 percent) reported handling the same amount of medical malpractice as five years earlier (before the 2003 cap). Most of these 250 respondents (211) handled no malpractice at either point in time. If we remove from our analysis the 211 respondents who reported not being in the medical malpractice market at either point in time, 16 percent of the remaining 249 respondents reported doing the same amount of medical malpractice, 24 percent reported doing more, and 61 percent reported doing less.[38]

---

38. The case distribution questions appeared early in the survey instrument and did not refer to any kind of legal change or tort reform. All questions dealing with

Perhaps more to the point are the responses from the 163 lawyers who completed both the 2000 and the 2006 surveys—the "repeaters" discussed in Chapter 5. Like the 2006 survey, the 2000 survey asked lawyers to indicate the distribution of their caseload by percent across twenty substantive areas. Because the surveys were done six years apart and each used the same list of substantive areas, we can compare the responses of those 163 lawyers about their caseload mix at the time of each survey and look for changes in mix of business. Doing so greatly minimizes the possibility that responses are driven by political opposition to damage caps in medical malpractice cases or other particular tort reform measures.

A comparison of individual responses for the repeaters in each survey regarding the percentage of caseload comprised of medical malpractice revealed that 57 reported handling no medical malpractice at the time of either survey. For the 106 lawyers who included some medical malpractice matters in their caseloads, 12 percent reported no change in the percentage of business made up by medical malpractice, 27 percent reported an increase, and 60 percent reported a decrease. In short, medical malpractice itself became less attractive to plaintiffs' lawyers after the implementation of damage caps.

The additional evidence from our surveys bolsters what the responses to the hypotheticals showed about the attractiveness of medical malpractice cases after the implementation of the 2003 cap. It is also consistent with the information cited at the beginning of the chapter on the decline of filings for medical malpractice cases in Texas trial courts and the changes in medical malpractice insurance claims.

CONCLUSION: CLOSING THE COURTHOUSE DOORS

This chapter set out to investigate the proposition that caps on noneconomic damages—like the low, hard caps enacted in Texas—will lead plaintiffs' lawyers to stop handling medical malpractice cases, especially those involving certain kinds of clients. There is strong evidence for that proposition in Texas.

---

tort reform came later in the survey. Lawyers were asked about the distribution at the time of the survey and five years earlier. Responses driven by political opposition to damage caps in medical malpractice cases, or other particular tort reform measures, are unlikely in this context.

The reason is that caps dramatically alter the incentive structure for plaintiffs' lawyers, who are constantly adjusting their practices in response to changes in the legal rules that shape their practices. As that East Texas lawyer said, "The juice simply isn't worth the squeeze."

Plaintiffs' lawyers function as the civil justice system's gatekeepers. Whether they keep the doorway open, and how wide if they do, will depend on the profitability of plaintiffs' lawyers' practices. Because they are effectively a limit on fees, damage caps directly affect profitability. This chapter shows how important understanding this idea is for assessing the effects of tort reform. A specific change in the formal law can limit damages to a degree that significantly alters the incentive structure at the heart of the contingency fee system. If damages are limited too severely in light of the costs and risks for a particular type of case, plaintiffs' lawyers may well avoid those cases—despite the normative values. A higher cap, of course, would not have the same kind of effect, and this may be the reason why the favored cap for medical malpractice cases is set at $250,000.

One important consequence of such a reform is diminished access to the civil justice system, and this is what the reformers intended. Particularly troubling is what this means for the people who resemble Finley's hidden victims. They will be hit the hardest, but they will not be alone in finding it more difficult to find representation—especially the most effective representation by lawyers who specialize and are best suited to handle a particular type of case, such as complex medical malpractice matters. In light of the supercharged rhetoric about the medical malpractice crisis and tort reform in the United States, perhaps more than anything else, the unique plight of the hidden victims reminds us that fundamentally important normative issues are at stake when we talk about access.

8. Conclusion

"Unless There's a Way to Make Money Practicing Law, Rights Don't Make Any Difference"

ACCESS, THE CONTINGENCY FEE, AND PLAINTIFFS'
LAWYERS

On the opening page of his book on the contingency fee written fifty years ago, F. B. MacKinnon matter-of-factly notes, "Although economic considerations are not (by definition) paramount for the professional man, they are essential, under modern conditions, for his existence."[1] His observation is quite important for a key theme of our book—access to the courts or, more fundamentally, access to the rights and remedies the law allows. The connection is plaintiffs' lawyers, who rely almost exclusively on the contingency fee. They are the civil justice system's gatekeepers. For access to be meaningful, to be anything but window dressing, a person needs a lawyer. As MacKinnon's point suggests and as our conclusion's title simply states, if plaintiffs' lawyers cannot make a living practicing law, they will not be playing that gatekeeping role and providing meaningful access.

Access, of course, is not free. Those lawyers need to be paid. When we think of problems concerning access with this in mind, we usually have in mind the very poor. Nonetheless, one does not need to be poor to find the cost of legal services beyond reach, especially if we're talking about litigation. Our legal system's response to this situation for matters involving injury or loss and damages is the contingency fee and the lawyers who build their practices on it. A lawyer we quoted in Chapter 1 put it best:

> Ninety percent of the people out there make their living, they pay for their kids to go to school, they pay to take care of their kids, they pay for their mortgage, they pay for their one or two cars, and at the end of the month, they may have $100 left over if they're the lucky ones. . . . And so,

---

1. F. B. MacKinnon, *Contingent Fees for Legal Services: A Study of Professional Economics and Responsibilities* (Chicago: Aldine, 1964), 3–4.

for someone to have the ability to go hire a lawyer on anything other than
a contingency, you know, I think it's a fiction.

The contingency fee is not a perfect answer to the problem of access for
people without substantial means. A key reason is that it is also a business
model for plaintiffs' lawyers who build most—if not all—of their practice
around the representation of people injured in some way. It is a business
model with its own unique challenges and incentives. Clients pay no fee and
typically pay none of the costs unless the lawyer is successful in obtaining
a monetary settlement or award. This means the lawyer—to at least some
degree—must be a rational business actor. The lawyer needs a steady stream
of clients with injuries or losses the civil justice system (in action, not just in
theory) will compensate adequately, meaning sufficient to compensate the
client for his or her injuries, cover the costs involved, and provide a fee. This
fee also needs to be enough to cover the time and costs for matters in which
the lawyer is not successful.

Given these requirements, a lawyer cannot blindly take every case and client. A plaintiffs' lawyer would quickly go out of business if he did. He must
balance, in Herbert Kritzer's words, risk, cost, and reward.[2] As the lawyer we
quoted in Chapter 5 plainly stated, "We're getting increasingly selective. I front
the costs, and if we lose I eat the costs." We saw that even high-volume, aggressively advertising lawyers are likely to turn away many potential clients.
This could mean turning away cases in which liability is quite problematic. As
MacKinnon found, what we call gatekeeping works both ways: "The lawyer's
reluctance [to take a case] is frequently based upon the lack of merit in the
claim,"[3] or it could be that the lawyer won't take cases in which the defendant
is unable to pay damages or in which insurance is not involved.

As Chapter 7 shows with regard to medical malpractice cases, it could also
be a situation in which the amount of damages is legislatively limited. The
limits can be severe enough in relation to the costs involved in bringing certain kinds of cases that lawyers cannot profitably do so. This could mean
avoiding certain clients even in cases with clear liability—the so-called hid-

2. Herbert Kritzer, *Risks, Reputations, and Rewards: Contingency Fee Legal Practice
in the United States* (Stanford, CA: Stanford University Press, 2004), 9–19.

3. MacKinnon, *supra* note 1, at 206; *see also* Herbert Kritzer, *Contingency Fee Lawyers as Gatekeepers in the Civil Justice System*, 81 Judicature 22 (1997).

den victims of tort reform. Or it could be more blunt, like the 1991 changes in workers' compensation discussed in Chapter 2 that directly limited fees to such a degree that most lawyers simply stopped handling these matters. This is a reminder of David Hyman and Charles Silver's concise summary of the business model: "It's the incentives, stupid."[4] It is also a reminder that reformers understand this business model, too. As Governor Perry said with regard to the caps on damages, "We are now removing the incentive that personal injury trial lawyers have to file frivolous lawsuits and run health care providers out of business."[5]

The balancing of risk, cost, and reward can go to certain clients and/or cases in situations not involving formal limits on damages or fees. In Chapter 5, we saw that lawyers were becoming more reluctant to handle lower-value automobile accident cases involving soft tissue injuries, even with liability running to another party and insurance. In our 2006 survey, only one-half of the BB1 lawyers we discussed in Chapter 5 (the lawyers whose practices are built largely on small auto accident cases) would take such a case. In our 2000 survey, two-thirds would take the case. Reminiscent of MacKinnon's observation that "sometimes a meritorious but difficult claim may be rejected, indicating some limits of the coverage of the fee system based on the self-interest of the lawyer,"[6] lawyers were becoming more reluctant because of their sense of what juries would do in such cases as a result of the reformers' public relations campaigns.

That reluctance extends even further. In our 2006 survey we asked lawyers who said they *would* take such a case whether they would still take it if the client is unemployed, has a criminal record, or has been a plaintiff before in a personal injury suit. For the BB1 lawyers we discussed in Chapter 5, the percentages who would take such clients are 79, 68, and 73, respectively. But remembering that only one-half of the 2006 BB1 lawyers said they would take the soft tissue injury case in the first place, this means that each of these clients is looking at a situation in which more than half of the lawyers would *not* take their case, even with good liability and an insured client.

4. David Hyman & Charles Silver, *Medical Malpractice Litigation and Tort Reform: It's the Incentives Stupid*, 59 Vanderbilt L. Rev. 1085, 1085 (2006).

5. *Gov Perry Speaks at Med Mal Bill Signing*, July 11, 2003, http://governor.state .tx.us/news/speech/10637/.

6. MacKinnon, *supra* note 1, at 206.

The reason, as a Houston lawyer we quoted in Chapter 5 said, is: "What they [jurors] don't want to see is Joe Blow who has a soft tissue back injury but also had a soft tissue back injury two years ago, and four years ago, and doesn't work and is unemployed, has three kids, and is on welfare. And those are a lot of the cases that get tried [and lost]. . . . You see it week after week in our Blue Sheets [the local verdict reporter]." To return to our letter writer in the Preface: "I believe tort reform was a major factor in my decision to close my practice. I found jury verdicts decreased due to the propaganda disseminated by insurance companies and big business, and this resulted in insurance adjusters offering less money to settle cases. I began to decline representation in cases I used to accept and was working harder and receiving less money on cases I took." This is the reality of balancing risk, cost, and reward. Again, it seems that the reformers with their public relations campaigns aimed at changing "the way people think about personal responsibility and civil litigation" understand the business model quite well.[7] This is one message from the plight of our letter writer who opened the book.

Despite the imperfections, plaintiffs' lawyers with a business model based on the contingency fee still provide substantial access. There is a demand for their services, and there is no realistic alternative available that would provide an equal or greater amount of meaningful access. Given this fact, the real questions are why, given the challenges, someone would choose to be a plaintiffs' lawyer and why someone would continue in the face of the tort reform movement. Nonetheless, a substantial bar has developed in Texas around the contingency fee and the clientele it serves. It is one with a long history and its own professional organizations. In many respects, it is rather like a profession within a profession that has a complex structure with specialization and an identifiable hierarchy.

Especially important for answering those two questions, we think, is an identifiable professional identity that goes to what it means not just to be a lawyer but also to what it means to be a plaintiffs' lawyer in Texas. As the lawyer we quoted in the Preface told us:

> You have true believers. . . . I put myself in that category. What has appealed to me is a family with kids whose life gets turned upside down

---

7. American Tort Reform Association, *ATRA's Mission: Real Justice in Our Courts*, http://www.atra.org/about/.

because someone in the family gets seriously hurt or killed, and they're facing a greater than David and Goliath battle, and they need someone to fight for them . . . I'll be in this business until the bitter end. And I hope that the bitter end is not five years from now.

The real challenge for these lawyers is in navigating the tension between this professional identity and business necessity—with the latter becoming even more acute as their practice environment becomes more problematic.

How a lawyer does so affects access. We found some lawyers who left the practice area or who, like our letter writer, closed their businesses and retired. Others were holding tightly to their sense of themselves as professionals, and not always with success. One lawyer we saw in Chapter 4 said he had thought of trying some other kind of legal work as his practice declined, but he concluded, "I'm not sure I could do it, I mean work for industry. . . . [I'd] be working for principles that I really don't believe in, and that would be hard to do. I may have to, but it would be difficult. It might cause a terminal clinical depression." He closed his practice not long after our interview.

Most, however, have persisted while trying to find ways to adjust their practices—some being quite entrepreneurial in looking for ways to prosper in a changing environment. We do not mean entrepreneurial in the sense of commercialism, with both concepts cast in a negative light as antithetical to professionalism. To provide an example to help clarify our point, Carroll Seron used a traditional professionalism/commercialism dichotomy as a framing device in her study of solo and small-firm practitioners in metropolitan New York City. In describing the lawyers she characterized as entrepreneurs, she said, "Their expectations revolved around a concern to use their training to develop a *business* in legal services."[8] In saying there are entrepreneurs among the lawyers we studied in Texas, we do not have this old dichotomy in mind. It does not seem appropriate.

Entrepreneurs look for new ways of doing things in the face of change. They look for opportunities in a changing environment that will allow them to

8. Carroll Seron, *The Business of Practicing Law: The Work Lives of Solo and Small-Firm Attorneys* (Philadelphia, PA: Temple University Press, 1996), 10 (emphasis in original). The entire opening chapter is devoted to the dichotomy: "Chapter 1: Professionalism versus Commercialism."

exploit the changes or insulate themselves from the changes.[9] They are innovators who develop new services, markets, or technologies that allow them to prosper rather than merely survive—or worse.[10] One of the reasons the plaintiffs' bar in Texas endures is the entrepreneurial spirit and success of many of its members in seizing opportunities in ways that others could emulate. The Jones firm described in Chapter 3 succeeded because its members were able to exploit changes in the law and in the local economy and offer a service for which there was a clear demand. The same could be said of the Mullinax, Wells firm or the other firms discussed in Chapter 3. The San Antonio lawyer quoted in Chapter 3 who built his practice on the 1970s changes in the law concerning consumer fraud, especially the trebling of damages and payment of attorney's fees, provides still another example. As he put it, "I tried the shit out of those DTPA [Deceptive Trade Practices Act] cases when I was a young lawyer."

Opportunity may come without a formal change in the law. We saw this in the discussion of 18-wheeler cases in Chapter 7, where we quoted one lawyer as saying, "Everybody seems to be able to connect with an 18-wheeler that's out of control. You know, we hit one for $20 million that we got paid on, and you know, even Republicans were voting for us on that one." We saw a similar logic with regard to commercial litigation. It is less costly and appears to be an area largely immune to the public relations campaigns—at least some plaintiffs' lawyers think so. Said one, "I'm doing some of that . . . just as a hedge against what might be happening in the PI business." Colorfully, he explained why:

> Commercial cases . . . those are easier cases than plaintiffs' personal injury.
> . . . We do it on a contingency fee basis. They are easier because . . . for
> some reason, people don't think those plaintiffs are scumbags. They don't
> think business plaintiffs are scumbags. They just think they have been
> wronged in a business deal. They have no problem with Southwestern Bell
> suing Greater Atlantic Bell. They don't like Alexander Bell and his wife
> suing for an injury. . . . It's a weird play out there right now.

9. Perhaps the simplest definition of an entrepreneur is Joseph Schumpeter's: one who carries out new combinations of production. For him, it is about change and new ways of doing things. *See* Joseph A. Schumpeter, *The Theory of Economic Development* (New York: Oxford University Press, 1961), 74–94.

10. Peter F. Drucker, *Innovation and Entrepreneurship: Practice and Principles* (New York: Harper Business, 1985), 27–28.

Lawyers moving in this direction may narrow their focus. Some, for instance, are looking for cases related to Texas's resurgent oil and gas industry. One said, "I let my referring attorneys know that I was handling some oil and gas—property damage involving oil and gas wells, downhole casings, things of that sort. . . . I handled a large royalty case for a New Orleans gas company and just sort of put the word out." He handles these matters on a contingency fee basis. Another said, "We're into oil and gas big time now. We were not five years ago; we didn't have any. . . . Now I'm into it big time. . . . There are big dollars in it. . . . We do everything on contingency fee."

Oil and gas is not the only area into which some lawyers are moving. Some are moving into the high-tech arena (especially in the Austin area), and others are seeking out smaller niches or targeting smaller businesses or professionals. One is representing doctors in suits again breast implant manufacturers. Another, again on a contingency fee basis, represents media professionals who have their works used without permission or royalties. Like a number of others, this lawyer has recognized that for some smaller businesses, hiring a lawyer on a contingency fee basis may be the only way to pursue a claim.

We could go on with other examples of new markets being explored by plaintiffs' lawyers or with examples of new ideas about getting clients. What is important is that many plaintiffs' lawyers are constantly looking for and trying to exploit opportunities—sometimes with success and sometimes not. Unlike the deeper past, there is a robust infrastructure with plaintiffs' lawyers' own professional organizations that can help. These organizations, especially the state and local ones, provide networking opportunities (including social media), conferences, continuing education programs, materials, and the like that allow—if not encourage—innovations to spread. The question is what kind of access, and for whom, there will be as plaintiffs' lawyers navigate the tension between their professional identity and business necessity.

"REFORM"

Along with access, we have also talked a great deal about the tort "reform" movement. One cannot discuss access and the contemporary practice of plaintiffs' law outside the "reform" context. We put "reform" in quotation marks as a reminder of two of our starting points in the Preface. One is the idea of what we mean by "reform." As we noted, the term carries a certain connotation about the common good and needed changes. The advocates for certain changes in the tort system have invested heavily in portraying their desired changes as "reform." They have skillfully and strategically used the term to take advantage of its symbolic value. As used, the concept of tort reform is generally understood to assume, rather than demonstrate, that the current state of the civil justice system is in dire need of improvement. It points to the misdeeds of particular sets of actors as the cause of the problem—plaintiffs' lawyers chief among them.

As used, *tort reform* directs attention away from any need for critical examination. Instead there is a carefully constructed picture of what is presented as common sense—an accepted, obvious wisdom of a system run amok for which "we all pay the price." Proposed changes are then presented not as those favoring the narrow self-interests of the "reform" advocates but as a needed step forward toward some more ideal or superior civil justice system that will benefit the common good. As Sherman Joyce, President of the American Tort Reform Association, asserts, "There is clearly broad support for tort reform as a means to rein in greedy personal injury lawyers that are manipulating our legal system for personal financial gain at the expense of the average consumer."[11]

Putting "reform" in quotation marks also brings us back to a second of our starting points—the matter of perspective. In light of the "reform" advocates' efforts, our intent has been to provide a different and critical perspective grounded in the insights of political science; informed by the best work in the law and social science literature; and based on extensive, systematic empirical research. We wanted to look deeper and not take the "reform" advocates' accepted wisdom at face value. Rather, we wanted to look under the hood, kick the tires, and not be fooled by the shiny new paint job. After all, it is about who gets what, when, and how—and that means it is about politics.

Plaintiffs' practice has always been a precarious business dependent on the substance of the law and the environment in which a lawyer works. The law can provide fewer or more opportunities, the environment can provide more raw material or less, and the cultural context can be more hospitable or more

---

11. *Voters Say "Too Many Lawsuits," According to New National Poll on Tort Reform,* www.atra.org/newsroom/voters-say-too-many-lawsuits-according-new-national-poll-tort-reform.

hostile. Among (and underlying) the justifications for tort "reform," cutting back the opportunities and altering the cultural context are at the top of the list. Again, as Professor Lester Brickman plainly says, "That, of course, is precisely the purpose of tort reform: to curtail tort litigation."[12] And we are not simply talking about the supposedly ubiquitous frivolous litigation. In Brickman's words, we are also talking about "claimants [who] would have prevailed had their cases gone to trial."

Former Texas Supreme Court Justice (and previous reform supporter) Deborah Hankinson would probably agree but sees things in a rather different light. As we saw in Chapter 2, her concern is about meaningful access. The legislation imposing the cap on noneconomic damages in medical malpractice cases and the constitutional amendment that allowed it (the amendment allows for such limitations in areas beyond medical malpractice) "would be closing the doors to a great many citizens." Knowing full well what the change means for plaintiffs' lawyers, she says it "wasn't designed to cut off bad—that is frivolous—lawsuits; it was designed to cut-off lawsuits by people with legitimate claims by restricting access to the courthouse. . . . This tort reform went too far. . . . I view this as something that deprives people of their constitutional rights."[13] Her remarks are a stark reminder of what is more generally at stake under the guise of "reform" and what it may mean for the role plaintiffs' lawyers play. Again, as we were told by that one Texas plaintiffs' lawyer, "Unless there's a way to make money practicing law, rights don't make any difference."

12. Lester Brickman, *Lawyer Barons: What Their Contingency Fees Really Cost America* (New York: Cambridge University Press, 2011), 121.

13. Mimi Swartz, *Hurt? Injured? Need a Lawyer? Too Bad!*, Tex. Monthly, Nov. 2005, www.texasmonthly.com/content/hurt-injured-need-lawyer-too-bad.

Methodological Appendix: Interviews and Surveys

At the heart of our research are in-depth interviews with Texas plaintiffs' lawyers and two detailed mail surveys of Texas plaintiffs' lawyers. The most important interviews were done during two different time periods. The original 100 interviews were done between 1995 and 2000, and the second set was done in 2005–2006. Of the 100 initial interviewees, 23 were from Austin, 28 were from the Dallas/Fort Worth area, 24 were from Houston, 23 were from San Antonio, and 2 were from small towns in East Texas. The four urban centers represent the largest concentrations of lawyers in the state, and we presume that they also include the largest numbers of plaintiffs' lawyers. Only thirteen lawyers declined to give us an interview. We also had informal discussions with a small number of judges and other lawyers.

To create the initial pool of plaintiffs' lawyers to interview, we started with two lists. The first was created through discussions with past and present officials of the Texas Trial Lawyers Association (TTLA). We asked them to identify lawyers whom they recognized as leaders in the plaintiffs' bar as well as a range of plaintiffs' lawyers with differing practices, abilities, reputations, etc. These conversations were supplemented by similar discussions with leaders of local plaintiffs' lawyers' groups. The second list came from published sources: Yellow Pages directories, Martindale-Hubbell, West's Legal Directory, the Texas Legal Directory, and the Texas Board of Legal Specialization Directory. Where available, published jury verdict reporters were also used to identify lawyers. Names were then randomly chosen from these two lists. Additional interview subjects were identified through a "snowballing" technique of asking interviewees for the names of others worth interviewing (as we put it, "the names of the good, the bad, and the ugly").

Fifty-one interviews were done in 2005–2006, and we broadened our geographic coverage by including lawyers from other parts of Texas as well as the major urban areas: Abilene, Amarillo, Beaumont, Brownsville, El Paso, Jacksonville, Longview, Lubbock, Nacogdoches, San Angelo, and Tyler. Twenty-one of these fifty-one 2005–2006 interviews were re-interviews with lawyers we had interviewed in the initial round. New names were chosen from a variety of sources as well as through a snowballing procedure. Because the reforms enacted in Texas in 2003 dealt with health care cases, we also targeted lawyers who were or had been specialists in this area. There were thirteen, some of whom were also among the twenty-one re-interviews. Finally, five additional interviews were done in 2012–2013: two with lawyers near retirement, two with new lawyers, and one with a mid-career lawyer previously interviewed in 2005.

We used a disparate set of sources for choosing interview subjects because our goal was to interview as wide an array of plaintiffs' lawyers as possible and not just the big, well-known names handling the newsworthy cases or the members of plaintiffs' lawyers' organizations. The attorneys interviewed devote a substantial proportion of their practices (50 percent or more, with a number as high as 90 percent) to handling plaintiffs' cases for a contingency fee. The interviews were in-depth and semi-structured, lasting on average for about 1.5 hours. In addition to their perceptions of tort reform and its impact on their practices, the lawyers were asked about their personal and professional backgrounds; their reasons for choosing a plaintiffs' practice; the nature of their practice; the nature of their clients; how their clients are obtained; their views on advertising and other ways of attracting clients; their firm or office organization; their approach to case screening, case resolution, and case financing; and their professional or political activities.

Based on the findings from the initial set of interviews, we designed and conducted a mail survey of Texas plaintiffs' lawyers in early 2000. A second mail survey was conducted in 2006, with many questions in common with the 2000 survey to allow for comparisons across the two time periods. Each survey relied on a list of lawyers provided by TTLA. It is important to emphasize that each survey relied on a separate list generated at the time each survey was fielded. Each list (2000 and 2006) included current (as of the time the list was created) TTLA members, former TTLA members, and lawyers identified by TTLA as "prospects"—lawyers thought to be practicing at least some amount of plaintiffs' work who had never been TTLA members. The nature of the two TTLA lists worked very well for our purposes, and the lists represent the best available estimate of the population of Texas plaintiffs' lawyers. Although Texas is a mandatory bar state, the State Bar of Texas does not have a listing of members who would specifically identify themselves as plaintiffs' lawyers.

The 2000 survey was sent to 2,642 lawyers chosen from a list of 5,284 (every other name—50 percent of the full 2000 TTLA list). We received 552 usable responses—that is, responses from lawyers whose practices were at least 25 percent devoted to plaintiffs' work on a contingency fee basis at the time of the survey or in the five previous years. After the sample size was reduced (to 1,902) when respondents and nonrespondents not meeting the 25 percent threshold were removed, the 552 responses represent an adjusted response rate of 29 percent. These 552 responses fall within a confidence interval of plus or minus 3.9 percentage points at the 95 percent confidence level.[1]

The 2006 survey included many of the same questions as the 2000 survey, with the main differences between the two surveys reflecting the relevant reforms—the 1995 reforms for the 2000 survey and the 2003 reforms for the 2006 survey. In addition, the 2006 survey also included a series of questions on referral practices in light of the efforts of the Texas Supreme Court in 2004 (outlined in Chapter 2) to fundamentally change the rules governing the referral system. After a reduction in the sample size (to 1,792) made for respondents and nonrespondents not meeting the 25 percent threshold, the 460 responses represent an adjusted response rate of 26 percent. These 460 responses fall within a confidence interval of plus or minus 4.3 percentage points at the 95 percent confidence level.

Having data from two independent surveys sharing certain key questions about the basic characteristics of plaintiffs' lawyers, each survey generating a substantial number of respondents, provides a unique check for bias in the survey results. While there is some overlap in terms of lawyers included, the two samples were not identical (again, TTLA provided a separate list for each survey), and neither were the two sets of respondents. A total of 424 lawyers appeared in both samples, which have a combined total of 3,694 names (using the adjusted numbers from above). There were a total of 163 repeaters—lawyers responding to both surveys—out of a total of 1,012 respondents for the two surveys combined.

Given the six years between surveys, we might expect some minor aggre-

---

1. We conducted a check of the nonrespondents using electronic sources (State Bar of Texas website, Martindale, Findlaw, and basic Internet searches) to see if they did not meet the threshold and should be removed from the sample. The decision rule was a conservative one—a nonrespondent would be left in the sample unless there was evidence of no contingency fee work at the time of the survey or within the five previous years, they were designated as ineligible to practice by the State Bar of Texas, or they had moved from the address or firm we had and no forwarding address was available (meaning most likely that the lawyer moved out of state or was no longer in practice).

TABLE A.1. *Respondents to the 2000 Survey and Respondents to the 2006 Survey Compared: Shared Questions in Each Survey on Practice Characteristics*

	2000	2006
Business contingency fee (%)	Mean 75; Median 90	Mean 75; Median 95
Typical case value (2006)	Median $43K	Median $38K
Caseload	Mean 66; Median 30	Mean 71; Median 25
Board certified in either personal injury trial or civil trial (%)	36	40
Income (estimate in 2006$)	Median: $161K	Median: $163K
Top four types of cases (% of caseload)	Auto accidents 33	Auto accidents 32
	Medical malpractice 11	Medical malpractice 11
	Commercial litigation 7	Commercial litigation 8
	Products liability 7	Products liability 8
Top four sources of business (%)	Lawyer referrals 37	Lawyer referrals 38
	Client referrals 29	Client referrals 24
	Other referrals 13	Advertising 13
	Advertising 13	Other referrals 11
Top three law schools attended (%)	Texas 19	South Texas 17
	South Texas 17	Texas 16
	Houston 11	Houston 12
White (non-Hispanic) (%)	85	86
Female (%)	13	11
Age at time of survey	Mean 46; Median 45	Mean 49; Median 49
Number of years as lawyer	Mean 15; Median 13	Mean 19; Median 18

gate differences in various demographics and practice traits across the respondent pools, but they should look relatively similar if they are capturing a reasonably accurate picture of the plaintiffs' bar in recent years. Table A.1 presents comparisons between the respondent pools from the two surveys on a series of questions on basic characteristics asked in both surveys.

The patterns across these characteristics among respondents are quite similar despite the six-year gap between the two surveys. For each set of respondents, the vast majority of business is plaintiffs' contingency fee work. Case value, income, size of firm, and number of open cases are all quite similar, as are the top four types of cases worked on and the top four sources of business. Racial and gender composition are also similar. It is worth noting that the plaintiffs' bar in Texas exhibited a much greater gender imbalance than the State Bar as a whole at the time, which was 30 percent female in 2005–2006.[2] The 2006 respondents have been licensed to practice for a few more years than the 2000 respondents, and correspondingly, they are a bit older. This reflects, in part, a more general trend among Texas lawyers. State Bar data show that in 2005–2006, the median age was forty-six and median years licensed was sixteen, up from forty-two and thirteen ten years earlier.[3]

Finally, there is no evidence of a bias toward negativity—that respondents are not doing as well as their peers. For instance, the estimated median income for respondents to the 2006 survey is $156,000. According to the State Bar of Texas, the 2005 median income for all lawyers in private practice in Texas was $120,000.[4]

2. *See* State Bar of Texas Department of Research and Analysis, *State Bar Members: Attorney Statistical Profile*, 1 (*2005–2006*), May 19, 2006, at 1, www.texasbar.com/AM /Template.cfm?Section=Archives&Template=/CM/ContentDisplay.cfm&ContentID =11457.

3. *Id.*

4. *See* State Bar of Texas Department of Research and Analysis, *2005 Private Practitioner Income Report*, State Bar of Texas Department of Research and Analysis, 2 (2006), Sept. 21, 2006, at 2, www.texasbar.com/AM/Template.cfm?Section=Demographic_and_ Economic_Trends&Template=/CM/ContentDisplay.cfm&ContentID=8819.

Index

Adler, Jim, 5, 115, 140
Aetna Insurance, 24–25
American Association for Justice, 72, 73
American Bar Association (ABA), 61–62, 72
  prohibition of pure referral fees, 61, 178
  standards for shared work or joint
    responsibility, 180
American Bar Foundation
  on legal specialization, 173
American Federation of Labor (AFL), 81, 83
American Tort Reform Association
    (ATRA), 3, 27, 238
  mission statement, 2, 11, 21–22, 23
  public relations campaigns, 25–26
asbestos and silica cases, 54
Auerbach, Jerold, 7
auto accident cases, 107, 132, 233
  bread-and-butter lawyers and, 142–143,
    148–149, 155, 233
  case value and referrals, 199
  fee size and referrals, 202–203
  heavy hitter lawyers and, 155, 171–172
  lawyer reputation and referrals, 190
  medical malpractice referrals and,
    195–196
  referral system and, 181, 186, 192
  specialization, 174
  specialization and referrals, 195–196
  tort reform and, 163, 169 (table), 169–170

Baker & Botts, 70–71
  insurance companies as clients of, 75
  railroads as clients of, 75, 87–88, 90
Baker Botts, LLP. See Baker & Botts
Baker Botts Amicus Fund, 104
Baker, James A., 47

Baldwin, Scott, 80
  TTLA and, 81, 94
Barber, Will, 35–36, 42
Baron, Fred, 86
Bates v. State Bar of Arizona (1977), 86, 113
billboard advertising in Texas, 67–68, 133
Blind Justice, 6n18, 56. See also Case, Ken
Bosworth, Rachel, 180n10, 181n11
Branson, Frank, 140
bread-and-butter lawyers (BB1 and BB2),
    142
  advertising, 152–153, 155, 164
  auto accident cases and, 147, 155, 170, 174
  caseloads, 146 (table), 147–148, 164, 170
    (table)
  certification of, 153
  characteristics of, 146 (table), 147
  client acquisition, 146 (table), 151–152,
    154
  client referrals, 151–152, 154, 164
  geographical market, 164
  hierarchy of Texas plaintiffs' bar and,
    143
  income, 154, 164, 170
  medical malpractice cases and, 147, 170
  noneconomic damages and, 150–151
  referrals, 153, 154
  solo practitioners, 154, 164
  See also plaintiffs' lawyers; Texas
    plaintiffs' bar
Brickman, Lester, 1, 13, 27
  on contingency fee lawyers, 24
  on contingency fees and access to legal
    system, 10–11
  Manhattan Institute and, 8
  on tort reform, 139, 239

Bullock, Bob, 45
Burke, Thomas, 2, 16–17, 34
 on national plaintiffs' lawyers'
  organization, 100
Bush, George W., 42, 46–47
Bush, George H. W., 18

Calve, Joseph, 67n96, 142n5
Campbell, Robert, 58
Case, Ken, 6n18, 56n54, 57n57. *See also Blind
 Justice*
case screening, 148, 148n11, 149, 212
 heavy hitter lawyers and, 155–156,
  158–159
 See also medical malpractice cases
certification
 bread-and-butter lawyers and, 153
 heavy hitter lawyers and, 161, 165
 legal expertise and, 194
 Texas State Bar Association members
  and, 154
 See also specialization
Champagne, Anthony, 6n18, 55n50, 59
Chapman, Willie, 83
Cheek, Kyle, 6n18, 55n50, 59
Chicago plaintiffs' bar, 177–178
cigarette litigation, 37
Citizens Against Lawsuit Abuse (CALA),
 26, 38, 43, 66, 150
Clements, William, 36
 Texas Supreme Court appointments, 38,
  58
client acquisition
 auto accident cases and, 120
 bread-and-butter lawyers and, 146
  (table), 151–152
 ethics and, 113, 119–120
 lawyer advertising and, 114
 lawyers' professional identity and, 126
 non-lawyer runners and, 130
 referrals and, 117, 125
 rules of, 112–113
 sources of, 116 (table), 117–118

Texas Disciplinary Rules of Professional
 Conduct, Rule VII and, 114–116
client attractiveness
 assessing, 216–219, 219n27, 220
 bread-and-butter lawyers and, 233–234
 damage caps effects on, 222
 hidden victims and, 216, 220–223, 221
  (table)
 gender and, 224
Cockrill, Ashley, 7, 70
collateral source rule, 17
Collins, John E., 107, 152
Combs, Arthur, 82, 87
 client referrals, 85
 communist accusation, 84
 labor law, 81–83
 NACCA and, 93
 TTLA and, 82, 94
 training young plaintiffs' lawyers,
  85
Congress of Industrial Organizations
 (CIO), 81
Conservative Legal Movement, 27
contingency fees, 17, 187, 189, 211
 access to courts and, 10, 10n29, 231–232,
  234
 bread-and-butter lawyers and, 148, 154,
  164
 business model, 232
 commercial cases and, 237
 damage caps effects on, 214
 elite lawyers and, 12
 heavy hitter lawyers and, 155, 157–158
 plaintiffs' lawyers' reliance on, 106, 112,
  141–142, 231
continuing legal education, 92–93, 95–99

damages
 caps on, 17, 17n51
 case screening and, 148, 160
 See also noneconomic damage caps;
  noneconomic damages
Davidson, Chandler, 79

Democratic Party, in Texas, 45, 59, 73, 83, 102

Edwards, George, Jr., 84
Edwards, George, Sr., 87
  Ku Klux Klan kidnapping of, 84
Edwards, John, 6

Federal Employers Liability Act (FELA), 78
Finley, Lucinda, 53n45, 225
  on hidden victims, 214–215, 216, 219n27
  on gender disparity, 224
Friedman, Lawrence, 7–8, 16
  on expansion of tort system, 105
  on nineteenth-century tort law, 75
frivolous litigation, 46, 54, 209, 211, 238

Galanter, Marc, 12, 14–15, 42
  on legal specialization, 174–175
gender
  client attractiveness and, 124
  Texas plaintiffs' lawyers, 143n8
"going rates," 14n38
  jury verdicts and, 14–15, 77
  settlements and, 15, 77
Gonzalez, Raul, 59
Goulden, Joseph, 70
Grisham, John, 4–5
Gwynne, S. C., 56

Haltom, William, xiii, 5–6, 16, 24
Hankinson, Deborah, 47, 239
Hardberger, Philip, 59–60
heavy hitter lawyers (HH1 and HH2)
  advertising, 157, 160–161
  auto accident cases and, 155, 158, 171–172, 174
  caseloads, 146 (table), 155, 158, 164–165, 171 (table)
  case screening, 155–156, 158–160
  case values, 165
  certification of, 161, 165
  characteristics of, 146 (table)

geographical markets and, 145, 157–158, 165
  hierarchy of Texas plaintiffs' bar, 142–143
  income, 161
  lawyer referrals and, 146 (table), 156–157, 160–161
  mass tort cases and, 158
  medical malpractice cases and, 155–156, 158–159, 171–172, 174
  products liability cases and, 155, 158
  solo practitioners, 165
  specialization, 158
  See also plaintiffs' lawyers; Texas plaintiffs' bar
Hecht, Nathan, 46
Henley, Hudson, 106–107
Hile, Richard, 64, 65n87, 116
Hill, John, 58
Hornsby, William, 113
Horowitz, Michael, 27
Howell, Timothy, 32
Hyman, David, xv, 9–11, 211
  on lawyers' business model, 233

"insurance crisis" and tort reform, 38–39, 57
Insurance Information Institute, 22, 25
internet advertising. *See* lawyer advertising

Jacob, Herbert, 9
Jamail, Joe, 140
joint and several liability rules, 17, 44n26
  Texas changes to, 44, 180
Jones firm, 236. *See also* Jones, Franklin, Jr.; Jones, Franklin, Sr.; Jones, Solomon
Jones, Franklin, Jr., 78
  law practice, 80
  in medicolegal short course, 99
  TTLA and, 81, 94
Jones, Franklin, Sr., 70, 87, 105
  on hostile climate for plaintiffs' lawyers, 91
  law practice, 80

Jones, Franklin, Sr., *continued*
in medicolegal short course, 99
on railroads and railroad lawyers,
89–90
TTLA and, 80–81, 94
on TTLA and politics, 102–104
Jones, Solomon, 70, 78, 105
Jost, Kenneth, 16
Joyce, Craig, 35–37
Joyce, Sherman, 238
juries
geographical markets and, 144
lawyer advertising and, 131, 133–134
tort reform and, 149–151
jury verdicts
"going rates" and, 14–15
tort reform and, 234
"Justice for Sale" (*60 Minutes*), 6

Kingdon, John, 19–21, 31
Kritzer, Herbert, xv, 148n11, 151n14, 232
on contingency fees and access to
courts, 10
on contingency fees and lawyer
reputation, 187, 189
on contingency fees and risk, 211
Ku Klux Klan, 84

labor law, in Texas, 81–83
Lanier, Mark, 73, 103, 140
Language for the 21ˢᵗ Century. See Luntz,
Frank
lawyer advertising
aggressive advertisers and litigation,
128–129
Bates v. State Bar of Arizona (1977) and,
113
bread-and-butter lawyers and, 152–153,
155
competition and, 133–134
Constitutional protection of, 86
cost of, 137
heavy hitter lawyers and, 157, 161

image enhancement and, 135–136
jurors and, 131, 133–134
lawyer referrals and, 160–161
marketing firms and, 137
necessity of, 132–137
plaintiffs' lawyers' criticism of, 121–122,
131
professionalism and, 133, 136
television, 5
Texas Disciplinary Rules of Professional
Conduct, Rule VII guidelines on,
114–115
tort reform and, 131
young lawyers and, 132–134
Lawyer Barons. See Brickman, Lester
lawyer referrals. *See* referral system
lawyers
as business persons, 203
as gatekeepers, 9, 33
jurors' perceptions of, 5
media coverage of, 6
public perceptions of, 2–3, 20
referral market and, 184–185
referral system of, 181, 203
See *also* plaintiff's lawyers
legal education, 79. *See also* continuing
legal education
legal specialization. *See* specialization
liability
and case selection, 148, 232–233
Lipartito, Kenneth, 75, 88–90
litigation, 231
lawyers' professional identity and,
128–130
plaintiffs' lawyers and, 157
as regulation, 13
Litigation Explosion, The. See Olson, Walter
Litigators, The. See Grisham, John
Loftus, Elizabeth, 22
Loncar, Brian, 140
Luban, David, 12, 15, 42
Luntz, Frank, 1–2, 28
Lucas v. United States, 34n10, 47n33

MacKinnon, F. B., 231, 232, 233

Maloney, Pat, Sr., 6, 57, 99, 140

Mandell and Combs, 81
  labor law in Texas, 81–82

Mandell, Arthur, 82
  NACCA and, 93
  TTLA and, 82, 94

Manges, Clint, 57

Manhattan Institute, 1, 8, 23, 27

Maryland Casualty v. Head, 167

mass tort cases
  heavy hitter lawyers and, 158
  Texas Senate Bill 15 and, 53–54

Mather, Lynn, 109–110
  on lawyer reputation, 177, 189

Maverick, Maury, Sr., 73, 93, 99, 103

McCann, Michael, 5–6, 16, 26

McDonald's coffee case, 6

medical malpractice cases, 188
  bread-and-butter lawyers and, 147
  case screening, 155–156, 158–159, 212
  case value and referrals, 199
  client attractiveness and, 220–221, 221
    (table), 222–224
  costs of, 212
  damage caps effects on, 168, 211, 213,
    221–222, 226–227, 229, 232
  damage caps effects on client
    attractiveness in, 224–225
  decline in Cook County, Illinois, 206,
    206n5
  decline in Texas, 205–206, 206n4
  difficulty winning, 211, 211n21
  fee size and referrals, 202
  gender and client attractiveness in,
    224
  heavy hitter lawyers and, 155–156,
    171–172
  lawyer reputation and referrals, 190
  referral system and, 160, 181, 186, 192
  specialization, 174
  specialization and referrals, 195
  Texas House Bill 4 and, 51–53

tort reform's effect on, 169 (table),
    169–170

medical malpractice reform, 17
  in Texas, 18, 44–46, 53 (*see also* Texas
    House Bill 4)

Mencimer, Stephanie, 58

Montford, John, 35–36, 42

Mullinax, Otto, 72, 139
  on labor law, 83–84
  law practice, 81–85
  legal education, 81
  at Mandell and Combs, 81–82
  at Mullinex, Wells, 82–83
  professional ethos of, 111, 122, 128
  Red Scare in Texas and, 81
  training of young plaintiffs' lawyers, 85
  on workers' injury cases, 77, 83

Mullinax, Wells firm, 236. *See also*
    Mullinax, Otto

National Association of Claimants'
    Compensation Attorneys (NACCA),
    82
  continuing legal education and, 92–93,
    96
  founding and history, 92
  Texas plaintiffs' lawyers and, 93–94

National Maritime Act, 77

negligence standard
  auto accident cases, 76–77
  common law defenses and, 77
  Federal Employers Liability Act (FELA)
    and, 78
  Texas changes in, 33–34, 76–77
  TTLA political involvement and, 101

New Deal, 73

noneconomic damage caps, 207–208
  affordable health care and, 208
  client access to legal system and effects
    of, 297
  client attractiveness and effects of, 222,
    225
  contingency fees and, 214

noneconomic damage caps, *continued*
    18-wheeler case and, 221
    elderly as victims of, 225
    hidden victims of, 216, 221
    in Illinois, 206
    injured people as victims of, 214
    medical malpractice cases and effects of,
        168, 207, 211, 213, 222, 226–227, 229,
        232
    non-working people as victims of, 225
    plaintiffs' lawyers' incentive structure
        and, 207, 211, 214
    plaintiffs' lawyers' professional identity
        and, 207
    purported benefits of, 208
    in Texas, 205–206, 209, 219n28
    See also Texas House Bill 4
noneconomic damages, 18, 149–151
    access to legal system and, 239
    bread-and-butter lawyers and, 151
    facial disfigurement as, 219
    See also noneconomic damage caps
Noteboom, Chuck, 62
nurse-paralegals, 158–159

Olson, Walter, xii, 2, 13
    at Manhattan Institute, 23–24
O'Neill, Harriet, 64
O'Quinn, John, 6, 119, 140
    attempts to disbar, 130

Paik, Myungho, xvin7, 18, 210
Parikh, Sara, 124, 177–178, 188
Pena, Richard, 64n84, 180n8
Perry, Rick, 46, 60, 206
    on damage caps, 233
    proclaims "Lawsuit Abuse Awareness
        Week," 67
    on Texas House Bill 4, 208–210, 211
    on tort reform in Texas, 19–20
personal injury cases
    case screening and, 148–149, 155–156
    certification and referrals, 194

    fee size and referrals, 202
    referrals, 183, 191
personal injury law, 54
    contingency fees and, 232
    labor unions in Texas and, 85
    railroads in Texas and, 79
Phillips, Thomas, 56, 58
physician-lawyers, 158–159
"Pit and the Pendulum, The." *See* Poe,
    Edgar Allan
plaintiffs' lawyers
    business model of, 232–234
    as business people, 121–122, 166–168, 207,
        232
    caseloads, 163
    case screening by, 148, 148n11, 149
    client acquisition by, 112, 121, 138 (*see
        also* client acquisition)
    as "community of practice," 109
    competition and, 118–119
    contingency fees and, 231
    criticism of aggressive advertising,
        123–125
    damage caps and incentive system,
        230
    definition of, 141–143, 143n8
    demonizing of, 28–29, 55
    economic considerations of, 231
    education and socialization of, 85–86
    empathy and, 127
    ethics and, 110, 113, 125–126
    as gatekeepers, 8–11, 33, 140, 178, 207,
        230–232
    "going rates" and, 14–15
    hierarchy, 140–141, 174
    historical view of, 7
    history of, 74
    litigation and, 128–129, 157
    market opportunities for, 86–87
    medical malpractice cases and, 215
    networks, 13
    as political actors, 105
    portrayal on *60 Minutes*, 6, 58

professional identity, 72, 91, 107–108, 138, 162
professional identity, definitions of, 109–111
professional identity, and litigation, 129–130
professional identity, and referral system, 176
professionalism, 109–111, 113, 122–123, 126
public good and, 126–128
public perceptions of, 3–8, 28, 136
public relations campaigns against, 91
referral system, 125, 176–178, 184–185, 203–204
reshaping of law, 11–15, 79
specialization and, 173–175
surveys of, 168
tort reform's effect on, 166–168, 169 (table)
See also Texas plaintiffs' bar; Texas plaintiffs' lawyers; Texas plaintiffs' lawyer survey (2006)
Platt, Joseph, 75, 88–90
Poe, Edgar Allan, 32
political progressives, 72–73, 85
Pope, Jack, 57–58
on Hubert Winston Smith, 96
Priest, George, 27
products liability cases
case value and referrals, 199
heavy hitter lawyers and, 158
lawyer reputation and referrals, 190
referrals, 186, 192
specialization and referrals, 196
products liability law, 12
expanding opportunities in Texas, 83
as legal specialization, 174
punitive damages, 12, 17

Quayle, Dan, 18

railroads
opposition to plaintiffs' law, 87–91
personal injury law and, 78

Ray, C. L., 57
Reagan Revolution, 18, 35
referral fees, 61–65
Texas caps on, 64
Texas Disciplinary Rules of Professional Conduct and, 179–180
Texas Rules of Civil Procedure, Proposed Rule 8a and, 178–179
referral system, 184–185
acceptance of paid referrals, 186
bread-and-butter lawyers and, 146 (table), 153, 203
case value and, 189
client access to legal system and, 202
fees as incentives, 203
financial interest and, 186–187, 189
heavy hitter lawyers and, 146 (table), 160–161
lawyer participation in, 203
lawyer reputation and, 187, 189–191, 190 (table)
plaintiffs' lawyers and other lawyers compared, 201–202
reasons for choosing a target lawyer, 190 (table)
service to client and, 189
as source of business, 203–204
specialization and, 186
specialization and certification, 194
specialization and reputation, 194
Texas plaintiffs' bar and, 176, 181–182, 197
See also Texas plaintiffs' lawyer survey (2006); Texas Referral Survey
reform
definitions of, 15–16, 237
See also tort reform
Report of the Tort Policy Working Group, 18
Republican Party, 18, 29
ascendancy in Texas, 38, 42, 46–47, 55–60
in Texas, 17, 31, 73, 104, 218, 236
Ricci, David, 21

Richards, Ann, 42, 73
Rise of the Conservative Legal Movement,
   The, 27
Robertson, Ted Z., 57
Rosenblum, Victor, xvii, 110–111
Rove, Karl, 42, 55–56, 59
Rule of Lawyers, The. See Olson, Walter

Sanders, Joseph, 35–37
Scruggs, Richard (Dickie), 6
Seron, Carroll, 235
settlement, 15, 77
"Shyster Lawyer, The." *See* Cockerill, Ashley
Silver, Charles, xv, 9–11, 211
   on lawyers' business model, 233
Smith, Hubert Winston, 72
   continuing legal education and, 95–99
   Law Science Institute at University of
      Texas at Austin, 96
   medicolegal short course for NACCA,
      96, 97–99
Smith, J. E., 79–80, 102
   associate editor of *NACCA Law Journal,*
      93
   legal apprenticeship, 86
   TTLA and, 80
solo practitioners, 154, 164–165
specialization
   medical malpractice cases and, 174, 195
   plaintiffs' lawyers and, 173–175
   referral system and, 186, 193–197
Spivey, Broadus, 130
Stern, Howard, 107
Stone, Deborah, 21
Swartz, Mimi, 45, 48n36, 50–51, 239n13

Teles, Steven M., 27
television advertising. *See under* lawyer
   advertising
Texans Against Lawsuit Abuse, 23, 26, 66
Texas Board of Legal Specialization, 153,
   173, 194
Texas Civil Justice League, 36, 38, 66

Texas Commission for Lawyer Discipline,
   6, 130
Texas Constitutional Amendment
   Proposition 12, 47
Texas Disciplinary Rules of Professional
   Conduct, 62–63, 179–180
   paid referral rules, 179–180
   Rule VII, 114–115
Texas House Bill 4 (2003), 46–49, 53, 205
   affordable health care and, 210
   elderly as victims of, 206–207
   hidden victims of, 53
   medical malpractice cases and, 51, 53
   physician shortage and, 209–210
   plaintiffs' lawyers and, 52–53
Texans for Lawsuit Reform (TLR), 38, 43,
   50, 61, 66
Texas plaintiffs' bar, 141, 234
   case values and hierarchy, 143, 143nn6–7
   geographical markets, 143–145, 145
      (table)
   hierarchy in, 142–145, 146 (table),
      161–162
   hierarchy and referral system, 176,
      197–198, 198 (table), 199
   history of, 71–75
   professional identity and referrals, 176
   referral system, 176, 181–182, 197
   reputation and referrals, 193
   segmentation of, 140–141
   specialization and referrals, 193
   structure of, 143–145, 172–173
   tort reform's effect on, 162–166
   See also bread-and-butter lawyers;
      heavy hitter lawyers; plaintiffs'
      lawyers; Texas plaintiffs' lawyers;
      Texas plaintiffs' lawyer survey (2006)
Texas plaintiffs' lawyers
   adaptation to change, 235–237
   commercial cases and, 236–237
   gender, 143n8
   hidden victims and, 215–216
   history of, 79–87

as innovators, 235–237
medical malpractice cases and, 215–216
new markets for, 236–237
in oil and gas industry, 237
opposition by railroads, 87–91
political identity of, 73
professional identity of, 234–235
violence against, 84
Texas plaintiffs' lawyer survey (2006)
    auto accident referrals and fee size,
        202–203
    auto accident specialists and referrals,
        195–196
    caseload and referrals, 198
    case value and referrals, 198–199
    certification and referrals, 194
    client attractiveness, 223–224
    client compatibility and referrals, 200,
        201 (table)
    damage caps effects on client
        attractiveness, 221 (table), 222,
        224–225, 225n35, 226–228, 227
        (table)
    damage caps effects on hidden victims,
        221
    damage caps effects on medical
        malpractice cases, 221–222, 222n30,
        228–229
    fee size and referrals, 200, 201 (table),
        202–203
    gender and client attractiveness, 224
    geographic location and referrals, 198,
        199n29
    hypothetical situations for comparing
        case types, 217–218, 220
    hypothetical situations for comparing
        client types, 216–219, 219n27, 220
    medical malpractice case costs, 212n22,
        212–213
    medical malpractice referrals and fee
        size, 202
    medical malpractice specialists and
        referrals, 195, 195n24

    lawyer reputation and referrals, 193–194,
        200, 201 (table)
    personal injury referrals and fee size,
        202
    products liability referrals and fee size,
        202
    products liability specialists and
        referrals, 196
    reasons for choosing a target lawyer,
        200–201, 201 (table)
    reasons for referring cases, 197, 198
        (table), 199–200
    reciprocity and referrals, 200, 201
        (table)
    referral acceptance rates, 197
    referrals by case type, 191–192, 192
        (table)
    referring lawyers, 192–193
    responses to hypothetical situations re
        attractiveness of clients, 220–221, 221
        (table)
    responses to hypothetical situations
        regarding attractiveness of medical
        malpractice cases, 220–221,
        221(table)
    self-interest and referrals, 200
    specialization and referrals, 193–197
    view of 18-wheeler cases, 217–218
Texas Referral Survey, 181, 182, 191
    auto accident cases, 181, 190
    caseload and referrals, 198
    case value and referrals, 189
    financial interest and, 186–187, 189
    geographical location and referrals, 188,
        198
    lawyer reputation and referrals, 189–191,
        190 (table), 200
    lawyers' participation in referral
        market, 184–185, 184n16, 185 (table)
    medical malpractice cases, 181, 188,
        190
    personal injury cases, 183
    products liability cases, 190

Texas Referral Survey, *continued*
reasons for choosing a target lawyer, 190
(table)
reasons for referring cases, 187–188, 188
(table)
referrals by case type, 183 (table)
service to client and referrals, 189
specialization and referrals, 188, 193
Texas Residential Construction
Commission Act (HB 730), 48–51
builder protection and, 50
failed reauthorization, 51
impact on lawyers' fees, 49
Texas Rules of Civil Procedure, Proposed
Rule 8a, 178–179
Texas Senate Bill 15, 54
mass tort cases and, 53–54
prohibition of consolidation in asbestos
and silica cases, 54
Texas State Bar Association, 71
certification among members, 154
plaintiffs' lawyers in, 141, 141n4
Texas Supreme Court, 55–65
election scandal, 56–58
Proposition 12 and, 47–48
referral fee rules and, 60–65, 178–180
Republican control of, 55–60
third party bad faith eliminated, 167
Texas Tort Reform Laws (1987), 34–38
comparative negligence and, 37
lawyers' reactions to, 37
product liability and, 37
Texas tort reform legislation (1995),
43–46
plaintiffs' lawyers and, 43–46
Texas Trial Lawyers Association (TTLA),
xviii, 36, 65, 72
continuing legal education and, 95–99
creation of, 93–94
Democratic Party politics and, 102
founders of, 80–81, 82, 94
Hubert Winston Smith's medicolegal
short courses and, 99

on lawyers' advertising, 115–116
membership, 141
membership rules, 111
opponents of, 91
PAC, 73, 103
in Texas politics, 100–104
Texas Workers' Compensation Act (1989),
38–42
Texas Workers' Compensation
Commission, 39
Thompson, David, 110–111
Tonahill, Joe, 100
in medicolegal short course, 99
NACCA and, 93
TTLA and, 93, 101
tort reform
access to legal system and, 230, 239
billboard advertising and, 67–68
Conservative Legal Movement and,
27
critical perspectives on, 237–239
elderly as victims of, 206–207
funding for, 24–26
GOPAC and, 29
hidden victims of, 205, 230, 232–233
history of, 17–18
juries and, 149–151
jury verdicts and, 234
medical costs and, 18
physician shortages and, 18
plaintiffs' law practices and, 162–165,
166–168
plaintiffs' lawyers as targets of, 1–2,
28–30, 238
as a political movement, 15–20, 50, 65
as a political movement, in Texas,
46–50, 55–60, 123
public discourse and, 20–24
public discourse and, in Texas, 65–68
public relations campaigns and, 38,
67–68, 149–150, 233–234
Republican Party and, 18–19, 46 (*see also*
Republican Party)

See also Texas House Bill 4 (2003); Texas
Senate Bill 15; Texas Tort Reform
Laws (1987); Texas tort reform
legislation (1995)
Turley, Wendell, 140

University of Texas School of Law, 72

Wells, Nat, 82–83
Williams, John Eddie, 140
worker injury cases, 77, 83
labor unions and, 81

workers' compensation
tort reform and, 38–39, 233
TTLA and, 101
See also Texas Workers' Compensation
Act (1989)
Wright, Herman, 82, 94

Yarborough, Don, 102
Yarborough, Ralph, 73, 99
yellow page advertising. *See* lawyer advertising

Zemans, Francis, xvii, 110–111